A TRAIN OF POWDER

A TRAIN
OF POWDER

BY REBECCA WEST

Our God is not out of breath, because he
hath blown one tempest, and swallowed a
Navy: our God hath not burnt out his
eyes, because he hath looked upon a Train
of Powder.   —JOHN DONNE

IVAN R. DEE
CHICAGO

Library of Congress Cataloging-in-Publication Data:
West, Rebecca, Dame, 1892-
    A train of powder / by Rebecca West.
      p. cm.
    Originally published: New York : Viking Press, 1955.
    ISBN 978-1-56663-319-2 (pbk: alk. paper)
    1. Criminals—Biography. 2. Trials. 3. Nuremberg Trial of Major
German War Criminals, Nuremberg, Germany, 1945-1946. I. Title.
    HV6245 .W4 2000
    364—dc21
                                                              00-043038

To Margaret Rhondda with deep affection

CONTENTS

Greenhouse with Cyclamens I

(1946)

GREENHOUSE WITH CYCLAMENS I

◆◆ 1 ◆◆

There rushed up towards the plane the astonishing face of the world's enemy: pine woods on little hills, grey-green glossy lakes, too small ever to be anything but smooth, gardens tall with red-tongued beans, fields striped with copper wheat, russet-roofed villages with headlong gables and pumpkin-steeple churches that no architect over seven could have designed. Another minute and the plane dropped to the heart of the world's enemy: Nuremberg. It took not many more minutes to get to the courtroom where the world's enemy was being tried for his sins; but immediately those sins were forgotten in wonder at a conflict which was going on in that court, though it had nothing to do with the indictments considered by it. The trial was then in its eleventh month, and the courtroom was a citadel of boredom. Every person within its walk was in the grip of extreme tedium. This is not to say that the work in hand was being performed languidly. An iron discipline met that tedium head on and did not yield an inch to it. But all the same the most spectacular process in the court was by then a certain tug-of-war concerning time. Some of those present were fiercely desiring that that tedium should come to an end at the first possible moment, and the others were as fiercely desiring that it should last for ever and ever.

The people in court who wanted the tedium to endure eternally were the twenty-one defendants in the dock, who disconcerted the spectator by presenting the blatant appearance that historical characters, particularly in distress, assume in bad pictures. They looked what they were as crudely as Mary Queen of Scots at Fotheringay or Napoleon on St. Helena in a mid-Victorian

Academy success. But it was, of course, an unusually ghastly picture. They were wreathed in suggestions of death. Not only were they in peril of the death sentence, there was constant talk about millions of dead and arguments whether these had died because of these men or not; knowing so well what death is, and experiencing it by anticipation, these men preferred the monotony of the trial to its cessation. So they clung to the procedure through their lawyers and stretched it to the limits of its texture; and thus they aroused in the rest of the court, the people who had a prospect of leaving Nuremberg and going back to life, a savage impatience. This the iron discipline of the court prevented from finding an expression for itself. But it made the air more tense.

It seemed ridiculous for the defendants to make any effort to stave off the end, for they admitted by their appearance that nothing was to go well with them again on this earth. These Nazi leaders, self-dedicated to the breaking of all rules, broke last of all the rule that the verdict of a court must not be foretold. Their appearance announced what they believed. The Russians had asked for the death penalty for all of them, and it was plain that the defendants thought that wish would be granted. Believing that they were to lose everything, they forgot what possession had been. Not the slightest trace of their power and their glory remained; none of them looked as if he could ever have exercised any valid authority. Göring still used imperial gestures, but they were so vulgar that they did not suggest that he had really filled any great position; it merely seemed probable that in certain bars the frequenters had called him by some such nickname as "The Emperor." These people were also surrendering physical characteristics which might have been thought inalienable during life, such as the colour and texture of their skins and the moulding of their features. Most of them, except Schacht, who was white-haired, and Speer, who was black like a monkey, were neither dark nor fair any more; and there was amongst them no leanness that did not sag and no plumpness that seemed more than inflation by some thin gas. So diminished were their personalities that it was hard to keep in mind which was which, even after one had sat and looked at them for days; and those who stood out defined themselves by oddity rather than character.

4

Hess was noticeable because he was so plainly mad: so plainly mad that it seemed shameful that he should be tried. His skin was ashen, and he had that odd faculty, peculiar to lunatics, of falling into strained positions which no normal person could maintain for more than a few minutes, and staying fixed in contortion for hours. He had the classless air characteristic of asylum inmates; evidently his distracted personality had torn up all clues to his past. He looked as if his mind had no surface, as if every part of it had been blasted away except the depth where the nightmares live. Schacht was as noticeable because he was so far from mad, so completely his ordinary self in these extraordinary circumstances. He sat twisted in his seat so that his tall body, stiff as a plank, was propped against the end of the dock, which ought to have been at his side. Thus he sat at right angles to his fellow defendants and looked past them and over their heads: it was always his argument that he was far superior to Hitler's gang. Thus, too, he sat at right angles to the judges on the bench confronting him: it was his argument that he was a leading international banker, a most respectable man, and no court on earth could have the right to try him. He was petrified by rage because this court was pretending to have this right. He might have been a corpse frozen by rigor mortis, a disagreeable corpse who had contrived to aggravate the process so that he should be specially difficult to fit into his coffin.

A few others were still individuals. Streicher was pitiable, because it was plainly the community and not he who was guilty of his sins. He was a dirty old man of the sort that gives trouble in parks, and a sane Germany would have sent him to an asylum long before. Baldur von Schirach, the Youth Leader, startled because he was like a woman in a way not common among men who looked like women. It was as if a neat and mousy governess sat there, not pretty, but with never a hair out of place, and always to be trusted never to intrude when there were visitors: as it might be Jane Eyre. And though one had read surprising news of Göring for years, he still surprised. He was so very soft. Sometimes he wore a German Air Force uniform, and sometimes a light beach suit in the worst of playful taste, and both hung loosely on him, giving him an air of pregnancy. He had thick brown young hair, the coarse bright skin of an actor who has used grease paint for decades, and the preternaturally deep wrinkles of the drug addict. It added up to something like the head of a ventriloquist's dummy. He looked infinitely corrupt, and acted naïvely. When the other defendants' lawyers came to the door to receive instructions, he often intervened and insisted on instructing them himself, in spite of the evident fury of the defendants, which, indeed, must have been poignant, since most of them might well have felt that, had it not been for him, they never would have had to employ these lawyers at all. One of these lawyers was a tiny little man of very Jewish appearance, and when he stood in front of the dock, his head hardly reaching to the top of it, and flapped his gown in annoyance because Göring's smiling wooden mask was bearing down between him and his client, it was as if a ventriloquist had staged a quarrel between two dummies.

Göring's appearance made a strong but obscure allusion to sex. It is a matter of history that his love affairs with women played a decisive part in the development of the Nazi party at various stages, but he looked as one who would never lift a hand against a woman save in something much more peculiar than kindness. He did not look like any recognized type of homosexual, yet he was feminine. Sometimes, particularly when his humour was good, he recalled the madam of a brothel. His like are to be seen in the late morning in doorways along the steep streets of Marseille, the professional mask of geniality still hard on their faces though they stand relaxed in leisure, their fat cats rubbing against their spread skirts. Certainly there had been a concentration on appetite, and on elaborate schemes for gratifying it; and yet there was a sense of desert thirst. No matter what aqueducts he had built to bring water to his encampment, some perversity in the architecture had let it run out and spill on the sands long before it reached him. Sometimes even now his wide lips smacked together as if he were a well-fed man who had heard no news as yet that his meals were to stop. He was the only one of all these defendants who, if he had the chance, would have walked out of the Palace of Justice and taken over Germany again, and turned it into the stage for the enactment of the private fantasy which had brought him to the dock.

As these men gave up the effort to be themselves, they joined to make a common pattern which simply reiterated the plea of not guilty. All the time they made quite unidiosyncratic gestures expressive of innocence and outraged common sense, and in the intervals they stood up and chatted among themselves, forming little protesting groups, each one of which, painted as a mural, would be instantly recognized as a holy band that had tried to save the world but had been frustrated by mistaken men. But this performance they rendered more weakly every day. They were visibly receding from the field of existence and were, perhaps, no longer conscious of the recession. It is possible that they never thought directly of death or even of imprisonment, and there was nothing positive in them at all except their desire to hold time still. They were all praying with their sharp-set nerves: "Let this trial never finish, let it go on for ever and ever, without end."

The nerves of all others present in the Palace of Justice were sending out a counter-prayer: the eight judges on the bench, who were plainly dragging the proceedings over the threshold of their consciousness by sheer force of will; the lawyers and the secretaries who sat sagged in their seats at the tables in the well of the court; the interpreters twittering unhappily in their glass box like cage-birds kept awake by a bright light, feeding the microphones with French and Russian and English versions of the proceedings for the spectators' earphones; the guards who stood with their arms gripping their white truncheons behind their backs, all still and hard as metal save their childish faces, which were puffy with boredom. All these people wanted to leave Nuremberg as urgently as a dental patient enduring the drill wants to up and leave the chair; and they would have had as much difficulty as the dental patient in explaining the cause of that urgency. Modern drills do not inflict real pain, only discomfort. But all the same the patients on whom they are used feel that they will go mad if that grinding does not stop. The people at Nuremberg were all well fed, well clothed, well housed, and well cared for by their organizations, on a standard well above their recent experience. This was obviously true of the soldiers who had campaigned in the war, and of the British and French civilians at work in the court; and it was, to an extent that would have surprised most Europeans, true of the American civilians. It never crossed the Atlantic,

7

the news of just how uncomfortable life became in the United States during the war: what the gasoline shortage did to make life untenable in the pretty townships planned on the supposition that every householder had an automobile; how the titanic munitions programme had often to plant factories in little towns that could not offer a room apiece to the incoming workers; what it was like to live in an all-electric house when electric equipment was impossible to replace or repair. By contrast, what Nuremberg gave was the life of Riley, but it was also the water-torture, boredom falling drop by drop on the same spot on the soul.

What irked was the isolation in a small area, cut off from normal life by the barbed wire of army regulations; the perpetual confrontation with the dreary details of an ugly chapter in history which the surrounding rubble seemed to prove to have been torn out of the book and to require no further discussion; the continued enslavement by the war machine. To live in Nuremberg was, even for the victors, in itself physical captivity. The old town had been destroyed. There was left the uninteresting new town, in which certain grubby hotels improvised accommodation for Allied personnel, and were the sole places in which they might sleep and eat and amuse themselves. On five days a week, from ten to five, and often on Saturday mornings, their duties compelled them to the Palace of Justice of Nuremberg, an extreme example of the German tendency to overbuild, which has done much to get them into the recurring financial troubles that make them look to war for release. Every German who wanted to prove himself a man of substance built himself a house with more rooms than he needed and put more bricks into it than it needed; and every German city put up municipal buildings that were as much demonstrations of solidity as for use. Even though the Nuremberg Palace of Justice housed various agencies we would not find in a British or American or French law court, such as a Labour Exchange, its mass could not be excused, for much of it was a mere waste of masonry and an expense of shame, in obese walls and distended corridors. It recalled Civil War architecture but lacked the homeliness; and it made the young American heart sicken with nostalgia for the clean-run concrete and glass and plastic of modern office buildings. From its clumsy tripes the personnel could escape at the end of the working day to the tennis courts and the swimming pools, provided that they were doing only routine work. Those who were more deeply involved had to go home and work on their papers, with little time for any recreation but dinner parties, which themselves, owing to the unique character of the Nuremberg event, were quite unrefreshing. For the guests at these parties had either to be co-workers grown deadly familiar with the passing months or VIPs come to see the show, who, as most were allowed to stay only two days, had nothing to bring to the occasion except the first superficial impressions, so apt to be the same in every case. The symbol of Nuremberg was a yawn.

The Allies reacted according to their histories. The French, many of whom had been in concentration camps, rested and read; no nation has endured more wars, or been more persistent in its creation of a culture, and it has been done this way. The British reconstituted an Indian hill station; anybody who wants to know what they were like in Nuremberg need only read the early works of Rudyard Kipling. In villas set among the Bavarian pines, amid German modernist furniture, each piece of which seemed to have an enormous behind, a triple feat of reconstitution was performed: people who were in Germany pretended they were people in the jungle who were pretending they were in England. The Americans gave those huge parties of which the type was fixed in pioneering days, when the folks in the scattered homesteads could meet so rarely that it would have been tiring out the horses for nothing not to let geniality go all up the scale; and for the rest they contended with disappointment. Do what you will with America, it remains vast, and it follows that most towns are small in a land where the people are enthralled by the conception of the big town. Here were children of that people, who had crossed a great ocean in the belief that they were going to see the prodigious, and were back in a small town smaller than any of the small towns they had fled.

For a small town is a place where there is nothing to buy with money; and in Nuremberg, as in all German towns at that time, purchase was a forgotten faculty. The Nurembergers went to work in shabby streetcars hooked three together; so presumably they paid their fares. They bought the few foodstuffs available to them in shops so bare that it was hard to associate them with the satisfaction of an appetite. They bought fuel, not much, as it was summer, but enough to cook by and give what they felt to be, much more urgently than might have been supposed, the necessity of light. In the old town a twisted tower leaned backward against the city wall, and of this the top floor had miraculously remained roofed and weather-tight. To get to it one had to walk a long way over the rubble, which exhaled the double stench of disinfectant and of that which was irredeemably infected, for it concealed thirty thousand dead; and then one had to walk up the sagging concave exterior of the tower, and go in through a window. It would seem that people who had to live in such a home would not care to stay awake when darkness fell; but at night a weak light burned in the canted window. Such minuscule extravagance was as far as expenditure could go, except for grubby peddling in the black market. One could not buy a new hat, a new kettle, a yard of ribbon, a baby's diaper. There was no money, there were only cigarettes. A judge's wife, come out for a visit, said to a woman staying in the same villa, who had said she was going into the town, "Will you buy me some silver paint? I want to touch up my evening shoes," and everyone in earshot, even the GI guards at the door, burst into laughter.

It was hysterical laughter. Merely to go into a shop and buy something is to exercise choice and to enjoy the freedom of the will; and when this is checked it hurts. True, the Allied personnel in Nuremberg could go into their own stores and buy what they wanted; but that was not the full healthy process, for they knew with a deadly particularity every item in their own stores, and the traveller does not feel he has made terms with the country he visits till the people have sold him their goods. Without that interchange he is like a ghost among the living. The Allied personnel were like ghosts, and it might have been that the story would have a supernatural ending. If Allah of the Arabian Nights had governed this dispensation an angel would have appeared and struck dead all the defendants, and would have cried out that the rest of the court might do what it willed, and they would have run towards the East, towards France, towards the Atlantic, and by its surf would have taken off from the ground and risen into the air on the force of their desire, and travelled in a black compact cloud across the ocean, back to America, back to peace, back to life.

It might seem that this is only to say that at Nuremberg people were bored. But this was boredom on a huge historic scale. A machine was running down, a great machine, the greatest machine that has ever been created: the war machine, by which mankind, in spite of its infirmity of purpose and its frequent desire for death, has defended its life. It was a hard machine to operate; it was the natural desire of all who served it, save those rare creatures, the born soldiers, that it should become scrap. There was another machine which was warming up: the peace machine, by which mankind lives its life. Since enjoyment is less urgent than defence it is more easily served. All over the world people were sick with impatience because they were bound to the machine that was running down, and they wanted to be among the operators of the machine that was warming up. They did not want to kill and be grimly immanent over conquered territory; they wanted to eat and drink and be merry and wise among their own kind. It maddened them further that some had succeeded in getting their desire and had made their transfer to peace. By what trickery did these lucky bastards get their priority of freedom? Those who asked themselves that bitter question grew frenzied in the asking, because their conditions became more and more exasperating. The prisoners who guarded the prisoners of Nuremberg were always finding themselves flaring up into rage because they were using equipment that had been worn out and could not be replaced because of the strain on the supply lines. It could not be credited how often, by 1946, the Allies' automobiles broke down on German roads. What was too old was enraging; and who was too new was exasperating too. The commonest sight in a Nuremberg office was a man lifting a telephone, giving a number, speaking a phrase with the slurred and confident ease that showed he had used it a thousand times before to set some routine in motion, and breaking off in a convulsion of impatience. "Smith isn't there? He's *gawn?* And you don't know anything about it? Too bad. . . ." All very inconvenient, and inconvenient too that it is impossible to imagine how, after any future war,

11

just this will not happen—unless that war is so bad that after it nothing will happen any more.

The situation would have been more tolerable if these conquerors had taken the slightest interest in their conquest; but they did not. They were even embarrassed by it. "Pardon my mailed glove," they seemed to murmur as they drove in the American automobiles, which were all the Nuremberg roads then carried save for the few run by the British and French, past the crowds of Germans who waited for the streetcars beside the round black Nuremberg towers, which were hollow ruins; or on Sundays, as they timidly strolled about the villages, bearing themselves like polite people who find themselves intruding on a bereaved family; or as they informed their officers, if they were GIs, that such and such a garage proprietor or doorman was a decent fellow, really he was, though he was a kraut. Here were men who were wearing the laurels of the vastest and most improbable military victory in history, and all they wanted was to be back doing well where they came from, whether this was New York or the hick towns which comedians name to raise a laugh at the extreme of American provincialism. Lines on a young soldier's brow proclaimed that he did not care what decoration he won in the Ardennes; he wanted to go home and pretend Pearl Harbor had never been troubled and get in line for the partnership which should be open for the right man in a couple of years' time. A complexion beyond the resources of the normal bloodstream, an ambience of perfume amounting almost to a general anaesthetic for the passer-by, showed that for the female the breaking of traditional shackles and participation in the male glory of military triumph cannot give the pleasure to be derived from standing under a bell of white flowers while the family friends file past.

Considering this huge and urgent epidemic of nostalgia, the behaviour of these exiles was strangely sweet. They raged against things rather than against one another. At breakfast in the Grand Hotel they uttered such cries as, "Christ, am I allergic to powdered eggs with a hair in 'em!" with a passion that seemed excessive even for such ugly provocation; but there was very little spite. The nicknames were all good-humoured, and were imparted to the stranger only on that understanding. When it was divulged that

12

one of the most gifted of the interpreters, a handsome young person from Wisconsin, was known as the Passionate Haystack, care was taken to point out that no reflection on her was implied, but only a tribute to a remarkable hair-do. This kindliness could show itself as imaginative and quick-witted. The Russians in Nuremberg never mixed with their Allies except at large parties, which they attended in a state of smiling taciturnity. Once a young Russian officer, joyously drunk, walked into the ballroom of the Grand Hotel, which was crowded with American personnel, and walked up to a pretty stenographer and asked her to dance. The band was not playing, and there was a sudden hush. Someone told the band to strike up again, the floor was crowded with dancing couples, a group gathered round the Russian boy and rushed him away to safety, out of the hotel and into an automobile; and he was dumped on the sidewalk as soon as his captors found an empty street. It is encouraging that those men would take so much trouble to save from punishment a man of whom they knew nothing save that he belonged to a group which refused all intercourse with them.

This sweetness of atmosphere was due chiefly to the American tradition of pleasantness in superficial social relations, though many of the exiles were constrained to a special tenderness by their personal emotions. For some of them sex was here what it was anywhere else. There is an old story which describes a native of Cincinnati, returned from a trip to Europe, telling a fellow townsman of an encounter with a beautiful girl which had brightened a night he had spent in Paris. On and on the story goes, dwelling on the plush glories of the restaurant, the loveliness of the girl and her jewels and her dress, the magic of a drive in the Bois de Boulogne, the discreet luxury of the house to which she took him, till it rises to a climax in a bedroom carpeted with bear skins and lined with mirrors. "And then?" "Well—then it was very much like what it is in Cincinnati." To many, love in Nuremberg was just as they had known it in Cincinnati, but for others the life of the heart was lived, in this desolate place given over to ruin and retributive law, with a special poignancy.

Americans marry young. There was hardly a man in the town who had not a wife in the United States, who was not on the vigorous side of middle age, and who was not spiritually sick from a surfeit of war and exile. To the desire to embrace was added the desire to be comforted and to comfort; and the delights of gratification were heart-rending, like spring and sunset and the breaking wave, because they could not last. The illusion was strong that if these delights could go on for ever they would always remain perfect. It seemed to many lovers that whatever verdicts were passed on the Nazis at the end of the trial, much happiness that might have been immortal would then be put to death. Those wives who were four thousand miles away haunted Nuremberg like phantasms of the living and proved the sacredness of what was to be killed. "He loves me, but he is going back to her out of old affection and a sense of duty to his children. Ah, what I am losing in this man who can still keep a woman in his heart, when passion is gone, who is a good father." These temporary loves were often noble, though there were some who would not let them be so. There were men who said, "You are a good kid, but of course it is my wife I really love," when these terms were too perfunctory, considering his plight and the help he had been given. There were also women who despised the men who needed them. Through the Bavarian forests, on Saturdays and Sundays, there often drove one of the more exalted personalities of Nuremberg, accompanied by a lovely and odious female child, whom he believed, since he was among the more elderly exiles and was taking exile badly, not to be odious and to be kind. She seemed to be sucking a small jujube of contempt; by waving her eyelashes and sniffing as the automobile passed those likely to recognize its occupants, she sought to convey that she was in company that bored her.

Those who loved the trial for the law's sake also found the course of their love running not too smoothly. This was not because they were uncomfortably impressed by the arguments brought forward by the declared opponents of the Nuremberg prosecutions. None of these was really effective when set against the wholeness of the historical crisis which had provoked it. It was absurd to say that the defendants were being tried for *ex post facto* crimes when the Briand-Kellogg Pact of 1928 had made aggressive warfare a crime by renouncing the use of war as an instrument of policy; and it was notable that even those opponents who had a special insight into that pact because they had helped to frame it were unable to meet this point, save by pleading that it had not been designed to be used as a basis for the prosecution of war criminals. But that plea was invalid, for in 1928 the necessary conditions for such prosecutions did not exist. There was then no country that seemed likely to wage war which was not democratic in its government, since the only totalitarian powers in Europe, the Soviet Union and Italy, were still weak. It would not be logical to try the leaders of a democracy for their governmental crimes, since they had been elected by the people, who thereby took the responsibility for all their actions. If a democracy breaks the Briand-Kellogg Pact, it must pay by taxation and penalties that fall on the whole people. But the leaders of a totalitarian state seize political power and continually declare that they, and not the people, are responsible for all governmental acts, and if these be crimes according to international law, their claim to responsibility must make them subject to trial before what tribunal international law decrees. This argument is so much in accordance with reality that, in the courtroom itself, it was never doubted. All the defendants, with one exception, seemed to think that the Allies were right in indicting not the German people, but the officers and instruments of the Nazi Government, for conspiring together to commit crimes against peace and the rules of war and humanity; and in most cases their line of defence was that not they, but Hitler or some other members of the party, had taken the actual decisions which led to these crimes. This line of defence, by its references to Hitler alone, concedes the basis of the Nuremberg trials. The one dissenter who would not make this concession was Schacht, who behaved as if there had been a democratic state superimposed on the Nazi state, and that this had been the scene of his activities.

There was obviously more in the other argument used by the opponents of the trial: that even if it were right to persecute the Nazi leaders on charges of conspiracy to commit crimes against peace and the rules of war and humanity, it could not be right to have a Soviet judge on the bench, since the Soviet Union had convicted itself of these crimes by its public rape of Finland and

Poland and the Baltic Provinces. Truly there was here often occasion for shame. The English judges sat without their wigs, in plain gowns like their American colleagues, as a sign that this was a tribunal above all local tribunals. The Russian judges sat in military uniform as a sign that this was no tribunal at all, and when Vishinsky visited Nuremberg in the early months of the trial, he attended a banquet at which the judges were present, and proposed a toast to the conviction of the accused, a cantrip which would have led to the quashing of the trial in any civilized country.

This incident appeared to recommend the obvious idealistic prescription of trying the Nazi leaders before a tribunal which should exclude all representatives of the belligerent powers and find all its judges in the neutral countries. But that prescription loses its appeal when it is considered with what a laggard step would, say, the Swedish judge have gone home from Nuremberg, after having concurred in a verdict displeasing to the Soviet Union. But that there had to be a trial cannot be doubted. It was not only that common sense could predict that if the Nazis were allowed to go free the Germans would not have believed in the genuineness of the Allies' expressed disapproval of them, and that the good Germans would have been cast down in spirit, while the bad Germans would have wondered how long they need wait for the fun and jobbery to start again. It was that, there in Germany, there was a call for punishment. This is something that no one who was not there in 1946 will ever know, and perhaps one had to be at Nuremberg to learn it fully. It was written on the tired, temporizing faces and the bodies, nearly dead with the desire for life, of the defendants in the dock. It was written also on the crowds that waited for the streetcars and never looked at the Allied personnel as they drove past, and it was written on Nuremberg itself, in many places: on the spot just within the walls of the old town, outside the shattered Museum of Gothic Art, where a vast stone head of Jehovah lay on the pavement. Instead of scrutinizing the faces of men, He stared up at the clouds, as if to ask what He himself could be about; and the voices of the German children, bathing in the chlorinated river that wound through the faintly stinking rubble, seemed to reproach Him, because they sounded the same as if they had been bathing in a clear river running between meadows. There was a strange pattern printed on this terrain; and somehow its meaning was that the people responsible for the concentration camps and the deportations and the attendant evocation of evil must be tried for their offences.

It might seem possible that Britain and America might have limited their trials to the criminals they had found in the parts of Germany and Austria which they had conquered, and thus avoided the embarrassment of Soviet judges on the bench. But had they done so the Soviet Union would have represented them to its own people as dealing with the Nazi leaders too gently, to the Germans in the Eastern Zone as dealing with them too harshly. So there had to be an international tribunal at Nuremberg, and the Americans and the British and the French had to rub along with it as best they could. The Nuremberg judges realized the difficulty of the situation and believed that the imperfection could be remedied by strict adherence to a code of law, which they must force themselves to apply as if they were not victors but representatives of a neutral power. It was an idealistic effort, but the cost was immense. However much a man loved the law he could not love so much of it as wound its sluggish way through the Palace of Justice at Nuremberg. For all who were there, without exception, this was a place of sacrifice, of boredom, of headache, of homesickness.

Here was a paradox. In the courtroom these lawyers had to think day after day at the speed of whirling dervishes, yet were living slowly as snails, because of the boredom that pervaded all Nuremberg and was at its thickest in the Palace of Justice. They survived the strain. The effect on the defendants could be tested by their response to the cross-examinations of Göring. They were frightened when Sir David Maxwell Fyfe, the chief acting British prosecutor, cross-examined him and in a businesslike way got him against the wall and extorted from him admissions of vast crime; and they were amused when Mr. Justice Jackson, the chief American prosecutor, could not cross-examine Göring at all well, because he had a transatlantic prepossession that a rogue who had held high office would be a solemn and not a jolly rogue, and was disconcerted by his impudence. But to the Russian cross-examination of Göring neither they nor anyone else in the court could bend their attention, because it was childish; it might have been part of a mock trial organized by a civics teacher in a high school. This was perhaps a superficial impression. It might be that the Russians were pursuing a legal aim other than ours. "It seems to me, when I look back on the last few months," said one of the journalists who sat through the whole trial, "that again and again I have seen the Russians do the most mysterious things. I don't think I dreamed that one of the leading Russian lawyers, all togged up in his military uniform, stepped up to the rostrum and squared his shoulders as if he were going to do some weight-lifting and shouted at whatever defendant it was in the box, 'Did you conspire to wage an aggressive war against the peace-loving democracies? Answer yes or no.' When the defendant said 'No,' the Russian lawyer thought for a long time and said, 'I accept your answer.' I cannot work that one out." The men in the dock did not try.

But they were inert before the French. These were veiled from us by a misleading familiarity, an old and false association of images. They wore the round caps and white jabots and black gowns we have seen all our lives in Daumier drawings, and we expected them to be the wolves and sharks and alligators that Daumier drew. But they were civilized and gentle people, who gave a token of strength in their refusal to let what had happened to them of late years leave marks on their French surface. The judge, Monsieur Donnedieu de Vabres, was like many men that are to be seen all over France, and in many old French pictures, and in the plays of Molière and Marivaux: small and stocky, with a white moustache, and a brow kept wrinkled by the constant offences against logic perpetrated by this chaotic universe; a man whom one might have suspected of being academic and limited and pedantic, though sensible and moderate; a man whom one would not have suspected of having been, only two years before, released from a term of imprisonment in a German jail, which would have left many of us incapable and fanatic. From the slightly too elegant speeches of all these French lawyers it could be divined that when they were little boys they were made to learn Lamartine's *Le Lac* by heart. From the speeches of none of them could it be divined that France had lately been shamed and starved and tortured. But they could not press their case so that the men in the dock found themselves forced to listen to it. They were too familiar with that case; they had known all about it before the Nazis ever existed, from the lips of their fathers and their grandfathers; they had been aware that if the Germans practised habitually the brutalizing business of invasion they would strengthen the criminal element in their souls till they did such things as were now being proved against the men in the dock. Their apprehensions had been realized through their own agony. They had been so right that they had suffered wrongs for which no court could ever compensate them. The chief French prosecutor, Auguste Champetier de Ribes, had been the chief anti-Munich minister in Daladier's cabinet, and had followed his conscience before the war in full knowledge of what might happen to him after the war. The fire of their resentment was now burned to ashes. It did not seem worth while to say over again what they had said so often and so vainly; and the naïve element in the Nazis noted the nervelessness of their attack and wrote them off as weaklings. It was here that the Americans and the British found themselves possessed of an undeserved advantage. Through the decades they had refused to listen to the French point of view. Now they were like the sailor who was found beating a Jew because the Jews had crucified Christ. When he was reminded that that had happened a long time ago, he answered that that might be, but he had just heard about it.

So the Germans listened to the closing speeches made by Mr. Justice Jackson and Sir Hartley Shawcross, and were openly shamed by their new-minted indignation. When Mr. Justice Jackson brought his speech to an end by pointing a forefinger at each of the defendants in turn and denouncing his specific share in the Nazi crime, all of them winced, except old Streicher, who munched and mumbled away in some private and probably extremely objectionable dream, and Schacht, who became stiffer than ever, stiff as an iron stag in the garden of an old house. It was not surprising that all the rest were abashed, for the speech showed the civilized good sense against which they had conspired, and it was patently admirable, patently a pattern of the material necessary to the salvation of peoples. It is to be regretted that one phrase in it may be read by posterity as falling beneath the level of its context; for it has a particular significance to all those who attended the Nuremberg trial. "Göring," said Mr. Justice Jackson, "stuck a pudgy finger in every pie." The courtroom was not small, but it was full of Göring's fingers. His soft and white and spongy hands were for ever smoothing his curiously abundant brown hair, or covering his wide mouth while his plotting eyes looked facetiously around, or weaving impudent gestures of innocence in the air. The other men in the dock broke into sudden and relieved laughter at the phrase; Göring was plainly angered, though less by the phrase than by their laughter.

The next day, when Sir Hartley Shawcross closed the British case, there was no laughter at all. His speech was not so shapely and so decorative as Mr. Justice Jackson's, for English rhetoric has crossed the Atlantic in this century and is now more at home in the United States than on its native ground, and he spoke at greater length and stopped more legal holes. But his words were full of a living pity, which gave the men in the box their worst hour. The feminine Shirach achieved a gesture that was touching. He listened attentively to what Sir Hartley had to say of his activities as a Youth Leader; and when he heard him go on to speak of his responsibility for the deportation of forty thousand Soviet children he put up his delicate hand and lifted off the circlet of his headphones, laying it down very quietly on the ledge before him. It seemed possible that he had indeed the soul of a governess, that he was indeed Jane Eyre and had been perverted by a Mr. Rochester, who, disappearing into self-kindled flames, had left him disenchanted and the prey of a prim but inextinguishable remorse. And when Sir Hartley quoted the deposition of a witness who had described a Jewish father who, standing with his little son in front of a firing squad, "pointed to the sky, stroked his head, and seemed to explain something to the boy," all the defendants wriggled on their seats, like children rated by a schoolmaster, while their faces grew old.

There was a mystery there: that Mr. Prunes and Prisms should have committed such a huge, cold crime. But it was a mystery that girt all Nuremberg. It was most clearly defined in a sentence spoken by the custodian of the room in the Palace of Justice that housed all the exhibits relating to atrocities. Certain of these were unconvincing; some, though not all, of the photographs purporting to show people being shot and tortured had a posed and theatrical air. This need not have indicated conscious fraud. It might well have been that these photographs represented attempts to reconstruct incidents which had really occurred, made at the instigation of officials as explanatory glosses to evidence provided by eye-witnesses, and that they had found their way into the record by error. But there was much stuff that was authentic. Somebody had been collecting tattooed human skin, and it is hard to think where such a connoisseur could find his pieces unless he had power over a concentration camp. Some of these pelts were infinitely pathetic, because of their obscenity. Through the years came the memory of the inconveniently high-pitched voice of an English child among a crowd of tourists watching a tournament of water-jousting in a French port: "Mummy, come and look, there's a sailor who's got no shirt on, and he has the funniest picture on his back—there's a lady with no clothes on upside down on a St. Andrew's Cross, and there's a snake crawling all over her and somebody with a whip." There had been men who had thought they could make a pet of cruelty, and the grown beast had flayed them.

But it was astonishing that there had been so much sadism. The French doctor in charge of these exhibits pondered, turning in his hand a lampshade made of tattooed human skin, "These people where I live send me in my breakfast tray strewn with pansies, beautiful pansies. I have never seen more beautiful pansies, arranged with exquisite taste. I have to remind myself that they belong to the same race that supplied me with my exhibits, the same race that tortured me month after month, year after year, at Mauthausen." And, indeed, flowers were the visible sign of that mystery, flowers that were not only lovely but beloved. In the windowboxes of the high-gabled houses the pink and purple petunias were bright like lamps. In the gardens of the cottages bordering a road which was no longer there, which was a torn trench, the phloxes shone white and clear pink and mauve, as under harsh heat they will not do, unless they are well watered. It is tedious work, training clematis over low posts, so that its beauty does not stravaig up the walls but lies open under the eye; but on the edge of the town many gardeners grew it thus. The countryside beyond continued this protestation of innocence. A path might mount the hillside, through the lacework of light and shadow the pine trees cast over the soft reddish bed of the pine needles, to the upland farm where the wedding party poured out of the door, riotous with honest laughter, but freezing before a camera into honest solemnity; it might fall to the valley and follow the trout stream, where the dragonflies drew iridescent patterns just above the cloudy green water, to the edge of the millpond, where the miller's flax-haired little son played with the grey kittens among the meadowsweet; it would not lead to any place where it seemed other than plain that Germany was a beautiful country, inhabited by a people who loved all pleasant things and meant no harm.

Yet the accusations that were made against the leaders in the Palace of Justice at Nuremberg were true. They were proved true because the accusers did not want to make them. They would much rather have gone home. That could be seen by those who shamefully evaded the rules of the court and found a way into one of the offices in the Palace of Justice which overlooked the orchard which served as exercise ground of the jail behind it. There, at certain hours, the minor Nazi prisoners not yet brought to trial padded up and down, sullen and puffy, with a look of fierceness, as if they were missing the opportunity for cruelty as much as the company of women or whatever their fancy might be. They were watched by American military guards, who stood with their young chins dropped and their hands clasped behind them, slowly switching their white truncheons backwards and forwards, in the very rhythm of boredom itself. If an apple fell from the tree beside them they did not bend to pick it up. Nothing that happened there could interest them. It was not easy to tell that these guards were not the prisoners, so much did they want to go home. Never before can conquerors in charge of their captives have been less furious, more innocent of vengeance. A history book opened in the mind; there stirred a memory that Alexander the Great had had to turn back on the Hydaspes because his soldiers were homesick.

❖❖ 2 ❖❖

The journalists who reported the Nuremberg trial were lodged in a vast villa a couple of miles or so outside the city. It was the home of a pencil manufacturer, and, according to an old custom which persisted in Germany long after it had been abandoned in England and the United States, it was built beside the factory from which the family fortune was derived. The road to it ran across flat fields, and it was visible, though not credible, a long way off. It spoke of wealth in the same accents as the palaces of Pittsburgh, but it was twice the size of any of them and showed a more allusive fantasy. The spires and turrets, which looked particularly strange when the morning mists were thick about them, were fussy as lobster claws; its marble entrance hall and grand staircase were like a series of huge ascendant fish shops; it had a vast dining room decorated with a bosomy and gold-encrusted fresco representing the phases in the life of German womanhood, and a smaller dining room, used for less formal occasions, could at a pinch seat two hundred and fifty people. Much space was eaten up by spiral staircases and vaulted corridors, not for any functional reason but out of loyalty to the Meistersingers.

It would have been pedantic not to enjoy it in the same way that one enjoys an old-fashioned opera set. Yet it was a cruel house, for it had turned out of doors the founders of the firm which had paid for it. They could be discovered in the immense grounds, which were laid out as what is known in Germany as an "English park," though no park in England is so closely planted with shrubs and trees, and which contained a pleasant old-fashioned German villa with many wooden balconies, the original home of the family, and, in remoter spots, several pavilions. One, built like a temple, could be entered. Its heavy cedar door had been battered open. The interior was panelled with carefully chosen marble, some the colour of meat, some of gravy; and in an alcove, on a pedestal bearing the family coat of arms, was a mid-nineteenth-century group of life-size statues, representing the founder of the firm playing with a little son and daughter. On his abundant beard, on the little girl's ringlets, on everybody's buttons and boots, the sculptor had worked with particularly excited care. Two orange marble benches were provided on which his descendants could sit and, if they could forget the probable consequences of spending any length of time on such a chilly seat, contemplate the image and the memory of their progenitor. He looked a self-respecting old gentleman of vigorous character, and surely it was the meaning of this pavilion that he had loved these children very much. There were no signs here that the fruit of this old gentleman's loins would later fantasticate his prudently acquired acres with a mansion dropsical in whimsy, and would thus show themselves victims of a mania that was to force their country to the edge of an abyss.

For the German passion of overbuilding must have done much to bring the Nazis to power. It engendered high taxation and a quicksand instability in the financial structure of Germany, and it laid on German industry and commerce an obligation to pay their executives on a scale excessive by the standards of any other European country. It also meant an increasing burden on municipal finances, for the multiplication of villas standing in their own large grounds meant that the water and gas and electricity and sewage systems had to cover an extended area, and that transport and the upkeep of roads were a larger problem. These were curious results of an excessive preoccupation with fairy tales; for that was the dream behind all this villa-building. It revealed itself clearly in this *Schloss*. Its turret windows were quite useless unless Rapunzel was to let down her hair from them; its odd upper rooms, sliced into queer shapes by the intemperate steepness of the tiled roof, could be fitly occupied only by a fairy godmother with a spinning wheel; the staircase was for the descent of a prince and princess that should live happily ever after. It was perhaps the greatest misfortune of the German people that their last genius, Wagner, who flowered at the same time as their political integration, their military conquests, and their industrial hegemony, and who has never had his domination over them so much as threatened by any succeeding artist, should have kept so close to the fairy tale in his greatest works. It is as if Shakespeare had confirmed the hold of Dick Whittington and Jack and the Beanstalk on the English mind; and it means that the German imagination was at once richly fecundated and bound to a primitive fantasy dangerous for civilized adults.

"I remember this hall so well," said an old French writer, looking about him as he entered the Schloss. "I visited this house often. I know many Bavarian families, and these people were among the most agreeable of them. They were not Nazi, but the last time I came here a most unpleasant incident occurred. I was staying near here, and my friends brought me over to dinner, and I entered this hall at the same time as the young wife of a German whom I had known since he was a boy, whose father and grandfather I had known. They were remarkable people, with a fine record of academic distinction and public service. She stood there looking charming in a beautiful sable cape; and something she said at once reminded me that I had heard a rumour in Berlin that she had become the mistress of Goebbels, and made it seem certain that the rumour was true. I never came here again." One's mind went out into the English park, to the marble old gentleman who stood with his son and daughter in the memorial pavilion, the founder against his will of this fantastic house, and its violated victim.

Now the villa was taking its due punishment. During the trial it could count itself a haunted house; the handful of correspondents who reported the sittings day in day out grew as wistful as ghosts in their exile. But as the time for the verdicts and the sentences came nearer, it was invaded by a crowd of journalists of all nationalities, their spirits undiluted by tedium, who poured over its threshold, mocking the architectural fantasy that was to shelter them; and indeed it was ironical to cross a dreaded frontier in order to report the last convulsion of a German crime and find oneself housed in a German fairy tale. Many of them were shabbily dressed—indeed, only the Americans were not, for there were still no clothes in Europe—and they brought squalor with them, for there were so many of them that every bedroom had to be crammed with hospital beds for their use, and there were queues outside the bathrooms and the lavatories.

The Victorian villa in the grounds was not spared, and was as overfull. In its principal bedroom there slept nine women journalists, one a lovely North African girl, with crenellated hair and skin the colour of cambric tea; another a French girl, manifestly so ill that she ought to have been in hospital but quite unconcerned about herself, for she had spent all her adult life in the resistance movement and had no experience of well-being by which to check her state. Nothing can have been so offensive to the spirit of the Schloss as these women correspondents. Its halls had been designed for women who lived inside their corsets as inside towers, whose hair was made into a solid and intricate artifact halfway towards being a hat, whose feet were encased in shoes that prevented them from hurrying and advertised their enjoyment of infinite leisure. Now Madeleine Jacob burned the air in the corridors, she rushed so fast along them; her long black locks, so oddly springing from the circle of white hair in the centre of her scalp, hung about her shoulders; she wore a crumpled white blouse and a pleated skirt of a tartan which struck a Scottish eye like a misprint; there were beach sandals on her feet because there were still no leather shoes in France; her superbly Jewish face was at once haggard and bright with contentious intellectual gaiety. It would have been very hard for the builders of the Schloss to grasp the situation: to understand that these ink-stained gipsies had earned the right to camp in their stronghold because they had been on the side of order against disorder, stability against incoherence.

There was nowhere in the Schloss where one could be alone. Everyone's bedroom became full of people sitting about because their own bedrooms were full of people sitting about because they too had found their bedrooms full. There was much talking round the bar, though never about Germany, which was known to be dead and buried. It seemed good in the golden autumn evening to walk in the garden; and when the setting sun discovered a greenhouse roof, to go and see how the Germans had kept that form of luxury going. It would presumably be like most greenhouses in England, haunted by red spider, a desert place of shabby and unpainted staging, meagrely set out with a diminished store of seed boxes, for it was not large enough to have been used for any extensive scheme of food production. It seemed probable that the only view of it would be through the glass, since surely the door would be locked, as it was now late in the evening. But the door was open; and it admitted to a scene far distant in time and space. This might have been a greenhouse in one of the great English or Scottish nursery gardens, before 1939; or one might push the date back further, to a time when labour was still cheap. There was perfect cleanliness and perfect neatness here, and it was full of plants, each of which had that simple and integrated appearance which meant that the gardener who grew it understood many things and never wearied in applying his wisdom. There was a row of canna lilies, scarlet and orange and crimson, bright with health; there were many obconica primulas, which perfectly exhibited their paradoxical character of being open-faced and brilliant and yet recognizably members of a shy and cool family; and there were rows upon rows of beautifully grown cyclamen which would have done credit to a specialist firm. Amateurs of this plant often liken its flowers to butterflies, for the petals are like wings; and it could be imagined that these might suddenly flutter on the sober foliage and soar in a red and white and rose swarm. One of the white varieties, with large white ruffled petals that gave especially strongly this sense of arrested motion, was like a known face; and, indeed, one of the American lawyers had several of these in his office in the Palace of Justice. But of course one had seen these cyclamens all over Nuremberg; and when a girl of twelve or thirteen laid down her watering can and came forward, she had the air of a practised saleswoman and knew the names of the plants in English.

It might seem that it would never be very interesting that somebody had started a brisk business in potted plants. But this was Germany, this was 1946, and it was as if one were in a lock, and saw the little trickle of water between the gates which meant that the lock was opening. The war had burned trade off Germany as flame burns skin off a body. This greenhouse was on the outskirts of a large town in which it was impossible to buy anything at all except foodstuffs, except in the second-hand market; there was no way of acquiring even such necessities as shoes or kettles or blankets or chairs or tables. This had come about automatically when the civil structure of Germany collapsed and the transport and postal and power systems ceased to operate. It was obviously the aim of the Allies to restore German trade, for they had rejected the Morgenthau Plan for the reduction of Germany to a needy agricultural state; but at present the power of buying and selling consumer goods was exercised only by the occupying forces within the enclaves of PX and the English and French equivalents. But here in this greenhouse the trading genius of the Germans was reasserting itself in what was probably an amusing and impudent way. For it seemed likely that this greenhouse had been kept going during the war in defiance of Hitler's rules and regulations, and that it was now defying the Allies' rules and regulations, since certainly they could not wish that German fuel and labour should be used for flower-growing.

This greenhouse was of the spacious type to be found in old-fashioned private gardens, halfway to being a winter garden, where the owner could stroll with his friends under the golden flowers of a Maréchal Niel climbing rose and inspect his collection of lilies; and it was plainly inconvenient for commercial use. It looked as if there must be at least a couple of gardeners at work here, but there was only one man to be seen, who was closing a light at the other end of the greenhouse with a clumsiness which was explained when he stumped off on two crutches to another light. He had lost a leg. The twitch and roll, twitch and roll of his walk, recalled another difference between the British and the German lot. The Nazi government had shown a monstrous cruelty to its own people in two respects. They did not dig out their dead from the ruins after air raids. It was for this reason that all German towns stank on hot days in the summer of 1946, and that sometimes there would be seen on the rubble lit lanterns and wreaths, set out by mourners who were observing an anniversary. Neither did they make the proper effort to furnish artificial limbs for their war casualties, and an appalling number of one-armed and one-legged men were to be seen in the German streets. But surely post-Nazi cruelty was at work here. It seemed reprehensible of the other gardeners to have left this one-legged man to close up the greenhouse with only a child of twelve to help him.

But nobody was working in this greenhouse except this one-legged man and the child of twelve. He had been one of the gardeners at the Schloss before the war, and he had lost his leg on the Russian front, towards the end of the campaign. When he came out of hospital it had become known that the Nazi leaders were to be tried at Nuremberg, and that many Americans and some British and French would stay in the town for a long time. He had gone to the owner of the Schloss and suggested that the greenhouse should be used for raising potted plants to sell to the victors, and had been told that he might do what he could with it. It had not been used for a long time, and there were only a few plants in stock, but he got hold of as many others as he could find in the district, and started propagation at once, and got the winter heating going on wood from the grounds. To run a greenhouse furnace on wood must demand vigilance by night and by day; and to this man it meant hobbling and perilous bending. He had got quite a lot of cyclamens in flower at the end of May, but it afflicted him sorely that he had had only a few to satisfy the Christmas market. He betrayed a deep regret that the trial was not going on over next Christmas, so that he could have a chance to sell a really large number of his cyclamens. This was not altogether because he wanted the profit on them; it was also because he knew that they were good, very good, though not, he mentioned with disquiet, so good as some he had seen in Dutch nursery gardens. He was not an unhappy man. He was certainly in a state of continual physical discomfort, for before he could perform any task with his hands he had to manœuvre himself into a position where his balance was firm; and the child could help him only out of school hours. But he had escaped to another dimension where pain had no power over him. He had escaped into his work.

There are, of course, countless workmen in other countries who, like this man, are industrious to the point of nobility; but there was something different and peculiarly German and dynamic in his self-dedication. In these other countries a good or a bad workman will enjoy his leisure, take pride in proving his worth in his trade-union branch, and will be prepared to argue that he and every man ought to be many-sided. But this grower of potted plants saw himself simply as a grower of potted plants, and was more than satisfied with that limitation; indeed, it was to him not a limitation at all, it was enfranchisement. He would have had no sympathy with a British workman's innocent desire to win a football pool and leave his job and escape in the holiday of independent means, or with the French workman's recurrent impulse to break the bars of the rigid industrial system in which he feels himself imprisoned and escape into a strike. He did not want to escape from his greenhouse, he wanted to escape into it. This did not necessarily demonstrate that he had a more agreeable character. Indeed, it might be alleged that he wanted to take shelter in his labour only because he and his kind had shown an exceptional disability to make the rest of life agreeable. But it gave him as a grower of potted plants a certain advantage over other growers of potted plants with different ideas of liberation; and when he spoke it was not to pass the time of day, not to relax in gossip after the long working hours, not to inform himself how it was going with his former leaders, but to ask questions relating to the exploitation of this advantage. He wanted to know how many trials were likely to be held in Nuremberg now that this one was finished, and whether as many Americans and British and French officials would be here to conduct these others; and it was plain that though he was aware that he would be told that the number would be less, he longed to hear that it would be not much less. He inquired whether any of the English people now here would be likely to stop off in Holland on the way home and would be able to send him Dutch seeds. He would have had more to say, but the greenhouse was getting dark. Above it the gabled and turreted Schloss was steeply and mysteriously misshapen against the stars, and scores of yellow windows told where the conquerors would sit among smoke and talk away the night.

❖❖ 3 ❖❖

It was necessary, and really necessary, that a large number of persons, including the heads of the armed and civil services, should go to Nuremberg and hear the reading of the judgment, because in no other conceivable way could they gather what the trial had been about. Long, long ago, the minds of all busy people outside the enclave of Nuremberg had lost touch with the proceedings. The newspaper reports inevitably concentrated on the sensational moments when the defendants sassed back authority, and to follow the faint obtrusions of the serious legal issues which made their way into the more serious journals would have taken the kind of mind which reads its daily Scripture portion and never misses; and that kind of persistence carries one irresistibly to the top of the grocery store, and no further. The high positions fall to people with pliant minds, who drop every habit if it is not serviceable to their immediate aims, and thus it was that the most influential classes in 1946 knew little or nothing about the Nuremberg trial.

It was unfortunate that since the European railway systems were still disorganized the only way open to Nuremberg was by air. This would always have presented a tough transport problem, for planes carry so few passengers, but it was made worse by demobilization, for a great many pilots had been liberated to civil life. Hence, though Nuremberg is normally between three or four hours distant from London by air, those who wanted to be at Nuremberg on Monday, September 30, had to leave London in a series of flights that began on the previous Tuesday, and had, unless they were very distinguished, to undergo a journey through Kafka territory. They did not simply get a plane ticket and a *laisser passer* and a passport visa; they had to apply for their army papers at the offices of the German branch of the Foreign Office and Allied Control Commission. There was nothing to grumble about in this; for obviously people could not be allowed to wander about in recently occupied territory without proper identification papers and definitions of their permitted scope, but it was equally impossible for the officials in Germany to scrutinize these papers, because they had too much to do in coping with other problems created by the travellers.

One party had to go to Nuremberg by way of Berlin, where grave young men welcomed our plane in the belief that it contained a quite different set of persons. It was apparent that in England there was a superb system for dispatching visitors to Germany, and in Germany a superb system for receiving visitors from England, but just at that moment they had ceased to have any connection with each other. The grave young men irritably told the two correspondents among the passengers that they had better get on the next plane to London and start afresh, for they had no idea how to get them from Berlin to Nuremberg. They had no time— and this was true—they really had no time, to look at the correspondents' army orders, which contained an answer to that perplexity. The correspondents thought it wise to get into an automobile that was waiting for someone else, and since the driver was one of those eccentrics who in all branches of the services in Germany were replacing the more normal types as they were demobilized, he fell in with the fraud, not humorously, but because, he said carefully, like a hypochondriac, making a change now and then did everybody good; it didn't do to keep in a groove. Let such disorganization never be mocked. It is inevitable.

It was an excellent automobile for occupied Germany. It whizzed along the long sandy road beside the smiling suburban lakes, and then the individual horror of bombed Berlin suddenly declared its character. Different towns have different modes of desolation. There was at first sight no rubble here, and few waste lots, but mile after mile of huge hollow houses, winnowed by the wind and rain, mere diagrams of habitation. Piranesi, after a lifetime spent drawing the well-fleshed architecture of the Romans and their Renaissance descendants, was smitten in his later years with madness and drew buildings as majestic but stripped to the bare brick and dedicated to the harsh necessity of being prisons. Berlin had suffered just that change. It had boasted many gross avenues, lined with gross houses, grossly ornamented. The shells of these houses still stood. Often it could have been imagined that the whole house still stood, though stripped of all ornament, to serve some utilitarian purpose, to be a better workhouse or barracks. But the glassless windows looked inward through the roomless ruin to the other glassless windows on the farther side and showed the empty sky beyond, in a maniac stare.

It was not easy to know what the Berliners were feeling. The women walking in the streets wore better winter coats than we in England had seen for years. The theatres were open. There was an Oscar Wilde season; the photographs showed that the dresses were beautiful. But of course no individual and no institution was the same in this city which, while London had been chastised with whips, had been chastised with scorpions; and one was always being disconcerted by coming on a familiar form without its familiar content. The lower parts of the wrecked buildings were being restored as shops, and quite a number of them were being opened as bookshops. German bookshops had rarely, if ever, pleased like the best English and French and Finnish book-shops, but they had been the outlets of an immensely powerful and efficient publishing trade. Now, however, they merely contained Allied propaganda and a certain number of other volumes which offered some German authors a uniquely disagreeable form of fame. Each bookshop exhibited a great many copies of a few works by unknown German authors, and it was obvious that when these booksellers had started work again under licence from the Allies they had been forced to restock their shelves by exhuming remainders of books which had been published before the war, had fallen flat, and had therefore been warehoused. Such a remark as, "I say, old man, I see your study of Angelus Silesius all over the place these days," must have been suffused with an offensiveness which it would have lacked anywhere else in the world.

The cafés too were open, and they were crowded; the crowds were neither munching sausage nor forking up cream cake; they were sitting over glasses of pale liquid which obviously had not cheered them, staring at the traffic, a spectacle which could not cheer them, for it consisted solely of Allied automobiles bearing Allied personnel about the business of occupation. And shopping was still going on in streets where, in the good old days of the boom under the Weimar Republic, shoppers plump with power slowly strolled before huge plate-glass windows so inordinately stocked with goods that the vice of overshopping appeared before the mind not less disgusting than overeating; but now the shoppers never looked right or left of them, they hurried to the street corners, where there were screens plastered with announcements of goods offered in barter, and hurried on hungrily if they did not see what they hoped.

Most of the business of clearing up bomb damage was, for some obscure reason, done by ageing women. Looking down the road at the foundations of a fire-gutted building which had just been blown up, one saw a gang of them shovelling the bricks into hand carts. A superintendent would shout something jocular at them as he left them, and they would halt for a minute and scream mocking answers and then stand grinning in the sunlight, their grey hairs falling stiff as bootlaces round their leathery faces, their bodies a mixture of bones and crumpled stuffs like unrolled umbrellas, their lean hands hardly more like flesh than their tools. They were a true occasion for love.

In bombed cities the misadventures which overtake works of art are always extremely poignant, because obviously they are not to blame. It was possible to argue that nobody need weep for the citizens of Berlin, because they did not know enough to come in out of the rain, even when it turned into blood; but nobody expects a statue to know when to come in out of the rain, so pity could be freely extended to the statues of Berlin, which have had as extraordinary misadventures as any statuary in the world. At the end of the Unter den Linden was the Brandenburger Thor, with the Reichstag beside it, and in front of it the Tiergarten, a vast wooded park, far more thickly wooded than any park in New York or London or Paris. In this area sculpture had been given its head under the Kaisers, and it had proved that commissions to artists need not necessarily be stimulants to art. Opposite the Thor, by the Reichstag, there was a huge column commemorating the three victorious wars waged by the Germans in the nineteenth century, the wars against Denmark, Austria, and France. Nearby were two massive statues of von Moltke and General Roon, and a still more monstrous statue of Bismarck, with a number of women round the base, with breasts like artillery pieces. Not far away, in a part of the Tiergarten always full of nannies and children, because a prosperous residential district lay near, was the Sieges Allee, a gorgeous chaplet of dynastic piety. Sculptured in marble white like the icing on a wedding cake, the Margraves of Brandenburg and their descendants the Hohenzollerns stood in family groups in odd raised marble enclosures like open opera loges. There were enough of them to line a long promenade, and in the surrounding glades was a rose garden presided over by a statue of one of the Hohenzollern empresses, wearing scrupulously finished marble clothes, even to a marble hat and a marble veil. There was also a statue of a nude girl riding a horse, more naturalistic than nature but very pleasant to come on in a walk under the tall trees.

All these statues except the two women, the empress with the marble hat and the girl with none, were picked up and moved by

Hitler. He did not want anything to remind the people of the Hohenzollerns or their servants or their victories. The vast column commemorating the three wars he moved into the Tiergarten, almost a mile down the avenue, and he set down the statues of Bismarck and Moltke and Roon round it; and he transferred the Sieges Allee to an unfrequented part of the park. It may be argued that the German people showed culpable negligence in not taking this act of extravagance and folly as a warning and rising against Hitler. Even if the Germans did not know about the concentration camps they must have known about this transfer of statuary. Should an American President move the Washington Square Arch to Brooklyn and the Lincoln Memorial to a playground in Georgetown, or a British Prime Minister move the Albert Memorial to a public garden in Hammersmith, and did so for political reasons, even if the mass of the population did not suspect anything, the people who worked round him would, and restrictive action would be taken.

The statues gained by the change. They were set deeper among the trees, they lost their smugness, they looked as if they were part of the setting of a romantic drama. But at the end of the war they had suffered a further change which lifted them out of their poor place as artifacts into Lear's kingdom of loss. The trees of the Tiergarten had in 1946 been nearly all destroyed. Some were burned in the air raids, others were hit by Russian artillery during the battle for the capital, most of them were cut down by the freezing population during the first winter after the war. Now the great park was nothing but a vast potato patch, with here and there a row of vegetables and a plot of tobacco plants. From this naked land rose the statues in starkly inappropriate prominence. Above them the column of the three victorious wars was surmounted by the French flag, since this was in the French Sector, and the horizon was bounded by riddled cliffs which were once splendid villas and apartment houses. But, as well as this landscape-wide humiliation, they had suffered more private troubles. The charge that the Red Army is illiterate was forever disproved. The pedestals of Moltke and Roon, the bellies of the women who sprawl round the base of the Bismarck memorial, were scrawled with the names and addresses of Russian soldiers.

The Empress Victoria had lost her marble veil, her marble hat, her marble head. Decapitated, she stood among the pergolas. The Sieges Allee had suffered a peculiar loss of the same sort. The statues and busts were left intact; they belong to a kind of realistic art greatly admired by the Russians. But each of the marble loges is decorated on each side by a Hohenzollern eagle, and every one of these had been decapitated, very neatly, and evidently by a suitable instrument. Only the naked girl was as she had been, but there were marks of attempts to get her off her horse. She could be seen a long way off over the bare ground.

There is no statuary at all near the Brandenburger Thor, except a memorial to the Russian troops, which is surmounted by a realistic figure bearing a fantastic resemblance to Mussolini. The sentry who guarded it was, like so many of the Russian soldiers in Berlin, a ravishing small boy, with pink cheeks and a nose that turned up to heaven with the gravity of prayer. But one did not see a large number of troops in the streets of the Russian Sector; and, indeed, few troops were visible in any sector. The machinery of the Four Power control of Berlin was masked; but how many officials were labouring at their desks to coordinate what was too complex to be coordinated became manifest when the traveller found himself uncomfortably uncoordinated. This inevitably happened to those who took this route to Nuremberg, for authority in England had allowed travellers to the trial to take with them letters of credit, which, however, new currency regulations that had just come into effect made it extremely difficult to cash, a turn of events which seemed to surprise authority in Germany as much as the travellers. But even when finesse of a hardly defensible kind got the letters of credit cashed in British scrip money, there was the problem of buying a plane ticket to Nuremberg, which had to be paid for in dollars. Newspapermen in the hotel in the Kurfürstendam which was the Berlin press camp affirmed that British scrip could be turned into American scrip in a certain bar; and authority, asked for an assurance that this could safely be done without risk of deportation, looked embarrassed and pretended not to hear. In the bar the service was rendered by a number of persons whose manner was disconcerting, for they voluptuously drooped their lids and dilated their nostrils while haggling over the exchange value of British and American scrip, in obedience to habits formed before the war, when they lived by procuring cocaine and other pleasures of the flesh. It was an odd experience to owe to authority. But let none mock at such disorganization. No great international event can be efficiently organized. There are conceivable feats of coordination which are beyond performance.

There came an afternoon which, it seemed to the two correspondents who had met on the plane from London, might well be spent visiting the Führerbunker, the air-raid shelter under Hitler's Chancellery. But authority pronounced that impossible. It was in the Russian Sector, and the Russians had set their face against any more visitors, and had just recently flatly refused to let a very distinguished party of Britons see it. It was plain that there was complete understanding on this point between the Four Powers' administrations at a high level; and from this, given the incoherence of the general situation, a conclusion could be drawn. It proved to be sound. The place was quite easy to visit. From the shadows a courteous and informed presence detached itself, who knew the terrain well, who had visited it often from the very first days after the fall of Berlin, who was anxious to earn some cigarettes, which were then the only hand-to-hand German currency. He knew at what point it was prudent to stop the Allied automobile, which had come into service for the afternoon's expedition without anybody's consent or knowledge, but not against anybody's expressed wish. The Russian sentry at the portal, snub-nosed and squat and smiling, was glad to see visitors, glad to accept a carton of cigarettes.

The Chancellery was another of these Berlin shells, flooded with sallow light; and the yellow-skinned Russian sentries, standing about in its vast punctured halls, looked like so many submerged Buddhas. In Hitler's Hall of Mirrors, a specially genial soul, with several chins and jolly slit eyes, who had been impassively watching a party of workmen hacking down the slabs of marble and porphyry which lined the walls between the shattered mirrors or their empty sockets, complained that people were losing interest in the place and hardly ever came there now. Another soldier paced out the Banqueting Hall to show its excessive length, which

seemed to him a huge joke. It was obvious that none of them
had ever heard of any order that visitors must be excluded. It
might have been, however, that the Russians had meant to give
such an order. They may have wanted the world to forget the
bunker. This was probable because of the difference between the
Allies regarding Hitler's fate. It was the British and American
theory that Hitler had committed suicide in the bunker on April
30, 1945, and the Russian authorities publicly accepted this view.
But in Moscow at the end of May and in June, and again in July
at Potsdam, Stalin informed various American officials that he
believed Hitler to be still alive; and this was in 1946 (and indeed
up till Stalin's death) the Soviet doctrine.

The bunker, however, was wide open to anyone who cared to
call. The Chancellery filled a corner site, the two blocks containing the Gallery of Mirrors and the Banqueting Hall forming a
right angle, within which lay a garden, now overgrown with long
grasses. Under a tree which autumn had just touched two English
soldiers sat with two German girls on a pile of bricks. One was
rhythmically squeezing his girl's waist and the other was stroking
his girl's bosom with a slow, massaging movement, therapeutic
rather than voluptuous, which suggested that he might at one
time have been in the Royal Army Medical Corps, while they
carried on a repetitive argument about football. The girls' faces
were quite blank, as if they belonged to some contemplative order
of prostitutes. A young Russian soldier stood near them, watching
them as if there was a long chance, on which he was not counting
but which he had to admit existed, that they might do something
novel and unexpected. Behind him was the door into the *Führerbunker,* which he was delighted to open for visitors even before
they produced cigarettes. Like his comrades, he enjoyed company.

A steep staircase descended fifty feet to the rooms in which
Hitler and Eva Braun, Goebbels and his wife and six children,
had died. These rooms were extremely disconcerting because of
their proportions. Hitler's Chancellery, like all the buildings for
which he was responsible, was vast because it was the result of a
soiled and limited flight of the imagination. A man who sold patent
medicine at a carnival, and was an abortionist and a fortune-teller
on the side, might, if he had been granted power to build as he

would, have remembered pictures he had seen of Egyptian temples and Roman palaces and, not remembering them clearly enough, have given orders for such huge, featureless constructions. But the thirty rooms in the bunker, though Hitler had had the resources of Germany to lavish on it, were in shocking contrast with the swollen halls above them. For an air-raid shelter it was perversely sordid. The rooms were small squares, the size of bathrooms in an ordinary suburban house, with a central passage cut into three sections about the size of a compartment in an English railway train, which served as the general dining room and sitting room and the conference room. The walls were coated with some substance resembling lamp black, on which many soldiers had since the end of the war written their signatures. This was the time of Chads, when the English people's reaction to shortages was expressed on every blank space by drawings showing a bald head with a single upgrowing hair poking over the top of a wall, with the legend, "What, no soap?" or sugar, or whatever it was that was most drearily lacking. Here a British soldier had drawn a Chad who looked over the wall and said, "What, no Führer?" These signatures and his drawing came out ghostly white on the black wall. It was as if one stood in a train that was quietly running into hell.

The Russian soldier pointed to the Chad and laughed. He did not know what the Chad was saying but he knew that it was meant to be funny, and he wanted everything to be funny, and he imagined he was helping things along in that direction by laughing. The courteous German presence nodded his head and smiled at him, to show his good will, and said, "Look, this is very singular. This curious cupboard place was called the *Hundebunker,* the dog bunker. Hitler's bodyguard used to sit here, and so it might just have been a nickname, but I think not; it is so oddly shaped a room that I think it really was designed for some pet dog. And you will see it is far more generously planned than any of the accommodation for human beings."

Suddenly it became very unpleasant to be in this insanely devised rat hole, where six children had been murdered by their father and mother, for no particular reason, since surely the Goebbels must have had relatives to whom they could have confided their family. It seemed good to run upstairs into the garden, pushing past one of the British soldiers and his girl, who were standing against the bunker door being photographed by his comrade. The Russian soldier followed and, wagging his head and smiling, repeated something over and over again. He was saying that he too often got very frightened, terribly frightened, at being so deep underground. "They are often very kind," said the courteous German presence. He meant the Russians. Yet during the drive from the press camp he had been saying that because of what he had seen when the Red Army entered Berlin he wanted to leave the city, though he had been born here, and never see it again; and he was speaking the truth, for a wave of sickness turned him green as he spoke. He was always thinking of the Russians, whose might was a sea round the small island of safety where he had a foothold. All Berliners were always thinking of the Russians. It was that preoccupation which made them different from the Nurembergers.

◈◈ 4 ◈◈

The system, with all its failures, got the travellers to Nuremberg in good time. At once a split appeared between those who had come to the trial for, say, the opening and these last two days, and those who had a longer experience of the sessions. The court had issued a directive that no photographs were to be taken of the defendants at the times they were being sentenced. This seemed to some journalists who had just arrived a shocking interference with the rights of the press, and even some historians thought that it would leave the film record of the case regrettably incomplete. But those who had frequented the court over months were for the most part of a different mind.

The issue pricked deep because it was certain that some of the defendants would be sentenced to death. It seemed that when people had never seen a man, or had seen him only once or twice, they did not find anything offensive about the idea of photographing him while he was being sentenced to death, but that if people had seen him often the idea became unattractive. The correspondents who had attended the court day in, day out, knew how the defendants had hated the periods of each session when it was part of the routine for the cameras to be put on. Most of them reached for their black glasses when the sharp and acid lights were switched on, with a sullenness which meant that they were doing more than merely trying to save their eyes; and those who most often resorted to those black glasses were those who had manifested the greatest repentance. Dr. Frank, who had murdered Poland and had been driven by remorse into a Catholic conversion which the authorities believed to be sincere, was always the first to put out his hand to his spectacle case. It might be right to hang such men. But it could not be right to photograph them when they were being told that they were going to be hanged. For when society has to hurt a man it must hurt him as little as possible and must preserve what it can of his pride, lest there should spread in that society those feelings which make men do the things for which they get hanged.

But though it might be right to hang these men, it was not easy. A sadness fell on the lawyers engaged in the trial. They had all been waiting for this day when judgment would be delivered and the defendants sentenced, and they could get back to the business of living. They had all surely come to loathe the Nazi crimes and criminals more and more in the slow unfolding of the case. But now this day of judgment had come they were not happy. There was a gloom about the places where they lived, a gloom about their families. In these last days of the trial all automobiles were stopped on the main roads for search and scrutiny by the military police. At a search post two automobiles were halted at the same time, and a visitor travelling in one saw that in the other was the wife of one of the judges, a tall Scandinavian notable for her physical and spiritual graces. They exchanged greetings, and the visitor said, "I shall be seeing you in court tomorrow." The other looked as if she had been slapped across the high cheekbones. "Oh no," she said. "Oh no. I shall not be in court tomorrow." Yet she had attended almost all other sessions of the court. Around the house of another judge a line of automobiles waited all the evening before the day of judgment, and passers-by knew that the judiciary was having its last conference. The judge's wife came to the window and looked out over the automobiles and the passers-by into the pine woods which ringed the house. But as she stared out into the darkening woods it could be seen on her sensitive face that she was living through a desert of time comparable to the interval between a death and a funeral.

There was another house in the outskirts of Nuremberg where this profound aversion from the consequences of the trial could be perceived. This, like the press camp, was a villa which an industrialist had built beside his factory, but it was smaller and not so gross, and it had been the scene of a war of taste which had in the long run been won by the right side. The industrialist had furnished it in the style of a Nord-Amerikan liner; but he had had two sons, who, according to the patriarchal system of his class, lived in the villa, the older on the first floor, the younger on the top floor. One of them had married a Frenchwoman who was still in the house, silently and efficiently acting as butler to the conquerors, with an exquisite and chivalrous care not to detach herself from the conquered, since her marriage vows had placed her in their company. She had a deep knowledge and love of Greek art and of the minor Italian masters of the sixteenth and seventeenth centuries. Most of her collections had been taken from her at the beginning of the war by the German government and stored in caves. When defeat came the guards in charge of the caves ran away, and the stores were rifled. She went there to look for her goods, and found some shards of her Greek vases trodden into the earth at the mouth of the caves, and nothing else. But she had insisted on keeping with her some of her Greek sculptures, and they still stood in the house among monstrous Japanese bronzes and moustachioed busts of the men of the family. In one room there were two marbles which, in the Greek way, presented the whole truth about certain moments of physical existence. There was a torso which showed how it is with a boy's body, cut clean with training, when the ribs rise to a deep and enjoyed breath; and there was the coiffed head of a girl who knew she was being looked at by the world, and, being proud and innocent, let it look.

The approach to this house at night was melancholy. About it, as about all houses inhabited by legal personnel, armed guards paced, and searchlights shone into the woods. The white beams changed to crudely coloured cardboard the piebald trunks of the

birch trees, the small twisted pines, the great pottery jars over-
flowing with nasturtiums which marked the course of the avenues.
From the darkness above, moth-pale birch leaves fell slowly,
turned suddenly bright yellow in the searchlight beam, and drifted
slowly down to the illuminated ground. Autumn was here, winter
would be here soon. People concerned with the trial drove through
these sad avenues and were welcomed into the house, and sat
about in its great rooms, holding glasses of good wine in their
hands, and talked generously of pleasant things and not of the
judgment and the sentences, and looked at the Greek sculptures
with a certain wonder and awe and confusion. If a trial for murder last too long, more than the murder will out. The man in the
murderer will out; it becomes horrible to think of destroying
him.

❖❖ 5 ❖❖

Monday, September 30, 1946, was one of those glorious days
that autumn brings to Germany, heavy and golden, yet iced, like
an iced drink. By eight o'clock a fleet of Allied automobiles, collected from all over Western Germany, was out in the countryside
picking up the legal personnel and the visitors from their billets
and bringing them back to the Palace of Justice. The Germans
working in the fields among the early mists did not raise their
heads to look at the unaccustomed traffic, though the legal personnel, which had throughout the trial gone about their business
unattended, now had armed military police with screaming sirens
in jeeps as outriders.

This solemn calm ended on the doorstep of the Palace of Justice. Within there was turbulence. The administration of the court
had always aroused doubts, by a certain tendency toward the bizarre, which manifested itself especially in the directions given to
the military police in charge of the gallery where the VIPs sat. The
ventilation of the court was bad, and the warm air rose to the
gallery, so in the afternoon the VIPs were apt to doze. This struck
the commandant, Colonel Andrus, as disrespectful to the court,
though the gallery was so high that what went on there was

unlikely to be noticed. Elderly persons of distinction, therefore, enjoyed the new experience of being shaken awake by young military policemen under a circle of amused stares. If they were sitting in the front row of the gallery an even odder experience might overtake them. The commandant had once looked up at the gallery and noted a woman who had crossed her ankles and was showing her shins and a line of petticoat, and he conceived that this might upset the sex-starved defendants, thus underestimating both the length of time it takes for a woman to become a VIP and the degree of the defendants' preoccupations. But, out of a further complication of delicacy, he forbade both men and women to cross their ankles. Thus it happened that one of the most venerable of English judges found himself, one hot summer afternoon, being tapped on the shoulder with a white club by a young military policeman and told to wake up, stay awake, and uncross his legs.

These rules were the subject of general mirth in Nuremberg, but the higher American authorities neither put an end to them nor took their existence as a warning that perhaps the court should be controlled on more sensible lines. An eccentricity prevailed which came to its climax in the security arrangements for these two final days. There was a need for caution. Certainly in Berlin nobody would have lifted a finger to avenge the Nazis, but here in Bavaria there were still some people who had never had any reason to feel that the Nazi regime had been a bad thing for them, and among them there must have been some boys who had been too young for military service and had enjoyed their time with Hitler Youth. It might also have been that Martin Bormann, who at the end of the war had replaced Göring, and who was said to have been killed by Russian fire after escaping from the Chancellery, and who was being indicted *in absentia* at this trial, might now choose to reappear.

It therefore seemed obvious that there would be stringent precautions to see that no unauthorized person entered the Palace of Justice, and we had imagined that we would have to queue up before a turnstile, by which competent persons would sit and examine our passes under a strong light. There was a rumour that there was a mark on the passes which would show only under

X-rays. But, instead, authority jammed the vast corridors of the Palace of Justice with a mass of military police, who, again and again, demanded the passes of the entrants and peered at them in a half-light. It was extremely unlikely that these confused male children could have detected the grossest forgery, but the question was never posed, for the corridor was so dark that it was difficult to read large print. No attempt had been made to clarify the situation by posting at strategic points men who could recognize the legal personnel; and thus it happened that, outside the judges' entrance to the courtroom, a military policeman, switching his white club, savagely demanded, "And how the hell did you get in here?" of a person who was in fact one of the judges. In the midst of this muddle certain precautionary measures were taken which were at once not strict enough and too strict and quite ineffectual.

Men were forbidden to take briefcases into court, and women were forbidden to carry handbags or wear long coats. These prohibitions were undignified and futile. Women's suits are not made with pockets large enough to hold passes, script, fountain pens, notebooks, and spectacle cases, and few women went into court without a certain amount of their possessions packed away inside their brassieres or stocking tops. One French woman journalist, obedient to the ban on long coats, came in a padded jacket which she had last worn on an assignment in the Asiatic theatre of war, and when she was sitting in court discovered that in the holster pocket over her ribs she had left a small loaded revolver. It may look on paper as if those responsible for the security arrangements at Nuremberg could justify themselves by pointing to the fact that the Palace of Justice was not blown up. But those who were there know that there was just one reason for this: nobody wanted to blow it up. But although the problem raised by Nuremberg security need not have been approached so eccentrically, it never could have been brought to a satisfactory solution. There were no persons qualified by experience to take control at a high level, for there had never been a like occasion; and there was not such a superfluity of customs officials and police workers that a large number of them could have been abstracted from their usual duties and seconded to special duties without harm; and if there had been, the business of transporting them and housing them would have created fresh problems. This was a business badly done, but it could have been done no better.

It seemed natural enough that nobody should have been very anxious to blow up the Palace of Justice when the defendants came into the dock that Monday. The court had not sat for a month, while the judges were considering their verdicts, and during that time the disease of uniformity which had attacked the prisoners during the trial had overcome them. Their pale and lined faces all looked alike; their bodies sagged inside their clothes, which seemed more alive than they were. They were gone. They were finished. It seemed strange that they could ever have excited loyalty; it was plainly impossible that they should ever attract it again. It was their funeral which the Germans were attending as they looked down on the ground when they walked in the streets of the city. Those Germans thought of them as dead.

They were not abject. These ghosts gathered about them the rags of what had been good in them during their lives. They listened with decent composure to the reading of the judgments, and, as on any other day, they found amusement in the judges' pronunciation of the German names. That is something pitiable which those who do not attend trials never see: the eagerness with which people in the dock snatch at any occasion for laughter. Sometimes it seems from the newspaper reports that a judge has been too facetious when trying a serious case, and the fastidious shudder. But it can be taken for granted that the accused person did not shudder, he welcomed the little joke, the small tear in the tent of grimness that enclosed him. These defendants laughed when they could, and retained their composure when it might well have cracked. On Monday afternoon the darkened mind of Hess passed through some dreadful crisis. He ran his hands over his brows again and again as if he were trying to brush away cobwebs, but the blackness covered him. All humanity left his face; it became an agonized muzzle. He began to swing backwards and forwards on his seat with the regularity of a pendulum. His head swung forward almost to his knees. His skin became blue. If one could pity Ribbentrop and Göring, then was the time. They had to sit listening to the judgment upon them while a lunatic swayed and experienced a nameless evil in the seat beside them. He was taken away soon, but it was as if the door of hell had swung ajar. It was apparent now, as on many occasions during the trial, that the judges found it repulsive to try a man in such a state; but the majority of the psychiatrists consulted by the court had pronounced him sane.

The first part of the judgment did not refer to the defendants but to bodies they had formed. It had been argued by the prosecution that the seven Nazi organizations—the Gestapo, SD,SS, Reich Cabinet, Corps of Political Leaders, General Staff and OKW, and Storm Troops—should be declared criminal in nature and that membership in them should by itself be the subject of a criminal charge. The judges admitted this in the cases of the first three, on the grounds that at an early date these organizations had so openly aimed at the commission of violence and the preaching of race hatred that no man could have joined them without criminal intent. The image of a rat in a trap often crossed the mind at Nuremberg, and it was evoked then. No man who had ever been an SS member could deny it. The initials and the number of his blood group were tattooed under his arm. But, of course, that trap did not spring. There were too many SS men, too many armpits, for any occupying force to inspect. The Storm Troopers were not put in the same category, because they were assessed as mere hooligans and bullies, too brutish to be even criminals. Of the others it was recognized that many persons must have joined them or consented to remain within them without realizing what Hitler was going to make of them. This was reasonable enough, for it meant that members of this organization could still be prosecuted if there was reason to believe they had committed crimes as a result of their membership.

But the refusal to condemn all the seven organizations was greatly resented by some of the spectators. It was felt to be a sign that the tribunal was soft and not genuinely anti-Nazi. This was partly due to temperamental and juristic differences among the nations. The four judges took turns at reading the judgment, and this section was read by the English member judge, Lord Oaksey. His father before him was a judge, who was Lord Chief Justice in the twenties; and he had the advantage which the offspring of an old theatrical family have over other actors. He had inherited the technique and he refined on it, and could get his effects economically. He read this passage of the judgment in a silver voice untarnished by passion, with exquisite point; but to a spectator who was not English it might have seemed that this was just one of the committee of an English club explaining to his colleagues that it was necessary to expel a member. The resemblance need not have been disquieting. People who misbehave in such clubs really do get expelled by their committees, and they remain expelled; whereas the larger gestures and rhetoric of history have often been less effective. But this was not understood by those whose national habit it is to cross-breed their judges with prosecutors or to think that the law should have its last say with a moralist twang.

There was, in other quarters, a like unease about the verdicts on the Service defendants, on Field Marshal Keitel and General Jodl and Admirals Doenitz and Raeder. Keitel and Jodl were found guilty on all four counts of the indictment: first, of conspiracy to commit the crimes alleged in the other counts, which were crimes against peace, crimes in war, and crimes against humanity. Raeder was found guilty on the three counts, and Doenitz was found guilty on the second. There was some feeling among those who attended only the end of the trial, and a very great deal of strong feeling among people all over the world who did not attend the court, that these defendants had been put into the dock for carrying out orders as soldiers and sailors must. But there is a great deal in the court's argument that the only orders a soldier or a sailor is bound to obey are those which are recognized practice in the Services of the time. It is obvious that if an admiral were ordered by a demented First Sea Lord to serve broiled babies in the officers' mess he ought to disobey; and it was shown that these generals and admirals had exhibited very little reluctance to carry out orders of Hitler which tended towards baby-broiling. Here was another point at which there was a split between the people who had attended the trial, or long stints of it, and the people who had not. Much evidence came up during the hearings which proved these men very different from what the products of Sandhurst and Dartmouth, West Point and Annapolis, are hoped to be. Doenitz, for example, exhorted his officers to be inspired

48

by the example of some of their comrades who, confined in a camp in Australia, found that there were a few Communists among the other captured troops, managed to distract the attention of the guards, and murdered these wretched men.

But it was in the case of the admirals that the court made a decision which proved Nuremberg to be a step farther on the road to civilization. They were charged with violating the Naval Protocol of 1936, which reaffirmed the rules of submarine warfare laid down in the London Naval Agreement of 1930. They had, and there was no doubt about it, ordered their submarines to attack all merchant ships without warning and not stop to save the survivors. But the tribunal acquitted them on this charge on the grounds that the British and the Americans had committed precisely the same offence. On May 8, 1940, the British Admiralty ordered all vessels in the Skagerrak to be sunk on sight. Also Admiral Nimitz stated in answer to interrogatories that unrestricted submarine warfare had been carried on by the American Navy in the Pacific Ocean from the first day that the campaign opened. The fact was that we and the Germans alike had found the protocol unworkable. Submarines cannot be used at all if they are to be obliged to hang about after they have made a killing and throw away their own security. The Allies admitted this by acquitting the admirals, and the acquittal was not only fair dealing between victors and vanquished, it was a step towards honesty. It was written down for ever that submarine warfare cannot be carried on without inhumanity, and that we have found ourselves able to be inhumane. We have to admit that we are in this trap before we can get out of it. This *nostra culpa* of the conquerors might well be considered the most important thing that happened at Nuremberg. But it evoked no response at the time, and it has been forgotten.

But in this court nothing could be clear-cut, and nothing could have a massive effect, because it was international, and international law, as soon as it escapes from the sphere of merchandise (in which, were men good, it would alone need to be busy), is a mist with the power to make solids as misty as itself. It was true that the Nazi crimes of cruelty demanded punishment. There in Nuremberg the Germans, pale among the rubble, were waiting for that punishment as a purification, after which they might regain their strength and rebuild their world; and it was obvious that the tribunal must sit to disprove Job's lament that the houses of the wicked are safe from fear. A tyrant had suspended the rule of law in his country and no citizen could seek legal protection from personal assault, theft, or imprisonment; and he had created so absolute a state of anarchy that when he fell from power the courts themselves had disappeared and could not be reconstituted to do justice on him and his instruments. Finally he had invaded other territories and reproduced this ruin there. Plainly some sort of emergency tribunal had to take over the work of the vanished tribunals when it was possible, if the Nazis were not to enjoy a monstrous immunity simply because they had included among their crimes the destruction of the criminal courts. It was only just that the Nazis should pay the due penalty for the offences they had committed against the laws of their own land, the millions of murders, kidnappings and wrongful imprisonments, and thefts. "Of course," people said then and still say, "it was right that the Nazis should have been punished for what they did to the Jews. To the left wing. To the religious dissidents. To the Poles. To the Czechs. To the French deportees. To half Europe. But aggressive war, that was a new crime, invented for the occasion, which had never been written on the statute books before." They spoke the very reverse of the truth. The condemnation of aggressive war as a crime was inherent in the Kellogg-Briand Pact; whereas no international body has ever given its sanction to a mechanism by which crimes committed in one nation which had gone unpunished because of a collapse of civil order could subsequently be punished by other nations. It is to be doubted whether the most speculative mind had ever drawn up the specification for such a mechanism.

Here one sees the dangers of international law. It would seem entirely reasonable to give nations which had remained at the common level of civilization the right to exercise judicial powers in nations which have temporarily fallen below that level and are unable to guarantee their citizens justice. But we can all remember how Hitler prefaced his invasions by pretences that civil order had been destroyed wherever there was a German minority, how it was roared at the world over the radio that Germans in Czecho-slovakia and Poland and Yugoslavia were being beaten in the streets and driven out of their houses and farms and were denied all police protection. Such an article of international law would give both knight-errantry and tyranny their marching orders. This, at Nuremberg, was not a remote consideration, though Germany seemed to lie dead around us. Each of the judges read some part of the judgment; and when the Russian had his turn there was a temptation not to give the earphones the right switch to the English version, for the Russian language rolled forth from the firm fleshy lips of this strong man like a river of life, a river of genius, inexhaustible and unpredictable genius. To listen to Slav oratory is to feel that Aksakov and Dostoevski and Bishop Peter Nyegosh had half their great work done for them by the language they used. But soon the desire to know what he was talking about proved irresistible. It turned out that the Russian was reading the part of the judgment that condemned the Germans for their deportations: for taking men and women away from their homes and sending them to distant camps where they worked as slave labour in conditions of great discomfort, and were often unable to communicate with their families. There was here a certain irony, and a certain warning.

The trouble about Nuremberg was that it was so manifestly a part of life as it is lived; the trial had not sufficiently detached itself from the oddity of the world. It was of a piece with the odd things that happened on its periphery; and these were odd enough. Some visitors to the trial were strolling through a village outside Nuremberg after the Monday session had ended, to freshen their brains with the evening air, when a frizzled and grizzled head was popped over a garden fence. There are women whom age makes look not like old women but immature apes, and this was one of them. She was not unlikeable, she was simply like an ape. She demanded, in English, to know whether we were English. Two of us were. "I shot your King Edward," she assured us, her bright eyes winking among her wrinkles, her teeth clacking at a different rate from her speech. In view of the occasion that had brought us to Nuremberg this seemed a not unlikely fantasy to vex a failing mind grounded in its environs, and there was the coo of "Yes,

yes, yes," of which lunatics must grow weary. But she stepped through her garden gate into the road, and one of the party, a devoted student of the text and illustrations in such books as the autobiographical works of the sixth Duke of Portland, recognized a familiar accent in the drain-pipe tweed coat, the thin ankles and high-arched feet turned outwards at an angle of forty-five degrees. "You mean you went shooting with King Edward?" she suggested. "Yes, yes, in your Norfolk!" Chattering like the monkeys in Gibraltar at sundown, she cried out the names of great English houses, of great English families, but briefly, for she had a more passionate preoccupation. "Well, have you sentenced all the scoundrels? What have they done to them?" She stamped her little foot on the ground. "What have they done to Sauckel? To Sauckel? That, that is what I wish to know."

It was explained to her that that day the judges had delivered judgment only on the Nazi organizations and the validity and significance of the indictment, and that the verdicts and sentences on the Nazi leaders would not be pronounced till tomorrow. She was disappointed. "I wanted to hear from you that Sauckel is to be hanged. I hope that I might have that good news. I shall not sleep happy till I have heard that that scoundrel pays for his crimes. Never," she cried, standing on tiptoe as if she were about to spring into the branches above us, "never will we undo the harm he did by bringing these wretched foreign labourers into our Germany. I had a nice house, *a home,* yes, *a home,* inherited from my family, in the village that is ten miles along the road, and what did this Sauckel do but send two thousand foreign workers to the factories in the district, two thousand wretches, cannibals, scum of the earth, Russians, Balks, Balts, Slavs—Slavs, I tell you. What did they do when our armies were defeated but break loose? For three days they kept carnival; they looted and they ate and drank of our goods. I had to hide with my neighbours in their cellar, and they slept in my bed and they ate in my kitchen and there was not a potato left, and they took all my good china and my linen and all they could carry, the brutes, the beasts!"

Somebody murmured that the foreign workers would have preferred to stay at home, and she glittered agreement. "Yes, yes, of course they should have been left at home, the place for a pig is in the sty. Oh, hanging will be too good for Sauckel, I could kill him with my own hands. You are doing very well at that trial. You English do all things well; we Germans should never have had a war with you. I am glad that you are giving"—she laughed— *"what for* to the Nazis. They were *canaille,* all of them. Not one had one known before, in the old days. But there is one quarrel I have with you. I am not against the Jews—of course it was terrible what Hitler did to the Jews, and none of us had any idea of what was going on in the camps—but to have a Jew as your chief prosecutor—really, really now, was that quite *gentleman?"* She looked from face to face in coquettish challenge. Nobody said anything, she was so very old. After a pause she pressed, "Was it now?" and shook her forefinger at us, showing a palm embarrassing to the sight, because it was tiny and plum-coloured and pulpy like the inside of a monkey's paw. Someone said sadly, "But Sir David Maxwell Fyfe is not a Jew." She gave a trill of kind but derisive laughter. "Oh, but I have seen him." "All the same, he is not a Jew. Some dark types of Scotsmen are very difficult to tell from Jews." "But how, how, can you be so simple?" she gasped into her handkerchief. "Think, you dear people, of the name. The name. David. Who would call his son David but a Jew?" "Many Englishmen, many Scotsmen, and a great many more Welshmen," she was told. She could not contain her laughter; it blew away from her in a trail of shrillness. "Oh, you English are so simple; it is because you are aristocrats. A man who called his son David might tell you that he was English or Scotch or Welsh, because he would know that you would believe him. But we Germans understand a little better about such things, and he would not dare to pretend to us that he was not a Jew."

From this village an agreeable path ran beside a stream for a mile or two, by woods and meadows, to one of the villas where guests were billeted. It was strange to follow that path alone, a conqueror walking unarmed among the conquered, during his climax of conquest. But unless some lunatic boy had run amok there was no danger. The peasants in the fields were as indifferent as the fields themselves; after a single sidelong glance they bent their heads again to look at the work they were doing to feed their kind. This was the spectacle which Germany presented at this time: the people had lost the wherewithal by which human beings live, the food, the clothing, the fuel, and they were making it again for themselves by a process which seemed as instinctive as a cow's growth of a thick coat for the wintertime. But though the peasants were working on into the evening hours, the town dwellers kept an easier urban schedule. The stream took a hairpin bend, and the path mounted a little bluff above the curve, and there, below it on a sandy patch by the water's edge, a town dweller was going through his exercises. The stream was at its deepest here, and he had been swimming. His trunks and his towel were neatly stretched out on the grass, and he was standing in his khaki shorts, slowly flailing his arms above his head and down to the ground. It was patent that he came from the town, for his body was city-white and he had been worse fed than the peasants were. Indeed, rarely can there have been a body so thin that was in such a state of muscular cultivation. He had little flesh on his bones, but even so it could be noted that it was not through starvation but through exercise that he had no belly; and when one of his arms windmilled up above his head, transmitting by the miracle of nervous force a command to his stomach muscle, which responded proudly, the concavity was still more concave. He was so absorbed in what he was doing that he did not know when he was watched. Between him and his body there was a real love. It was not vanity. He had a long and bony face, with high cheekbones and a tortured three-cornered mouth, thoughtful but not intelligent, even silly; and a silly German face can be much more alarming than a silly English face. But there was no threat of perversity about his tranced and anxious stare. Simply he had come a long way to bathe in a stream which here was clean, as it would not be when it reached the fouled city where he had to live, and now he was affirming that though he had lost everything else, he still had his body, he still had that surely quite remarkable stomach muscle, he still was his unique self.

The villa could be seen a long way off through the pine woods; all the rooms were lit up because there was going to be a dinner party, given for those so closely concerned with the trial that they would not wish to dine alone that night. The lights of the factory belonging to the villa owner shone behind the tree trunks, and the twilight was shaken by the hum of its dynamos. Here fertilizers were extracted from the air, and so it was working day and night to restore the starved fields of Germany. Along the gravel path there hurried towards the village a sober shadow of a woman who often helped in the house when there were parties, the wife, neither young nor old, of a foreman. She never spoke, she was not like the other servants, who were young and unembarrassed by conquest, but now she stopped and asked grimly and tersely what sentence the court had passed on Streicher. When she heard that he was still unsentenced she did not move on but halted, staring at a great earthenware vase that stood by the gravel path, reflectively, as if the nasturtium growing from it had some meaning for her. Then she expressed the hope that he would be hanged. She had always hoped that something would happen to him ever since he had come to the village one Sunday before the war. They had been told that he was coming to speak at the Town Hall, and the police had come round to tell them that they must all go to hear him and take their children. So she and her husband had dressed up their sons and daughter and gone to the hall, and Streicher had got up on the platform and had spoken about politics for some time, which, she said, with holy simplicity, "did nobody any harm." But quite suddenly he had begun to talk filth, gibbering filth about the Jews, describing the sexual offences he pretended they committed and the shameful diseases he pretended they spread, using dreadful words. She and her husband, and several other couples, had got up and led their children to the doors, but SS men were standing there and ordered them to return to their seats. Yes, quite young boys had forced her and her husband to stay with their children in this bath of mud. Again she fell silent, and her face was a solid white circle in the dusk. Then she burst into a rage of weeping, and went away.

❖❖ 6 ❖❖

The next day, the last day of the trial, there was something like hatred to be seen on the faces of many Germans in the street. The Palace of Justice was even fuller than before, the confusion engendered in the corridors by the inefficient scrutiny system was still more turbulent. There were some bad officials at Nuremberg, and that day they got completely out of hand. One of them, an American, male and a colonel, had always been remarkable for having the drooping bosom and resentful expression of a nursing mother who has had a difficult parturition, and for having throughout the trial nagged at the correspondents as if they were the staff of the maternity ward that had failed him. Hitherto he had not been arresting; the mind had simply noted him as infringing a feminine patent. But standing this day at the entrance of the gallery, staring at obviously valid passes, minute after minute, with the moonish look of a stupid woman trying to memorize the pattern of a baby's bootee, he was strangely revolting in his epicene distress.

The defendants were, however, quiet and cool. They were feeling the relief that many of us had known in little, when we had waited all through an evening for an air raid and at last heard the sirens, and, ironically, they even looked better in health. In the morning session they learned which of them the court considered guilty and which innocent, and why; and they listened to the verdicts with features decently blank except when they laughed. And, miraculously enough, they found the standing joke of the judges' pronunciation of German names just as funny today as before; and the acquittals amused them no end. Three of the defendants were found not guilty. One of these was a negative matter which caused no reaction except comradely satisfaction: that Hans Fritzsche, the radio chief of Goebbels' Propaganda Ministry, should have been found innocent recalled the case of poor Elmer in the classic American comedy, *Three Men on a Horse*. Elmer, it may be remembered, was a gentle creature, who neither smoked nor drank nor used rough words, and when he was found in a compromising attitude with a gangster's moll, and the gangster was wroth, one of the gang inquired, "But even if the worst was true, what would that amount to, in the case of Elmer?"

But the acquittals of von Papen and Schacht were richly positive. The two old foxes had got away again. They had tricked and turned and doubled on their tracks and lain doggo at the right time all their lives, which their white hairs showed had not been

56

brief; and they had done it this time too. And it was absolutely right that they should have been acquitted. It would only have been possible to get them by stretching the law, and it is better to let foxes go and leave the law unstretched. Von Papen had never performed an official act, not even to the initialling of a faintly dubious memorandum, which could be connected with the commission of a war crime or a crime against humanity. He had intrigued and bullied his way through artificially provoked diplomatic crises with the weaker powers, he had turned the German Embassy in Vienna into a thieves' kitchen where the downfall of Schuschnigg was planned and executed; but this skulduggery could not be related to the planning of aggressive warfare, and if he had been found guilty there would have been grounds for a comparison, which would have been quite unfair but very difficult to attack on logical grounds, with Sir Neville Henderson. As for Schacht, he had indeed found the money for the Nazis' rearmament programme, but rearmament itself had never been pronounced a crime; and it is impossible to conceive an article of international law which would have made him a criminal for his doings and not given grounds for a comparison with Lord Keynes. Indeed, the particular jiggery-pokery he had invented to make Germany's foreign trade a profitable racket, particularly in the Balkans, was so gloriously successful, and would have produced such staggering returns if it had been uninterrupted, that he cannot have wished for war.

But, all the same, these were not children of light, and the association of innocence with their names was entertaining. When the verdict on von Papen was pronounced the other defendants gave him good-natured, rallying glances of congratulation; and he looked just as any Foreign Office man would look on acquittal, modest and humorous and restrained. But when the defendants heard that Schacht was to go free, Göring laughed, but all the rest looked grim. A glance at Schacht showed that in this they were showing no unpardonable malice. He was sitting in his customary twisted attitude, to show that he had nothing to do with the defendants sitting beside him and was paying no attention to the proceedings of the court, his long neck stretched up as if to give him the chance to breathe the purer upper air, his face red with indignation. As he heard the verdict of not guilty he looked more indignant than ever, and he tossed his white hairs. Had anyone gone to him and congratulated him on his acquittal he would certainly have replied that he considered it insulting to suppose that any other verdict could have been passed on him, and that he was meditating an action for wrongful imprisonment. There was, to be sure, nothing unnatural or illogical in his attitude. The court had cleared him with no compliments but with no qualifications, and the charges which had been brought against him were definitely part of the more experimental side of Nuremberg. Why should he feel grateful for the acquittal that was his right? There was no reason at all. But it must have been trying to be incarcerated over months in the company of one whose reason was quite so net and dry, who was capable of such strictly logical behaviour as Schacht was to show over the affair of the orange.

This was quite a famous affair, for it amused the other defendants, who laughed at it as they had not been able to laugh at his acquittal, and told their wives. That was how it got known, long before one of the court psychiatrists told it in his book. Each defendant was given an orange with his lunch; and of the three acquitted men two had the same inspiration to perform a symbolic act of sympathy with their doomed comrades by giving their oranges away. Von Papen sent his to von Neurath, and Fritzsche sent his to von Schirach. But Schacht ate his own orange. And why not? Why should a man give up an orange which he had a perfect right to eat and send it to somebody else, just because he had been acquitted of crimes that he had not committed and the other man had been found guilty of crimes that he had committed? The laughter of his fellow prisoners was manifestly unjust. But surely they earned the right to be a little unjust, to laugh illogically, by what happened to them later at the afternoon session.

Something had happened to the architecture of the court which might happen in a dream. It had always appeared that the panelled wall behind the dock was solid. But one of the panels was really a door. It opened, and the convicted men came out one by one to stand between two guards and hear what they had earned. Göring, in his loose suit, which through the months had grown looser and looser, came through that door and looked surprised, like a man

58

in pajamas who opens a door out of his hotel room in the belief that it leads to his bathroom and finds that he has walked out into a public room. Earphones were handed to him by the guard and he put them on, but at once made a gesture to show that they were not carrying the sound. They had had to put on a longer flex to reach from the ground to the ear of a standing man, and the adjustment had been faulty. His guards knelt down and worked on them. On the faces of all the judges there was written the thought, "Yes, this is a nightmare. This failure of the earphones proves it," and it was written on his face too. But he bent down and spoke to them and took a hand in the repair. This man of fifty-three could see the fine wires without spectacles. When the earphones were repaired he put them on with a steady hand and learned that this was not a nightmare, he was not dreaming. He took them off with something like a kingly gesture and went out, renouncing the multitudinous words and gestures that must have occurred to him at this moment. He was an inventive man and could not have had to look far for a comment which, poetic, patriotic, sardonic, or obscene, would certainly have held the ear of the court and sounded in history; and he was a man without taste. Yet at this moment he had taste enough to know that the idea of his death was more impressive than any of his own ideas.

A great mercy was conferred upon him. At this last moment that he would be seen by his fellow men it was not evident that he was among the most evil of human beings that have ever been born. He simply appeared as a man bravely sustaining the burden of fear. This mercy was extended to all the prisoners. It must be recorded that there was not a coward among them. Even Ribbentrop, who was white as stone because of his terror, showed a hard dignity, and Kaltenbrunner, who looked like a vicious horse and gave no promise of restraint, bowed quietly to the bench. Frank, the governor of Poland, he who had repented and become a good Catholic and wore black glasses more constantly than any of the others, gave an odd proof of his complete perturbation. He lost his sense of direction and stood with his back to the bench until he was spun round by the guards. But then he listened courageously enough to his sentence of death.

There was a deep unity in their behaviour as there was a unity in their appearance. The only diversion was the mad little slap Hess gave the guards when they tried to hand him his earphones. He would not wear them, so he did not hear his sentence. The Service defendants, too, were distinct in their bearing, for they had experience of courts-martial and knew the protocol, and bowed and went out when their sentences were delivered. The others seemed to believe that the judge would add to their sentences some phrase of commination, and waited for it, looking straight in front of them; and, curiously enough, they seemed to be disappointed when the commination did not come. Perhaps they hoped that it would also be an explanation. That was what all in the court required: an explanation. We were going to hang eleven of these eighteen men, and imprison the other seven for ten, fifteen, twenty years, or for life; but we had no idea why they had done what they did. All but Streicher had Intelligence Quotients far above the average, and most of them had not been unfavoured in their circumstances. We had learned what they did, beyond all doubt, and that is the great achievment of the Nuremberg trial. No literate person can now pretend that these men were anything but abscesses of cruelty. But we learned nothing about them that we did not know before, except that they were capable of heroism to which they had no moral right, and that there is nothing in the legend that a bully is always a coward.

Then the court rose. It did so in the strict physical sense of the word. Usually when a court rises it never enjoys a foot of real elevation; the judge stalks from the bench, the lawyers and spectators debouch through the corridors, their steps heavy by reason of what they have just heard. But this court rose as a plane takes off, as gulls wheel off the sea when a siren sounds, as if it were going to fly out of the window, to soar off the roof. The courtroom was empty in a minute or two, and the staff hurried along the corridors into one another's offices, saying good-bye, good-bye to each other, good-bye to the trial, good-bye to the feeling of autumn that had grown so melancholy in these latter days, because of the reddening creepers and the ice in the sunshine, and these foreseen sentences of death.

The great left at once, that very day, if they were great enough, and so did some who were not so very great, but who, avid for home, had plotted for precedence as addicts plot to get drugs. The less great and the less farseeing had to wait their turn, for again transport could not meet the demands of the occasion, and the going was worse than the coming. Fog took a hand, and it was usually noon before the planes could leave the ground. Visitors and correspondents waited at the airport for days, some of them for a week, and more and more people tried to go away by train, and some who succeeded ran into awkward currency difficulties. And in the Palace of Justice there were packing cases on the floor of every office: the typewriters had to go home, the files had to go home, the stationery had to go home. Those who had finished and were free ran in and bent down beaming to say good-bye to those still on their knees beside these packing cases, who beamed up at them because they were to be free themselves quite soon, and cried happy thanks for the parting gift, which if they were to remain any time was often a pot of those prodigious cyclamens grown by the one-legged gardener in the greenhouse at the press camp. It was a party, it was like going off for a cruise, only instead of leaving home, you were going home, going home, going home.

But for some on whom the burden of the trial had lain most heavily that happiness did not last intact after the sun went down. One lawyer said, in answer to nothing, after turning on the lights long before the dusk had fallen, "Damn it all, I have looked at those men for ten months. I know them as I know the furniture in my room. Oh, damn it all." Some of these who felt the tragedy of the trial most deeply had to remain there to fulfil certain legal formalities, which could not be performed till some days had passed; and it was discovered that, though it was hard to fly westward from Nuremberg, it was very easy to fly eastward, since nobody wanted to go in that direction. Some Americans and English and French filled in this time of waiting by going to Prague on a plane that had to run a diplomatic errand. The city astonished by its beauty: by its trumpeting baroque, by the little streets on its waterways, by clean farmlands that dropped in terraces to the heart of the capital. It astonished also by its catastrophic situation, which was going unrecorded in the press of the world.

The Sudeten Germans had been driven out of Czechoslovakia into Germany. On paper this looked good; they had allowed themselves to be made the pawns of Henlein, of Hitler. But the effect was not what might have been foreseen. There were many shops in the city filled with specimens of the glassware for which the country has been famous through the centuries; and an American lawyer went from one to another, trying to order a set of table glass. Each shopkeeper in turn admitted that it would take at least two years to fulfil the order, if it were possible to fulfil it at all. It seemed that this, like several other major industries, had been to a large extent manned by Sudeten Germans, and that the expulsions had thrown the machine out of gear. On the farms left empty by the expellees the unharvested crops were rotting; but it appeared that not much effort had been made to harvest them, since UNRRA was flooding the country with American grain. It was also flooding the country with gasoline, of which there was such an abundance that the Czechs were holding a touring automobile race. At that time, and for another four years or so, gasoline was still rationed in Great Britain and in France, and the meagreness of the supplies allowed officials in the British and French Zones of Western Germany was a serious handicap to the efficiency of the Control Commission. The American Ambassador, Laurence Steinhardt, spent his days and nights begging the State Department to stop the flow of raw and manufactured materials which UNRRA was pouring into the country without real regard for its needs. When the Germans were first driven out of Czechoslovakia the struggle of the armies left the people in a state of privation only to be medicined by large-scale relief work, and there was still some scope for soup-kitchen charity. But what the Czechs really needed by this time was aid in the reorganization of their existing economy, and the return of some Sudeten Germans and the training of substitutes.

The Treaty of Munich had inflicted on the country the pain and wrong of annexation and occupation, but it also had the unpredictable result that no Continental industrial power except Switzerland came out of the war with its industry less damaged. The plants were for the most part still standing, and greatly improved by the up-to-the-minute modernization that the Germans had given them for military purposes. That took us back to Nuremberg. In 1945 Hitler had ordered the destruction of Czechoslovakian industry: but he had given the order to Speer, whom we had just seen sentenced to twenty years' imprisonment for complicity in slave labor. He had quietly held his hand and done nothing.

The last thing this highly developed country required was the horde of amateur administrators imported by UNRRA. If Czechoslovakia could revive its foreign trade it would enjoy prosperity again, and there was no material obstacle to prevent this. The hotels were full of American businessmen who had come in the hope of reanimating agreements that had operated before the war, greatly to the benefit of the Czechs. But they were all in despair. Their claims were not denied, nor were they recognized. They were pigeonholed. These powerful economic friends of Czechoslovakia were allowed neither to enter into possession of their property, nor to take any other step that might lead to the resumption of the manufacture in which they were interested. The cunctative process at work was explained by the lists which most of them carried in their wallets: lists prepared for them by their Prague agents, which consisted of the names of civil servants and politicians whom they would have to approach in the prosecution of their claims, and what manner of men they were. This one was honest and would consider cases on their merits and strive to act appropriately. But this one could be bribed; he had a daughter in the United States for whom he wanted dollars, and perhaps he might be considering emigration. That one too could be bribed; in a concentration camp during the war, he now had poor health and had begun to drink, and cared only for the moment. This one could be bribed too, but it was believed that he was under Communist discipline and was ordered to accept bribes so that the party would ultimately be able to publish the facts of the transaction, to the discredit of transatlantic capitalist hyenas. The next one could not be bribed, and the papers would lie on his desk and never travel a foot farther. He was a Communist, and he was both preparing the ground for the expropriation which would follow the Russian engulfment of the country and making it clear to his colleagues what pattern of behaviour would earn the approval of the Russians. And the papers would lie long on this other man's desk though he was not a Communist. He was merely one of the colleagues who was willing to learn that lesson.

Morning broke over Czechoslovakia, and there was day, and then there was night; but the clock had stopped. The people of Prague knew it and, though free and walking where they chose in their own city, were of like mind with their enemies, the prisoners of Nuremberg, concerning time. They wished it for ever suspended, knowing that when the hands of the clock moved again their doom would fall on them. They even found it in their hearts to dislike the American businessmen who were stirring themselves to serve the supreme Czech interest of trade, because they were trying to start the clock again. Only in one place was it claimed that the hours were passing at their customary speed and that the future was not precisely known. In the Hradcani Palace there were four hundred and forty rooms; and among them was a splendid baroque chamber designed for the conduct of great business, which the autumn sunlight coloured as hock gilds the glass that holds it. There President Beneš sat and declared that all was going well with his country. His reason for this optimism? To him it was clear. This had been his room before the war. Then for a long time it was not his room. And now it was his room again. The little lame old man hobbled to the window and stood at it, with his back to Prague, and explained that it was at this very window that Hitler had stood and wept for joy because Prague was his. Well, where was Hitler? And where was he, Beneš? It is a sad sight, an old gambler boasting of his luck, for age is a proof that no luck lasts for ever.

But he was alone, alone as Lear; only it was the rest of the cast that wandered on a blasted heath, while he was within doors. All Prague was in fear of the Russians, as all Berlin was in fear of the Russians. The blankness of a new page of history was being inscribed with a black text; and even those who had come to Prague in order to escape from the Nuremberg trial rarely thought of it. Though sometimes it came back.

There was at that time in Prague a British Film Festival which the liberals and Social Democrats were attending as a demonstration of their faith. This was a sign of their extreme desolation.

They did not love Great Britain, for it had betrayed them at Munich. But at least Britain was not the USSR. So they stared loyally at the screen, even though what they saw was Mr. Noel Coward's *Brief Encounter,* a masterpiece which made little appeal to their sympathies. Sexual renunciation on secular grounds is not a theme which Central Europe understands; and the Czechs are forthright and matter-of-fact even for that territory. They looked at the doctor and the suburban housewife and supposed that they would sleep together if their desire to do so was sufficiently strong, and that they would not sleep together if their desire to do so was sufficiently weak. This reduced the element of conflict in the story to negligible proportions. They also asked themselves with some emotion whether it could really be true that in England there were no other places than railway buffets where lovers could meet. The drab and inhibited little drama seemed to unfold very slowly before this audience, which so plainly felt that if such cases of abstinence occurred in a distant country there was no need why it should have to know about them; and there was drowsiness in the air when an American voice spoke loudly out of the darkness. A minor character had crossed the screen and at the sight this voice was saying in horror, "By God, that man looks just like Göring." It was one of the American lawyers from Nuremberg, who had fallen asleep and had awakened to see the screen as a palimpsest with the great tragedy imposed on the small. The trial had begun its retreat into the past. Soon none of us, we thought, would ever think of it, save when we dreamed of it or read about it in books.

❖❖ 7 ❖❖

Yet we were soon to think often and gravely of Nuremberg and its prisoners. We had already had some warning in an uneasy incident. It had happened after the trial was over, when all the prisoners had been sentenced and the courtroom vacated. The correspondents were sitting in the press room, typing the last takes of their stories when there suddenly appeared before them the three men who had been acquitted: Fritzsche and von Papen and Schacht. They smiled at the astonished journalists with a soliciting amiability. The Russian judges had dissented from all three acquittals; and therefore all the Communist journalists were savagely incensed against these men and set up a howl at the sight of them. Some of the other journalists were of the same mind; and even those who accepted the acquittals as a logical consequence of the terms of the Nuremberg charter felt that they preferred the men who had done no hedging and trimming in their service of evil and were now to pay the penalty. So even the correspondents who felt the least hostility to them cried out mocking questions, which they answered, still smiling; and some threw apples and chocolate bars at them, which they picked up, as if taking part in a joke. The news spread through the Palace of Justice, and the correspondents who had been filing their pieces at the cable offices rushed down to the press room to see the fun, but the three men had suddenly turned their backs and gone back to the prison. The correspondents were left with the belief that they had witnessed an amazing feat of impudence. But actually the three men had been in terror of their lives.

Quite rightly, they had suspected that the German civil administration would arrest them as soon as they left prison and bring them before a denazification court on the charge of having betrayed the German people. This was not to be as severe an ordeal for them as they sometimes feared. It was a fact, and not a fiction of the Nuremberg court, that these men had succeeded in varying degrees in keeping themselves uninvolved in the major Nazi crimes; and the Allies succeeded sufficiently well in reimposing the rule of law on Germany to make their fears for their lives quite groundless. The denazification courts acquitted Schacht altogether and gave the other two sentences of imprisonment of which they served only part, von Papen being released in 1949 and Fritzsche in 1950. But their ordeal was to be severe enough. They were subjected to enormous fines, and their legal expenses ate up all their means; and the German authorities, uncertain how to apply the novel procedure, arrested them and released them and arrested them again. During their periods of freedom they had difficulty in getting a roof over their heads, and though their lives were to be safe, one of them at least was to suffer physical violence. Von Papen was set on by a fellow prisoner in a labour camp and had his head battered to a pulp, at seventy years of age. When the three men had been acquitted at Nuremberg they had foreseen their fate as worse than this, and they had come to see the journalists to test a demented hope that they had made an endearing impression of innocence in court and could rely on international opinion to protect them from their own people. They had turned their backs on the mockers and taken refuge in their cells because they saw that that hope was baseless. After three days of dread Fritzsche and Schacht left the prison under the cover of darkness and were soon arrested. It throws a light on Schacht that he was willing to try his luck with Fritzsche, who was many years younger. Von Papen had to be coaxed and bullied over weeks before he would face his freedom.

The authorities should have allowed none of these things to happen. It was worse than absurd to let the acquitted defendants stray about the Palace of Justice as they chose, when its corridors and halls were still thronged with excited people who were not merely spectators but, owing to the nature of the case, interested parties. A number of decent journalists were surprised into an act of cruelty which they would not have committed, however unappetizing they found the three, had it been known that they were frightened. And these men had reason for fear: they were exposed to unlawful outlawry, as the Allied Control Commission did not trouble itself to make an arrangement with the German authorities which would have ensured that these men were quietly arrested as soon as they were acquitted by the International Military Tribunal, kept in safe custody, and given an expeditious trial. During the first few days of October it became clear that the Allies had failed in common sense, and that the consequences of that failure might be ugly. As the month went on that apprehension joined uneasily with the visceral mournfulness excited by the knowledge of the condemned men's fate, that sympathy evoked by all doomed flesh, any doomed flesh, whatever the value of the spirit that infused it.

The executions were to take place on October 16. Some time during the preceding night Göring killed himself. The enormous clown, the sexual quiddity with the smile which was perhaps too wooden for mockery and perhaps not, had kicked the tray out of the hands of the servants who were bringing him the wine of humiliation, the glasses had flown into the air and splintered with a sound too much like laughter. This should not have happened. We are all hunters, but we know ourselves hunted by a mightier hunter, and our hearts are with the hunted, and we rejoice when the snared get free of the snare. In this moment visceral mournfulness changed to visceral cheerfulness; we had to applaud for the flesh that would not accept the doom that had been dealt to it but changed it to an expression of defiance. All those people who had fled from Nuremberg, British and American and French, who were scattered over the world, trying to forget the place of their immurement, would straighten up from whatever they had been bent over and burst out laughing before they could help themselves, saying, "That one! We always knew he would get the better of us yet." Surely all those Germans who walked through the rubble of their cities while their conquerors drove, they too would halt, and throw back their heads, and laugh, and say, "That one! We always knew he would get the better of them yet."

Göring should not have been permitted even this small amelioration of his doom. True, we now know some reasons for feeling that he might have been allowed to get a little of his own back. Like all the Nazis, he had been plagued by the attentions of the psychiatrists who haunted Nuremberg Jail, exercising a triple function of priest and doctor and warder hard to approve. They visited the men in the cells and offered themselves as confidants, but performed duties at the behest of the court authorities. When some of the defendants seemed to be taking an unrepentant pro-Nazi stand in their line of defence, one of the psychiatrists worked out, at the commandant's request, a plan for a new seating arrangement at the lunch table in order to break up this group and expose them to other influences. It is not easy to think of an accused person on trial before a national tribunal being subjected to such manipulation by prison officials. There was no silver lining to this cloud. One of these psychiatrists has related, without humorous intention, that when Göring asked him what a certain psychological test had revealed about his character, he replied that it had shown that he lacked the guts to face responsibility. Göring had also the benefit of spiritual care of a remarkably robust kind.

He asked the Lutheran chaplain to give him Holy Communion on the night before the executions, but the chaplain refused, on the ground that he was probably shamming.

Nevertheless Göring should not have been given the chance to use his courage to weaken public horror at his crimes, to which his courage was not relevant. The Nazis were maniacs who plastered history with the cruelty which is a waste product of man's moral nature, as maniacs on a smaller scale plaster their bodies and their clothes with their excreta. Since sanity is to some extent a matter of choice, a surrender to certain stimuli and a rejection of others, the nature of mania should never be forgotten. It is unfair, not only to Germans, but to all the world, if the vileness of the Nazis be extenuated; and it was unfair that this Nazi of all Nazis should have been allowed to disguise his gross dementia. This suicide meant a long-term danger to human standards, and it might have meant a short-term danger too, had it not been for the severity of the following winter. Germany was to be ice-bound and water-logged and had no time to think of reviving the Nazi party; and if that stretch of bad weather broke Europe's heart, it also broke the continuity of popular political thinking and forced it on to a fresh phase not shadowed by resentment at conquest. But the Allies had failed idiotically in a prime matter. All to no purpose had the military policeman in the V.I.P. gallery shaken the venerable Lord of Appeal and bidden him wake up and uncross his legs. All to no purpose had his colleague waved his club round the ears of the judge and asked him how the hell he had got in. All to no purpose had the maternal colonel shadowed our passes with his pendulous bosom. The cyanide had freely flowed.

But worse than that had happened. No wise person will write an unnecessary word about hanging, for fear of straying into the field of pornography. The strain of evil in us, which, given privileges, can take pleasure in the destruction of others by pain and death, takes delight in dreams about hanging, which is the least dignified form of death. That delight emits the strongest of all the stinks that hang about the little bookshops in the backstreets. Yet if there must be capital punishment, it had better take the form of hanging. That murderers should be killed by injections is a fatuous suggestion, for this could not be efficiently done without recourse to the aid of doctors, who could not give it without breaking the Hippocratic oath and losing their sacred characters as the preservers of life. In these days it is vitally important to maintain this traditional concept of medicine in its purity, since a totalitarian government might imitate the Nazi state in asking its doctors to exterminate an unfavoured class or perform lethal experiments on it, and it would be well that both doctors and the public should realize this to be an obscene retrogression. The electric chair has the disadvantage of raising in the vulgar a vision of regal stoicism; the half-witted gangster can feel it is his throne, and the current links him with the scientific cosmos of Superman. The firing squad is the happiest of executions, for it gives the condemned man a chance to gain the good opinion of his executioners; and for that reason it must be forbidden, like suicide, to those whose crimes are vile and must be remembered as vile. There remain decapitation and hanging; and the bloody act of decapitation, with the grace notes of horror that are added when the headsman is failed by his skill, is a huntsman's call to cruelty.

This long grim argument keeps the hangman in our lives. But this is a horrible necessity. It is not because we have grown too tender that we think it so. The mobs of the past, coarse-pelted as hogs, were distracted by the burden they had laid on another man's soul by making him a public servant and publicly abhorrent. They acted as simple people do under the consciousness of guilt and pretended that it was their victim who was guilty. The crimes of which so many eighteenth-century hangmen were convicted lie on the records with an oblique air. Either they were the consequences of these outcasts' frenzied misery or revengeful impostures practised by the community. When Dennis was accused of having joined in the Gordon Riots and stoked fires in the street with wood torn from Catholic houses, the Recorder believed his story that as he made his way through the burning city to his home the rioters had closed in on him, crying, "Here's bloody Jack Ketch, let's make him carry some to the fire," and had threatened to burn him if he refused. But the jury condemned him to death; though it was not to have its will, for the state needed him to do his work, since it was not easy to get another scapegoat.

In the nineteenth century the mob grew milder and intellectuals addressed themselves to the task of self-analysis. But neither the mob nor the intellectuals grew kinder to the hangman and continued to show cruelty to one whose offence was of their own creating. Old Jimmy Bottin, paralysed, got about Brighton by using a chair as a crutch and sitting down on it when he was exhausted; and at the sound of the chair legs scraping the ground the people crossed the street and left him to hobble along alone. They were unjust to hangmen but they were not merciful to those who were hanged. Hangings were public until 1869, and it was a matter of common knowledge that the victims on the scaffold often took a long time to die and suffered horribly. In fact, they died of slow strangulation. In the past that had been accepted as the way that hanged men died. A free end of the noose was passed through a ring on the scaffold pole, and while the victim dangled in the noose the executioner pulled on it and strangled him. The drop system had been introduced in the hope that the fall through the trapdoor would dislocate the victims' spines and cause instantaneous death; but still they died of strangulation.

No doctor, no lawyer, no professed humanitarian, took the trouble to inquire why this system had failed in its purpose. That was left to an illiterate cobbler from Lincolnshire named William Marwood, who was obsessed by hangings. He thought about them all day long as he worked on his boots and shoes; and he was visited by the idea that hanged men still suffered the pains of strangulation because the usual drop was not long enough to cause a fall of sufficient violence. He perceived also that to get a fall violent enough to dislocate the spine but not so violent that it tore the head from the body, the length of the rope must be in proportion to the weight of the body. Marwood succeeded in being appointed public executioner in 1871, and it was at once seen that his system went far to eliminate the risk of strangulation, but he never worked out any but an approximate formula for the length of the rope. This, however, was perfected by one of his successors, James Berry. These hangmen did a great work of mercy to the most defeated children of men, and they lifted from us all the guilt of torturing as well as killing. Yet we never thank them for it, their names are not written in gold like those of Shaftesbury and Schweitzer, and if we met them face to face few of us would immediately remember that we owe them reverence and gratitude; and it will be hardest for those to remember it who have stood outside a prison at the hour of a hanging. There is nothing to see there before the hanging except a white notice pinned on the great outer door of the prison, which bears an announcement that a man is to be hanged that morning; and after the hanging a warder comes out of a small door which is cut in the great door, and takes down the noticeboard and takes it inside, and brings it out again and hangs it up, with two other notices pinned on to it, one a sheriff's declaration that the man has been hanged, the other a surgeon's declaration that he has examined the hanged man and found him to be dead. But people come long distances to see this nearly invisible sight, often bringing their children, who have sometimes clamoured to be brought; and they go away with the satisfaction of those who have had their orgasm. There was never a lawful occasion which smelled so strongly of the unlawful.

When the Nuremberg tribunal came to deal with these delicate matters it proved to be as zanyish as we had feared it might be. It undertook the task of hanging eleven men with a dreadful innocence which made the reports of the journalists who witnessed the executions not nearly so unlike the testimony concerning Nazi atrocities which had brought these men to the gallows as one might have hoped. The hangman was an American sergeant who meant no harm but had not fully benefited by the researches of Marwood and Berry. The ten men slowly choked to death. Ribbentrop struggled in the air for twenty minutes. Yet it would be treachery against truth not to concede that justice had been done. Each one of these men who had been hanged had committed crimes for which he would have had to give his life under German law; and it would have then been an axe that killed him. But there are stenches which not the name of justice or reason or the public good, or any other fair word, can turn to sweetness.

Opera in Greenville

OPERA IN GREENVILLE

The note of Greenville, South Carolina, is rhetorical. Among the stores and offices on Main Street there is a vacant lot that suddenly pretends to be a mountain glade, with a stream purling over a neatly assembled rockfall; and in the foreground there is staked a plaque bearing the words:

GREENVILLE CITY WATER WORKS 1939.
The water supply of Greenville, South Carolina, pure, sparkling, life's most vital element, flows by gravity from an uncontaminated mountain watershed of nine thousand acres, delivered through duplicated pipe lines, fourteen million gallons capacity, a perfect water for domestic and industrial uses.

Not in such exuberant terms would the existence of a town water supply be celebrated in the North or in my native England, and no deduction can be drawn from this that is damaging to the South. The exuberance of the inscription is actually a sober allusion to reality. Here one remembers that water is a vital element, as it is not in the North or in England. One is always thinking about water, for one is always wanting to have a drink or take a shower or get some clothes washed. The heat of the South is an astonishment to the stranger. When the lynching trial in Greenville came to its end, late in May, it was full summer there, and the huge, pale bush roses that grow around the porches were a little dusty. Greenville was as hot as the cities that lie on the Spanish plains, as Seville and Córdoba. But in those cities the people do not live a modern life, they do not work too grimly, and they sleep in the afternoons; here they keep the same commercial hours as in New York, and practice the hard efficiency that is the price this age asks for money. On this point they fool the stranger. It is the

75

habit of the mills and other factories to build themselves outside
the city limits to dodge taxation. So Greenville has a naïve-look-
ing Main Street, with cross streets running, after a block or two,
into residential sections, where the white houses stand among
gardens that look as if they were presently going to pass into
woods and fields and the clear countryside; and it has a population
of 35,000. But outside Greenville city, in Greenville County,
there are 137,000 people, 123,000 of whom live within ten miles
of the city. In fact, the lynching for which thirty-one men were being tried in the court house was committed not, as might be imagined by an interested person who was trying to size the matter
up by looking at a map and gazetteer, in a backward small town,
but in a large modern city.

To sustain the life of a large modern city in this cloying, clinging
heat is an amazing achievement. It is no wonder that the white
men and women in Greenville walk with a slow, dragging pride, as
if they had taken up a challenge and intended to defy it without
end. These people would deny that it is the climate that has challenged them. They speak of the coolness of the nights almost before the stranger has mentioned the heat of the day. When they
name the antagonist against whom they have to pit themselves,
they simply and passionately and frequently name the North, with
the same hatred, the profounder because it is insolently unrequited,
that the Irish feel for the English. But the stranger will obstinately
continue to admire them for living and working in this land over
which the sun seems to be bending low, and for doing more than
that: for luxuriating in rhetoric, and topping rhetoric with opera.

Near the center of Greenville there stands an old white church,
with a delicate spire and handsome steps leading down from a
colonnade—the kind of building that makes an illusion of space
around itself. This is the First Baptist Church. In there, on Sunday evenings, there is opera. The lovely girls, with their rich hair
curling around their shoulders and their flowered dresses showing
their finely molded throats and arms, sit beside the tall young men,
whose pale shirts show the squareness of their shoulders and the
slimness of their waists, and they join in coloratura hymns with
their parents and their grandparents, who sing, like their children,
with hope and vehemence, having learned to take things calmly

no more than the older characters in opera. As they sing, the women's dresses become crumpled wraps, the men's shirts cling to them, although the service does not begin till eight o'clock at night. But, undistracted by the heat, they listen, still and yet soaring, to the anthems sung by an ecstatic choir and to a sermon that is like a bass recitative, ending in an aria of faith, mounting to cadenzas of adoration. In no other place are Baptists likely to remind a stranger of Verdi.

In the court house, also, there was opera. This is a singularly hideous building, faced with yellow washroom tiles, standing in Main Street, next the principal hotel, which, it should be noted for those who want to understand the character of Greenville, is cleaner and more comfortable and kinder to the appetite than most of the great New York hotels since the war. The courtroom is about the size of the famous Number One Court of the Old Bailey, in London.

In the body of the courtroom there were chairs for about three hundred white persons. The front rows were occupied by the thirty-one defendants who were being tried for lynching a Negro early on the morning of February 17, 1947. With the exception of three young men, one a member of a wealthy mill-owning family, one a salesman, and one a restaurant proprietor, these defendants were all Greenville taxi drivers. Many people, including a number of Greenville residents, some of whom desired them to be acquitted of all charges on the ground that lynching is a social prophylactic, talked of them as if they were patently and intensely degraded. As a matter of fact, they covered a wide range of types, most of them very far from repulsive. Some were quite good-looking and alert young men; most were carefully and cleanly dressed; some were manifest eccentrics. The most curious in aspect was a young man of twenty-five who must have weighed about three hundred pounds. The contours of his buttocks and stomach suggested that they were molded in some ductile substance like butter, and his face, which was smiling and playful, was pressed upward, till it turned toward the ceiling, by an enormous accumulation of fat under the chin and jaws. His name was Joy, and he was known as Fat Joy. The most conspicuous by reason of character was Roosevelt Carlos Hurd, Sr., who was a taxi driver also working as a taxi dispatcher, a man of forty-five with hair that stood up like a badger's coat, eyes set close together and staring out under glum brows through strong glasses, and a mouth that was unremitting in its compression. He looked like an itinerant preacher devoted to the worship of a tetchy and uncooperative God. In his statement he had declared that his education had stopped in the second grade. This did not necessarily imply that he was of weak intelligence. When he was a boy there were no laws against child labor in the State of South Carolina, and it is probable that he went to work. Several of the statements made by other defendants alleged that Mr. Hurd was the actual trigger man of the lynching, the man who fired the shot that killed the Negro.

Nearly all these defendants were exercising a right their state permits to all persons accused of a capital offence. They had brought their families to sit with them in court. Many had their wives beside them, young women, for the most part very young women, in bright cotton and rayon dresses, their curled hair wild about them. A number of these women had brought their children with them; one had five scrambling over her. All the children were plump and comely, and, though some were grimy, all of them were silent and miraculously court-broken. Mr. Hurd, though married and a father, was accompanied only by his own father, a thin and sharp-nosed man, his eyes censorious behind gold-rimmed spectacles, the whole of him blanched and shrivelled by austerity as by immersion in a caustic fluid. It was altogether plain that at any moment he and his son might become possessed by the idea that they were appointed God's arm and instrument, and that their conception of God would render the consequence of this conviction far from reasonably bland.

It was said by the anti-lynching element in the town that the families had been brought into court to sit with the defendants in order to soften the hearts of the jurors. But certainly they liked to be there, and the defendants liked to have them there. It is quite untrue to imagine, as was often said, that the defendants were sure of being acquitted. They were extremely afraid of what might be coming to them, and so were their families. Several of the wives sat in close embrace with their husbands, shaken from time to time by the inimitable convulsions of distress. One pregnant

girl in a green dress sat throughout the trial with an arm thrown
about her young husband's shoulder, rubbing her pudgy and
honest and tear-stained face against his arm. Many of the men,
including some who seemed to take no particular interest in their
wives, obviously enjoyed playing with their children. One tall and
dark young man with an intelligent face sat with his wife, who was
dressed with noticeable good taste, and two pretty little daughters.
During the recesses he spread his legs wide apart, picked up one
or the other of the little girls under her armpits, and swung her
back and forth between his knees. He would look down on her with
adoration as she gurgled with joy, but if she became too noisy he
would stop and set her down with a slight frown and a finger to his
lips. It was the oddest gesture to see in this trial, in this place. Mr.
Hurd's father was also there out of profound concern for the person whom he loved, though he made no physical manifestation except for occasionally biting his lips and lowering his head. His
part was to confirm his son's title to rectitude, his inheritance of
grace. It was so hot in the court that the women at the press table
all wore fresh dresses every day and almost every man except the
attorneys and officers of the court sat in their shirts. But Mr. Hurd's
father, from the beginning to the end of the case, wore a neat blue
coat and a conservative tie. Most of the defendants and their
relatives, but never Mr. Hurd or his father, chewed gum throughout the proceedings, and some chewed bubble gum. So, until the
press made unfriendly comment, did two of the attorneys.

Behind the defendants and their families sat something under
two hundred of such white citizens of Greenville as could find the
time to attend the trial, which was held during working hours.
Some were drawn from the men of the town who are too old or
too sick to work, or who do not enjoy work and use the court
house as a club, sitting on the steps, chewing and smoking and
looking down on Main Street through the hot, dancing air, when
the weather is right for that, and going inside when it is better
there. They were joined by a certain number of men and women
who did not like the idea of people being taken out of jail and
murdered, and by others who liked the idea quite well. None of
these expressed their opinions very loudly. There were also a
number of the defendants' friends.

Upstairs, in the deep gallery, sat about a hundred and fifty Negroes, under the care of two white bailiffs. Many of them, too, were court spectators by habit. It is said that very few members of the advanced group of coloured people in the town were present. There were reasons, reticently guarded but strongly felt, that they did not want to make an issue of the case. They thought it best to sit back and let the white man settle whether or not he liked mob rule. But every day there went into court a number of coloured men and women who were conspicuously handsome and fashionably dressed, and had resentment and the proud intention not to express it written all over them. They might be put down as Negroes who feel the humiliation of their race so deeply that they will not even join in the orthodox movements for its emancipation, because these are, to their raw sensitiveness, tainted with the assumption that Negroes have to behave like good children to win a favorable report from the white people. In the shadows of the balcony the dark faces of these people could not be seen. Their clothes sat there, worn by sullen space. The shoulders of a white coat drooped; a hat made of red roses tilted sidewise, far sidewise. The only Negroes who were clearly visible and bore a label were two young men who sat in the front row of the balcony every day, cheerful and dignified, with something more than spontaneous cheerfulness and dignity, manifestly on parade. They were newspapermen from two Northern Negro journals. They had started at the press table down in the front of the court, for the newspaper people there, Northern and Southern, national and local, had made no objection, and neither had the judge. But one of the defence attorneys said that it was as good as giving the case to him to have a nigger sitting at the press table along with white men and women, and this remark was repeated. Also, the local Negroes intimated that they would take it as a favor if the Northern Negroes went up into the gallery. So they took their seats up there, where, it may be remarked, it was quite impossible to get anything like a complete record of the proceedings. Then there was a very strong agitation to get them to come back to the press table. But that turned out to be inspired by the defence. Such was the complication of this case.

It was complicated even to the extent of not being a true lynching case, although the man taken from prison was a Negro and the men charged with killing him were white. Or, rather, it was not a pure lynching case. The taxi drivers of Greenville are drawn from the type of men who drive taxis anywhere. They are people who dislike steady work in a store or a factory or an office, or have not the aptitude for it, have a certain degree of mechanical intelligence, have no desire to rise very far in the world, enjoy driving for its own sake, and are not afraid of the dangers that threaten those who are on the road at night. They are, in fact, tough guys, untainted by intellectualism, and their detachment from the stable life of the community around them gives them a clan spirit which degenerates at times into the gang spirit. The local conditions in Greenville encourage this clan spirit. In every big town the dangers that threaten taxi drivers as they go about their work are formidable and shameful to society, and they increase year by year. In Greenville they are very formidable indeed. A great many people are likely to hire taxis, for there are relatively few automobiles in the region; two-thirds of the people who are likely to hire a Greenville taxi live in small communities or isolated homes; it is so hot for the greater part of the year that people prefer to drive by night. Hence the taxi drivers spend a great part of their time making journeys out of town after dark. In consequence a large number of taxi drivers have during the last few years been robbed and assaulted, sometimes seriously, by their fares. The number of these crimes that has not been followed by any arrest is, apparently, great enough to make the taxi drivers feel aggrieved. The failure to make an arrest has been especially marked in cases in which the assailants were supposedly Negroes, for the reason, it is said, that Negroes are hard to identify. The taxi drivers therefore had a resentment against fares who assaulted them, Negroes in general, and the police. In defence of the police, it is alleged that investigation of these crimes is made difficult because a certain number of them never happen at all. Taxi drivers who have got into money troubles have been known to solve them by pretending that they have been robbed of their money by fares, whom they described as Negroes in order to cash in on racial prejudice.

On February 15, 1947, an incident occurred which drew the taxi drivers of Greenville very close together. A driver named Brown picked up a Negro fare, a boy of twenty-four called Willie Earle, who asked him to drive to his mother's home in Pickens County, about eighteen miles from Greenville. Mrs. Earle, by the way, had given birth to Willie when she was fourteen. Both Willie Earle and Brown had been the victims of tragedy. Willie Earle had been a truck driver and had greatly enjoyed his occupation. But he was an epileptic, and though his mates conspired with him to conceal this fact from his employer, there came a day when he fell from the truck in a fit and injured himself. His employer, therefore, quite properly decided that he could not employ him on a job in which he was so likely to come to harm, and dismissed him. He could not get any other employment as a truck driver and was forced to work as a construction laborer, an occupation which he did not like so well and which brought him less money. He became extremely depressed and began to drink heavily. His fits became more frequent, and he developed a great hostility to white men. He got into trouble, for the first time in his life, for a sudden and unprovoked assault on a contractor who employed him, and was sent to the penitentiary, from which he had not been long released when he made his journey with Brown. Brown's tragedy was also physical. He had been wounded in the First World War and had become a taxi driver, although he was not of the usual type, because his state of health obliged him to take up work which he could leave when he needed rest. He was a man of thoughtful and kindly character. A Greenville resident who could be trusted told me that in the course of some social-service work he had come across a taxi driver and his wife who had suffered exceptional misfortune, and that he had been most impressed by the part that Brown had played in helping them to get on their feet again. "You could quite fairly say," this resident told me, "that Brown was an outstanding man, who was a good influence on these taxi boys, and always tried to keep them out of trouble. Lynching is just the sort of thing he wouldn't have let them get into."

Willie Earle reached his home that night on foot. Brown was found bleeding from deep knife wounds beside his taxi a mile or two away and was taken to a hospital, where he sank rapidly. Willie was arrested and put in Pickens County Jail. Late on the night of February 16 the melancholy and passionate Mr. Roosevelt Carlos Hurd was, it was said, about certain business. Later the jailer of the Pickens County Jail telephoned to the sheriff's office in Greenville to say that a mob of about fifty men had come to the jail in taxicabs and forced him to give Willie Earle over to them. A little later still, somebody telephoned to the Negro undertaker in the town of Pickens to tell him that there was a dead nigger in need of his offices by the slaughter pen in a by-road off the main road from Greenville to Pickens. He then telephoned the coroner of Greenville County, whose men found Willie Earle's mutilated body lying at that place. He had been beaten and stabbed and shot in the body and the head. The bushes around him were splashed with his brain tissue. His own people sorrowed over his death with a grief that was the converse of the grief Brown's friends felt for him. They mourned Brown because he had looked after them; Willie Earle's friends mourned him because they had looked after him. He had made a number of respectable friends before he became morose and intractable.

Thirty-six hours after Willie Earle's body had been found no arrest had been made. This was remarkable, because the lynching expedition—if there was a lynching expedition—had been planned in a café and a taxicab office that face each other across the parking lot at the back of the court house. On the ground floor of the court house is the sheriff's office, which has large windows looking on the parking lot. A staff sits in that office all night long. But either nobody noticed a number of taxi drivers passing to and fro at hours when they would normally be going off duty or nobody remembered whom he had seen when he heard of a jail break by taxi drivers the next day. When the thirty-six hours had elapsed Attorney General Tom C. Clark sent in a number of FBI men to look hard for the murderers of Willie Earle. This step evoked, of course, the automatic resentment against federal action which is characteristic of the South; but it should have been remembered that the murderers were believed to number about fifty, and Greenville had nothing like a big enough police staff to cope with such an extensive search. The sensitivity based on a concern for states' rights was inflamed by a rumour that Attorney General Clark had sent in the FBI men without consulting, or even informing, the Governor of South Carolina. Whether this rumour was true or false it was believed, and it accounted for much hostility to the trial which had nothing to do with approval of lynching. Very soon the FBI had taken statements from twenty-six men, who, along with five others whom they had mentioned in their statements, were arrested and charged with committing murder, being accessories before or after the fact of murder, and conspiring to murder. It is hard to say, now that all these defendants have been acquitted of all these charges, how the statements are to be regarded. They consist largely of confessions that the defendants were concerned in the murder of Willie Earle. But the law has pronounced that they had no more to do with the murder than you or me or the President. The statements must, therefore, be works of fiction, romances that these inhabitants of Greenville were oddly inspired to weave around the tragic happenings in their midst. Here is what one romancer invented about the beginnings of that evil:

Between ten and eleven p.m. on February 16, 1947, I was at the Blue Bird Cab Office and heard some fellows, whose identities I do not know, say that the nigger ought to be taken out and lynched. I continued to work until about two a.m., February 17, 1947, at which time I returned to the Blue Bird Taxi Office where R. C. Hurd was working on the switchboard. After I had been at the office for a few minutes, Hurd made several telephone calls to other taxicab companies in Greenville, including the Yellow Cab Company, the Commercial Cab Company, and the Checker Cab Company. He asked each company to see how many men it wanted to go to Pickens. Each time he called he told them who he was. When he finished making the calls, he asked me to drive my cab, a '39 Ford coach which is number twenty-nine (29), and carry a load of men to Pickens. I told him that he was "the boss." He then got a telephone call from one of the taxicab companies and he told them he would not be able to go until Earl Humphries, night dispatcher, got back from supper. After Earl Humphries returned from supper, Hurd, myself, Ernest Stokes, and Henry Culberson and Shephard, all Blue Bird drivers, got in Culberson's cab, which was a '41 Ford colored blue. We rode to the Yellow Cab Company on West Court Street followed by

Albert Sims in his cab. At the Yellow Cab Company we met all the other cab drivers from the cab companies. After all got organized, the orders given me by R. C. Hurd were to go back and pick up my cab at the Blue Bird Office. I would like to say here that Hurd had already made arrangements for everybody to meet at the Yellow Cab Company.

These sentences touch on the feature that disquiets many citizens of Greenville. A great deal was going on, at an hour when the city is dead, right under the sheriff's windows, where a staff was passing the night hours without, presumably, many distractions. They also touch on the chief peril of humanity. Man, born simple, bravely faces complication and essays it. He makes his mind into a fine wire that can pry into the interstices between appearances and extract the secret of the structural intricacy of the universe; he uses the faculty of imitation he inherits from the ape to create in terms approximating this intricacy of creation; so there arrive such miracles as the telephone and the internal-combustion engine, which become the servants of the terrible simplicity of Mr. Hurd, and there we are back at the beginning again.

A string of about fifteen automobiles lined up for the expedition. All but one of these were taxicabs. In their statements the taxi drivers spoke of the one that was not a taxi as a "civilian" automobile and of the people who were not taxi drivers as "civilians." When they got to Pickens County Jail, which lies on the corner of a highway and a side road, about twenty miles from Greenville, some of them parked on the highway and some on the side road. A taxi shone its spotlight on the front door, and they called the jailer down. When they told him they had come for the Negro, he said, "I guess you boys know what you're doing," and got the jail keys for them. The only protest that he seems to have uttered was a request that the men should not use profanity, in case his wife should hear it. He also, with a thoughtfulness of which nobody can complain, pointed out that there were two Negroes in the jail, and indicated which of the two had been guilty of nothing worse than passing a bad check. This surrender of Willie Earle by the jailer has been held by many people to be one of the worst features of the case. It is thought that the jailer showed cowardice in handing the Negro over to the mob, and that his protest about profanity meant that he had strained at a gnat but swallowed a camel. But a visit to Pickens County Jail, however, showed that the situation was not as it appeared at a safe distance.

The jail is a mellow red-brick building, planned with much fantasy by somebody who had seen pictures of castles in books and had read the novels of Sir Walter Scott and Mrs. Radcliffe, or had been brought up by people who had read them. It is a building that the Sitwells would enjoy. The front part is in essence like any home in the district, with two stories and a porch running around it. But at the corner looking on the highway and the side road there rises a rounded and crenellated tower, and over both the front door and the side door are arches and crenellations which suggest that the words "dungeon" and "oubliette" were running through the architect's mind, but that it was a kind mind, interested in the picturesque rather than in the retributive. This part of the jail, which seems to be the jailer's residence and office, is joined to a small oblong building, severe except for a continuance of feudal fantasy along the parapet, with six barred windows on the first story and six on the second. The cells must be extremely small, and it is probable that the jail falls far below modern standards, but there is a pleasantly liberal notice hanging on the side door which announces that visitors' hours are from nine to eleven in the morning and from two to four in the afternoon. The floor of the porch is crumbling. On a wooden table there is a scarlet amaryllis. Beside it stood the jailer's wife, and it could be well understood that her husband would not wish her to hear profanity. She wore spectacles, a pink cotton sunbonnet, a blue-flowered cotton frock, a brown apron streaked with absent-minded cooking. She spoke sweetly but out of abstraction; her bones were as fragile as a bird's; her eyes looked right through her spectacles, right through this hot and miserable world, at a wonder. She was a Methodist. God was about her as an enveloping haunt. Such of her as was on earth cooked for the prisoners, who usually numbered five or six, and for fifteen or sixteen people in the poorhouse up the road. She had a daughter to help her, but the daughter too was gentle and delicate, and had a child to care for. They were tired, gracious, manifestly not cherished by destiny.

Few of us, did unkind circumstance place us in charge of that jail and a mob come to demand a prisoner, would fail to hand him over without the smallest show of resistance. The jail is far beyond shouting distance of the center of Pickens town. On one side of it is a large vacant lot. On the other side, beyond a tumble-down fence, a long cabin that seems to be occupied by two or three families stands in a paddock where a couple of lean cows graze. Three women were standing about on the porch with their children, all pale and dispirited. (A startling hint as to the economics of the district was given by some particulars posted on the jail wall regarding the terms on which most people become inmates of this jail. In Pickens County a man who is run in for drunkenness is usually fined twelve dollars, with the alternative of going to jail for thirty days; if he has been drunk and disorderly he gets sixty days or twenty-four dollars; if he has driven an automobile while drunk he gets ninety days or fifty-two dollars.) Opposite the jail there are larger houses, which may be inhabited by more vigorous people, but the highway is wide and anybody answering the jail-er's call for help would have to come a considerable distance with-out cover. My misgivings about the possibility of showing ideal courage in Pickens County Jail were confirmed when the jailer, Mr. Ed Gilstrap, arrived. He was a stout man in his sixties, with that passive and pliant air of geniality that is characteristic of men who hold small political appointments. He wore khaki overalls with green suspenders, and a derby. When he removed this to greet his visitors, it was disclosed that there ran down his bald scalp a new scar, appallingly deep and about three to four inches long. He did not spontaneously mention the incident that had led to this injury, but, asked about it, he explained that on April 23, nine weeks after the lynching, three prisoners had tried to break out of the jail, and while he was preventing them, one had hit him over the head with an iron pipe. What had he done? He had shot at them and killed one and wounded another. The wounded one was still in the hospital. "I wish I had killed him," said Mr. Gilstrap, not unamiably, just with simple realism, "for he was the one who hit me with the pipe." And the third man? "He is still right here in jail," said Mr. Gilstrap. "We try to be fair to him. We're feeding him just the same as before."

The men who took Willie Earle away were in a state of mind not accurately to be defined as blood lust. They were moved by an emotion that is held high in repute everywhere and especially high in this community. All over the world friendship is regarded a sacred bond, and in South Carolina it is held that it should override nearly all other considerations. Greenville had at first felt some surprise that one of the defence attorneys, Mr. Thomas Wofford, had accepted the case. It was not easy for a stranger to understand this surprise, for the case might have been tailored to fit Mr. Wofford; but all the same, surprise was generally felt. When, however, it was realized that the group of defendants he represented included the half-brother of a dead friend of Mr. Wofford, his action was judged comprehensible and laudable. It is not to be wondered at, therefore, if in Greenville a group of very simple people, grieving over the cruel slaughter of a beloved friend, felt that they had the right to take vengeance into their own hands. They would feel it more strongly if there was one among them who believed that all is known, that final judgment is possible, that if Brown was a good man and Willie Earle was a bad man, the will of God regarding these two men was quite plain. It would, of course, be sheer nonsense to pretend that the men, whoever they were, who killed Willie Earle were not affected in their actions by the color of Willie Earle's skin. They certainly did not believe that the law would pursue them—at least, not very far or very fast— for killing a Negro. But it is more than possible that they would have killed Willie Earle even if he had been white, provided they had been sure he had murdered Brown. The romances in statement form throw a light on the state of mind of those who later told of getting Willie Earle into a taxi and driving him to a quiet place where he was to be killed. One says that a taxi driver sat beside him and "talked nice to him." He does not mean that he talked in a way that Willie Earle enjoyed but that the taxi drivers thought that what he was saying was elevating. Mr. Hurd described how Willie Earle sat in the back seat of a Yellow Cab and a taxi driver knelt on the front seat and exhorted him, "Now you have confessed to cutting Mr. Brown, now we want to know who was the other Negro with you." Willie Earle answered that he did not know; and it appears to be doubtful that there was another Negro

with him. The taxi driver continued, in the accents of complacent pietism, "You know we brought you out here to kill you. You
don't want to die with a lie in your heart and on your tongue."

Brown's friends were in the state of bereavement that is the
worst to bear. Brown was not dead. He was dying, and they could
do nothing to save him. They were in that state of frustration that
makes atheists at the deathbed of their loved ones curse God.
"They then drug the Negro out of the car," said Mr. Hurd in his
statement. ("Drug" is certainly a better word that "Dragged.")
Nobody speaks of doing anything there beside the slaughter pen;
they all speak of hearing things. One heard "the tearing of cloth
and flesh"; another heard "some licks like they were pounding him
with the butt end of a gun." Some heard the Negro say, "Lord, you
done killed me." Some saw as well as heard. "I saw," stated one,
"Hurd aim the single shotgun towards the ground in the direction
of where I judged the Negro was laying and pulled the trigger; I
then heard the shot fired. I then heard Hurd ask someone to give
him another shell." But Mr. Hurd also is among those who heard
but did not do. He did not even see. "When I seen they were going
to kill the Negro," he stated, "I just turned around, because I did
not want to see it."

People can become accustomed to committing acts of cruelty;
recent Europe proves that. But the first act of cruelty disgusts and
shames far past the unimaginative man's power of prevision. The
men who had joined the lynching party in the mood of righteous
men fulfilling a duty did not, according to their statements, enjoy
the actual lynching. "I only heard one report from a gun because
I immediately drove away," stated one. "I have worked only one
night since then," stated another. Fat Joy, another says, was overcome by terror on the way home and drove up to one of the taxis
and said, "Let's drive side by side; I think the law is coming." But
it was only the "civilian" car that had been with them all night. Of
their return to the town another states, "I got out at the Southern
depot and went into the Southern Café. I got a cup of coffee. The
man George, a Greek, behind the counter said, 'Did you get him?'
I said, 'Who do you mean?' He said, 'You know.' I said, 'I don't
know what you're talking about.'" It was so little like what they
had expected that even Mr. Hurd informed the FBI that he thought
89

it had all been a mistake, and recalled that he had never been in trouble for anything before. That the deed sickened them was proved beyond a shadow of doubt in the court house. When Sam Watt, the assistant but more conspicuous prosecuting attorney, read from the statements the details of what had been done to Willie Earle and described them as the detestable horrors that they were, the defendants were ashamed. They did not like their wives to hear them; and indeed their wives were also sickened. Mr. Hurd's father himself, whose loyalty to Mr. Hurd will be unshakable in eternity, looked down his long nose; so might an Inquisitor look, suddenly smitten with doubt of the purging flame. That hour passed. There were those at the trial who saw to that. But in that hour the defendants surely hated evil and loved good.

Years ago a poet in New York, babbling the indecencies of early parenthood, told a gathering that his child of two already enjoyed having poetry read to him. Someone asked what poetry he read to it. "Shelley and some of my own work," he answered. "That," said the false friend, "gives the kid the whole range." This trial gave the kid the whole range. The judge, J. Robert Martin, Jr., is very local. He knows all about rhetoric and opera. His speech arouses wonder as to how the best sort of stenographer, who takes down by sounds and not by sense, is not wholly baffled in the South, where "You gentlemen must apportion your time" is converted into "Yo' ge'men must appo'tion yo' taiaime," with a magnificent vibrato on the diphthongs and a strong melodic line to the whole. He is so good that though he is local he expands the local meaning, and recalls that the great Southerners are great men to the whole world. He has humour but hates a clown. He would have given much to have had the court fully decorous; when an important personage of the region took his seat on the dais and threw his raincoat over the law books on the judge's table, it irked him. His love of handsomeness and fine manners extends to the intellectual world. His charge to the jury was both powerful and beautifully shaped. Throughout the trial he stood on the skyline, proclaiming his hostility to lawlessness and his determination to keep his court uncontaminated, with a solid and unremitting positiveness that must have made him a personal enemy of every reactionary in the state.

The leader for the prosecution was nominally Robert T. Ashmore, the Greenville County solicitor, a gentle and courteous person. But the leading prosecuting attorney was Sam Watt, who comes from the neighboring town of Spartanburg, a lawyer of high reputation throughout the South, a much more dynamic person. He was assigned to the case by the Attorney General of the State of South Carolina at the suggestion of the Governor, about ten days after the FBI men had gone in. When he arrived the preliminaries of the case were over; and they had been conducted with some imprudence. The taking of statements from accused persons is one of the most delicate processes of police work. All over the world police forces are likely to become corrupt and tyrannous, and are then apt to coerce accused persons into making confessions. This is generally recognized. It is very hard to examine accused persons in places that are not more or less private, and therefore it is very hard to know when they have or have not been coerced. While there was no reason to believe that the FBI men used any illegitimate methods, it is true that they took these statements in circumstances that did not protect them from the charge that the defendants gave them under duress. It is also true that the statements amounted to frank confessions of participation in a capital crime. It is actually not at all uncommon for criminals who have committed acts which touch them deeply to make such confessions. But this is not so generally recognized. So this was very dubious material to bring before a jury, and indeed at least one of the defence attorneys flatly declared that they would be fools to believe that twenty-six men would incriminate themselves unless under compulsion.

But the mishandling went a great deal farther than that. The statements, which were not sworn, might have been supplemented when the defendants applied to be released under bond, for it was perfectly possible to demand that the applicants should again recite their connection with the crime in the form of sworn affidavits prepared by their own attorneys. This had not been done. The defendants had been turned loose unconditionally, and most of them, by the time Sam Watt came into the case, had returned to their duties as taxi drivers. Any stranger visiting the town of Greenville during late February, March, April, or early May of this year was as likely as not to be driven from the station by a person awaiting trial for murder and conspiracy to murder. But it is not necessary to bring the stranger into it. The citizens of Greenville also used these taxis, and it would be interesting to know how they liked the idea.

A prosecutor who introduced these statements in court would be a very lucky man if he could support them by strong corroborative evidence, and a very unlucky one if he could not. Mr. Watt and Mr. Ashmore had at their disposal nothing like the evidence that might convince a jury that these statements had not been obtained by duress, or, rather, prevent the jury from using a suspicion of duress as an excuse for an acquittal. It was true that one of the defendants had handed over to the police a gun that was damaged, and that the gun was of the same make as a gun that several men had described in their statements as being used by one of their number to beat the dying Negro until it broke under the force of his blows. This, however, was not such satisfactory evidence as it appears, because the man who was supposed to have broken the gun on the Negro's body did not himself admit in his statement that he had used it to beat the Negro, and each of the statements was evidence only against the man who made it and not against the men mentioned in it. This is not mere legal fussiness but a sensible provision, as the statements were not sworn and could not have been subjected to cross-examination by the attorneys of the mentioned persons unless the makers of the statements went into the witness box, which they did not do. There was also the testimony of one Roy Stansell, proprietor of a tourist camp on the Pickens highway, at which some of the taxis had stopped. This merely proved that the expedition had been on the road; it did not connect the men with the jail break or the murder. There was also the unfortunate U. G. Fowler, a taxi driver who gave evidence that he had been asked to join the party and had refused. But even he had heard the purpose of the expedition announced only by a voice to which he could not pin a name. There must have been a great many taxi drivers who could have given much more pointed evidence along these lines. Why they did not do so was revealed before the end of the trial. U. G. Fowler was set upon as he was driving along a country road, beaten, and threatened with death. He appeared before a local judge and made a complaint, but the judge refused to swear out a warrant for the arrest of the men who had beaten him. So Mr. Fowler left town.

It cannot be said, therefore, that the prosecution had put together a valid argument for a conviction. Timid muddling by someone or by some people who were not only muddlers but had an eye on the political weather had drawn most of its claws. As the case was handled, the jury cannot be blamed for returning an acquittal. If it had convicted on any of the indictments, even on the least, which related to conspiracy, either the verdict would have been reversed by a superior court or a very dangerous precedent would have been established. The trial had not the pleasing pattern, the agreeable harmony and counterpoint, of good legal process, however much the judge tried to redeem it. But whether the jury returned their verdict of not guilty because they recognized the weakness of the state's case, it was hard to guess. It was the habit of certain people connected with the case to refer to the jury with deep contempt, as a parcel of boobs who could be seduced into swallowing anything by anybody who knew how to tickle them up by the right mixture of brutish prejudice and corny sentimentality; and it was odd to notice that the people who most despised the jury were those who most despised the Negroes. To a stranger's eye, the jurymen looked well built and well groomed; and they stayed awake, which is the first and most difficult task of a juror, although they, like the attorneys, kept their coats on when the heat was a damp, embracing fever. What was marvelled at about this jury was its constitution. As Greenville is a town with, it is said, twenty-five millionaires and a large number of prosperous and well-educated people, it may have seemed peculiar that the jury should consist of two salesmen, a farmer, a mechanic, a truck driver, and seven textile workers. Some of the prosperous citizens had indeed appeared on the list of the veniremen from which the jurors were selected, but they had been singularly fortunate in being challenged by the attorneys. The unpopular task of deciding a lynching case therefore fell to an unfavored group who had

93

not the money to hire a bodyguard or to leave the town. They would, let us remember, have been in a most difficult position if they had returned a verdict of guilty. They might not have been murdered, like Willie Earle, or beaten up, like U. G. Fowler, but they would never have been able to take a taxi again with an easy mind, and that would be a considerable inconvenience in Greenville. It is one of the mysteries of this case that the trial was not shifted to another town.

Of the prosecuting attorneys, Mr. Ashmore made a speech that was not very spirited but was conscientious and accepted the moral values common to civilized people without making any compromise. Sam Watt, who has a deep and passionate loathing of violence and disorder, and who is such a good attorney that the imperfections of the case must have vexed him to his soul, handled the situation in his own way by using the statements to build up a picture of the lynching in all its vileness. It was while the defendants were listening to this speech that they hated evil and that they desired to remounce it. It was a great, if highly local, speech, and it made a mark on the public mind that was to last, though the close of the case cancelled it for the moment. That cancellation was due to the remarkable freedom of two of the defence attorneys from the moral values accepted by Mr. Ashmore and Mr. Watt. The two other defence attorneys accepted them; one wholly, the other partly. Mr. Bradley Morrah, Jr., accepted them wholly, Mr. Ben Bolt partly.

Mr. Bradley Morrah, Jr., was a young man who was a member of the state legislature. He was representing a strange defendant, his cousin, Mr. John B. Marchant, who was twenty-eight and the son of a widow of good family greatly loved in the town. Mr. Marchant was the driver of the "civilian car" that accompanied the string of taxicabs to the lynching. According to his story, he was leading the contemplative life in a café opposite the Yellow Cab office in the early hours of February 17 when he saw the expedition forming and joined it out of sheer curiosity. He was extremely disconcerted when he discovered its object, and though he did not dare leave the party, he did not approach the scene of action but waited some distance away. Mr. Marchant apparently spent much of his time accompanying the sheriff's men on their night work just as a hobby, and he certainly visited the sheriff's office next day and volunteered a statement before there was any need. There is no reason to disbelieve his account.

Both Mr. Marchant and Mr. Morrah gave the impression that they were stranded in the wrong century, like people locked in a train that has been shunted onto a siding. Mr. Morrah was as old-fashioned in appearance as Governor Dewey; he looked like a dandy of 1890. He was very likeable, being small and delicately made, yet obviously courageous; and there was nothing unlikeable in his oratory. He told the court that he had known his cousin for twenty-five years and knew that he had never had a vicious thought, and he wished that it was possible for him to take John Marchant's heart out of his breast and turn it over in his hand so that the jury could see that there was not an evil impulse in it. He was going on to say that he could picture John Marchant "with his mother, my aunt," when Sam Watt rose and said, "I object. There is no evidence about the Marchant family." The judge allowed the objection. Mr. Morrah altered the phrase to "I can picture him surrounded by his loved ones," and said that he "stood firmly bottomed, like a ship," and warned the jury that if they convicted him, the facts "would rankle in the hearts of men throughout the state, from the rock-ribbed brow of Caesar's Head to the marshes of Fort Sumter" and someplace else on the sea, and that "the ghosts of Hampton's men would rise to haunt you." But there was nothing barbarous in his speech. He was a transparently honest and kindly and dutiful person, and he depreciated no civilized standard, though it was startling when he ended his speech with the statement that the prosecution of Marchant reminded him of words spoken two thousand years ago, "Forgive them, Father, for they know not what they do." The comparison did not seem apt.

But great play was made with the Scripture; it might almost be called ball play. The Bible belonging to Greenville County Court House is in terrible shape. Like many Bibles, it has a flounce, or valance, of leather protecting its edges, and this is torn and crumbling, while its boards are cracked, and small wonder. Its quietest hours are when it is being sworn upon; at any other time it is likely to be snatched up from the small stand on which it rests, which is like that used for potted plants in some homes, and waved in the air, held to an attorney's breast, thrust out over the jury box, and hurled back to its resting place in a convulsion of religious ecstasy. Some of the Bible-tossing in this case was inspired by sincere conviction. But it looked as if a great deal was done in cold sacrilege to impress the jury, who were assumed to be naïvely pious. This was only one of the cynical efforts to exploit the presumed naïveté of the twelve men in the box. The subjects of these efforts were, as well as religion, alcohol, the hatred of the state for the nation, the hatred of the South for the North, and the hatred of the white man for the Negro. This last the judge had expressly ruled should not be mentioned in court. Of the four defence attorneys, Mr. Morrah obeyed this ruling, Mr. John Bolt Culbertson and Mr. Thomas Wofford openly defied it, and Mr. Ben Bolt, who stood somewhere in the scale between Mr. Morrah and the other two, skated round it.

Mr. Ben Bolt is a slow-moving, soft-voiced, grey-haired person of noble appearance, who is said to make many speeches about the common man. The industrial development of the South is evidently producing the same crop of liberal attorneys that were produced in England and the Northern states in the similar stage of their development. Mr. Bolt began his speech by a plea for racial tolerance, celebrating the life of dear old Aunt Hester, who aided his dear mother to guide his footsteps and who now lies in a grave that he often visits, always with the feeling that he ought to take his shoes off, since it is hallowed ground. Laying hold of the exhausted Bible, he changed the subject and recalled that the Supreme Court has ruled the Bible to be part of the common law of the State of South Carolina, and he pointed out that the Bible condemns conviction without several witnesses. It was not necessary to bring in the Bible to explain that, but Mr. Bolt was certainly performing his proper function when he proceeded to demonstrate the insufficiency of the evidence against the defendants. He passed on, however, to make an attack on the credibility of the witness U. G. Fowler that was embarrassing in its fatuity and seeming insincerity. This witness had been asked what his initials stood for, and had amazed the court by saying that he did not know, that they did not stand for anything but themselves. To people who questioned him outside court, he said that his mother had called him after a brother of hers and had never explained to him what his full name was. It was said by local experts that the uncle was probably called Huger, like many people in parts of South Carolina nearer the sea; it is the name of a Southern family of Huguenot origin, and it is pronounced "U.G." by the simple folk who have borrowed it. Mr. Bolt tried to disseminate another explanation. "That don't sound exactly Southern to me," he said. "Those initials certainly don't stand for Robert E. Lee or Stonewall Jackson." He was attempting to engender prejudice against this person by suggesting that his parents had christened him Ulysses Grant. This eminently sensible person was talking what he obviously knew to be humbug, out of his fathomless contempt for the jury. How little that school of thought realizes the dangers of contempt was demonstrated by a remark he made when he was representing the lynching as an episode that nobody but the meddlesome federal authorities would ever have thought of making a fuss over. When he was speaking of the FBI agents he said, "Why, you would have thought someone had found a new atomic bomb," but "all it was was a dead nigger boy." This is not a specifically Southern attitude. All over the world there are people who may use the atomic bomb because they have forgotten that it is our duty to regard all lives, however alien and even repellent, as equally sacred.

Mr. John Bolt Culbertson's speeches were untainted by any regard for the values of civilization. He went all the way over to the dead-nigger-boy school of thought. Mr. Culbertson is a slender, narrow-chested man with a narrow head. His sparse hair is prematurely white, his nose is sharp, and his face is colorless except for his very pink lips. He wears rimless spectacles, and his lashes are white. The backs of his hands are thickly covered with fine white hairs. In certain lights he gives the impression of being covered with frost. He has a great reputation in the South as a liberal. He is the local attorney for the CIO and has worked actively for it. He has also been a friend to the emancipation of the Negroes and has supported their demands for better education and the extension of civil rights. He recently made an address to Negro veterans, which took courage on his part and gave them great happiness. He is one of the very few white men in these parts who shake hands with Negroes and give them the prefix of Mr. or Mrs. or Miss. Not long ago an article in the *New Republic* hailed him as one of the true liberal leaders of the South. Many young people in Greenville who wish to play a part in the development of the New South look to him as an inspiring teacher, and many Negroes feel a peculiar devotion to him. Mr. Culbertson belongs to the school of oratory that walks up and down in front of the jury box. At the climactic points of his speeches he adopts a crouching stance, puts his hands out in front of him, parallel to each other, and moves them in a rapid spin, as if he were a juggler and they were plates. Finally he shoots one hand forward and propels his argument with it. His choreography was especially vigorous when he was putting in a little work on the jury's possible prejudice against alcohol. He was attempting to discredit the evidence of the tourist-camp proprietor who had identified the alleged lynchers. His knees went down. "Doesn't this man"—his hands went forward—"own a honky-tonk . . . a camp"—his knees went lower; his hands came further forward—"where they sell"—his right hand shot out; his voice caught in his throat with horror and then cracked across space like a whip—"BEER?" It is not illegal to sell beer in South Carolina. Nor is there any reason to think that Mr. Culbertson, though a man of most sober habits, is a teetotaller. Had the outburst been simply an unlovely piece of hypocrisy, based on a profound contempt for his fellow men, it would have sounded much the same; and it would have sounded equally irreconcilable with liberalism as that word is generally understood.

Mr. Culbertson pandered to every folly that the jurors might be nursing in their bosoms. He spoke of the defendants as "these So'th'n boys." Only two or three could be considered boys. The ages of the others ranged from the late twenties to the fifties. It was interesting, by the way, to note how all the attorneys spoke with a much thicker Southern accent when they addressed the jury than when they were talking with their friends. Mr. Culbertson attacked the FBI agents in terms that either meant nothing or meant that it was far less important to punish a murder than to keep out the federal authorities. He made the remark, strange to hear in a court of law, "If a Democratic administration could do that to us, what would a Republican adminstration do to us down here?" He appeared later to be declaring that the FBI had been sent in by the administration to provide an anti-lynching case to win the Northern vote, in a Democratic seat that was not likely to go Republican even after a lynching prosecution. He himself, it may be noted, was a former FBI agent, and was, it is said, famous for his zeal. He used his hope that the jury were xenophobes to make an attack on the freedom of the press. He pointed to the press table and declared that because of this fussy insistence on the investigation of a murder there was now a trial to which Northern papers had sent representatives; and the implication was that they had come for the purpose of mocking and insulting the South. *"Lai-ai-aife* and *Tai-ai-aime,"* he chanted with the accent that was so much stronger in the courtroom than it sounded in the hotel lobby or the drugstore, "have sent representatives." The judge pointed out that Mr. Culbertson had no evidence of the existence of these people and that they therefore could not be discussed.

The thread on which these pearls were strung appeared to be the argument that the murder of Willie Earle was of very slight importance except for its remote political consequences. Mr. Culbertson was to prove that he did not give this impression inadvertently. He went into his crouching stance, his hands were spinning, he shone with frosty glee, exultantly he cried, "Willie Earle is dead, and I wish more like him was dead." There was a delighted, giggling, almost coquettish response from the defendants and some of the spectators. Mr. Hurd and his father looked fortified. There was a gasp from others of different mind. Thunderously the judge called him to order: "You confine yourself to my ruling or I'll stop you from arguing to the jury." Culbertson, smiling at the defendants, almost winking at them, said, "I didn't refer to Willie Earle as a Negro." When the judge bade him be careful, he continued, still flirting with his audience, "There's a law against shooting a dog, but if a mad dog were loose in my community, I would shoot the dog and let them prosecute me." A more disgusting incident cannot have happened in any court of law in any time.

The attitude of Greenville towards this speech was disconcerting. Prosperous Greenville did not like it, but it likes very little that Mr. Culbertson does, and it explained that one could expect nothing better from him, because he was a liberal. If it was objected that this was precisely not the kind of speech that could be expected from a liberal, this Greenville answered that it was a horrid speech, and that liberals were horrid, an argument that cannot be pursued very far. The response of the liberal section of Greenville was not any easier to take. The liberals made no attempt to conceal the important fact that two of the defendants were close connections of a CIO official. But they insisted that Mr. Culbertson was sincerely liberal, and apparently, if they rejected him, there was no local liberal of anything like his energy to take his place. To rationalize their continued acceptance of him, they had to adopt a theory that would do them no moral good at all. They admitted that it would have been awkward for his relations with the local CIO if he had refused to appear for the defendants; and they claimed that he was right not to refuse, because nothing is of equal importance to the necessity of introducing the CIO into the South. When they were asked why he used such squalid arguments in court, they replied that it is a lawyer's duty to do everything he can to win his case for his clients, and that as he believed these arguments would appeal to the jury he was obliged to use them. That is, of course, pure moonshine. In no system of jurisprudence is there a moral obligation on a lawyer who accepts the task of defending an accused murderer to go so near justifying murder as John Bolt Culbertson did in his passage about Willie Earle and the mad dog. This recalls many like accommodations that were made by lawyers in Italy and Germany during the early days of the Fascist and Nazi parties. They relaxed their traditional principles and practice because the establishment of the party seemed a necessity that had precedence over all others. But it is not generally understood that the CIO is the kind of party that demands such sacrifices.

If Mr. Culbertson's conduct of the case confused and depraved the standards of young liberal Greenville, it did something just as unpleasant to the Negroes. The connection that linked the defendants and the CIO was known to every Negro in town. The uneducated Negroes invented their own legend on the subject. Mr. Culbertson's home, they believed, done belong to CIO, and CIO done say it put Mr. Culbertson's furniture right out on the sidewalk if Mr. Culbertson don't save their folks' good name. Then they laughed, with a roaring, jeering cynicism that was a humiliation to every white man and woman in the land.

It was for the speech made by the fourth defence attorney, Mr. Thomas Wofford, that Greenville apologized most unhappily, though most laconically. Mr. Wofford was a person whom the town liked, or, to put it more accurately, for whom it felt an uneasy emotional concern. He was a man in his late thirties, red-haired, lightly built and quick on his feet, intelligent, nerve-ridden, well mannered, with a look in his eyes like a kicking horse. He must have been a very attractive and hopeful boy. He had always been fortunate. His uncle and his father-in-law were famous lawyers, and he has had the brains to make the best of the opportunities these relationships have given him. He is said to have political amibitions. In the preliminary stages of the case, when the judge was compiling a list of questions to be put to the veniremen to determine their suitability as jurors in this case, Sam Watt desired that they should be asked if they were members of any "secret organization, lodge, or association." Mr. Wofford objected, on the ground that such a question might be "embarrassing."

All the defence attorneys exaggerated their Southern accents and assumed a false ingenuousness when they addressed the jury, but none more so than Mr. Wofford. This elegantly attired and accomplished person talked as if he had but the moment before taken his hands off the plough; and he was careful to mop the sweat from his brow, because it is well known that the simple admire an orator who gives out even from the pores. He excelled his colleagues not only in this play acting but in his contempt for the jury. He assumed that they hated strangers, as the stupid do. He assumed that they would be stingy about money, as the poor often are. So he referred to the FBI investigation as a "case of what I call 'meddler's itch,' " pointed out the FBI agents who were sitting in court, and cried out in indignation because the state had closed its case four days before, "and here they are, staying at government expense." He must have known quite well that the FBI would only be performing its duty if it ordered its agents to stay till the end of the case, so that they could hear the attorneys' comments on their activities. He was against the FBI; he was also

101

against the local representatives of the law. "If you're going to enforce all the laws, why don't you prosecute the jailer?" he asked. "It took," he cried scornfully, "a nigger undertaker to find out there had been a lynching." Everybody and everything was wrong, it seemed, except murderers and the idea of murder. Like Mr. Culbertson, he disregarded the judge's ruling that no alleged action of Willie Earle was to be mentioned as affording "justification, mitigation, or excuse" for the lynching. It was rumoured in the recess preceding Mr. Wofford's speech that he meant to flout this ruling, and he did so with evident deliberation. He said, "Mr. Watt argues, 'Thou shalt not kill.' I wonder if Willie Earle had ever read that statement." This was as flagrant a defence of the lynching as Mr. Culbertson's remark "Willie Earle is dead, and I wish more like him was dead" and the allusion to the mad dog. But it was much more dangerous, because it was not obviously disgusting. Mr. Culbertson was plainly seeking to please and enroll as allies people in court and outside who could not for one moment be thought of as representing the highest tradition of Greenville or the South. Mr. Wofford was careful to look and speak in such a manner that people who did not fully understand the implications of his defence might think he was upholding those traditions. When the judge checked him and ordered the remark stricken off the records, Mr. Wofford showed a remarkable lack of deference to the court, but again in such a way that many people might have thought that he was defending the cause of justice and democracy. And it would be interesting to know what he was really defending. "We people get along pretty well," he said, "until they start interfering with us in Washington and points North," and he spoke of the Northern armies that had laid waste the South in the Civil War. He abused the "Northern agitators, radio commentators, and certain publications" for interfering in this case. He said that "they refer to us as 'a sleepy little town.' They say we are a backward state and poor—and we are. But this state is ours. To the historian, the South is the Old South. To the poet, it is the Sunny South. To the prophet, it is the New South. But to us, it is *our* South. I wish to God they'd leave us alone." This would be an attitude that one would respect in the case of the ordinary citizen of Greenville.

But in view of Mr. Wofford's desire not to embarrass secret organizations, his hostility to all law-enforcement agencies, and his attitude towards murder, it would be interesting to know what he wanted to be left alone to do.

It would not be fair to chronicle the speeches of the last two defence attorneys without emphasizing that they were in no way representative of Greenville. Some hours after Mr. Wofford had spoken, a man that Greenville looks up to paused in the lobby of the principal hotel to say to me, "I would like you to know that we were very disappointed in Tom's speech. We hoped he would do better." A nice man was putting something nicely. Greenville was more at ease the next day, the tenth day of the trial, when Judge Martin made his charge to the jury. The courtroom was fuller than ever before. There were now heavy showers, but the heat had not broken, so the women were still in summer dresses and the men in their shirts, while the rain fell in rods past the windows. In the front row of the seats, within the bar of the court, were the judge's wife and three daughters, all spectacular beauties, with magnificent black eyes and silky black curls. The youngest child, who is not yet in her teens, was dressed in a pink-checked muslin frock and had a special charm. The judge's charge to the jury struck oddly on the ears of strangers, for by the law of South Carolina the judge cannot comment on the evidence; he must do no more than analyze the law applying to the evidence and define the verdicts that it is possible to return against the accused persons. It is not easy to see the purpose of the law. If the intention is to prevent the common man from being hoodwinked by his superiors, there is equal reason for forbidding the prosecuting and defending attorneys from making closing speeches. For what it was, Judge Martin's charge was masterly, but it represented a legal position very favorable to the defendants. They were charged with murder and conspiracy, and there was very little evidence except their own statements. No man had in his statement confessed to murder. Nearly all had confessed to conspiracy. But, as the judge put it, "the state cannot establish a conspiracy by the alleged statements of the individual defendants alone." However, the judge also seemed at some pains to make the jury understand that if they acquitted the defendants on the charges relating to murder and found them guilty of conspiracy, the sentences passed on them could not exceed ten years.

Shortly after three o'clock the jury went out to consider their verdict and the judge left the bench. He had directed that the defendants need not be taken out, and might sit in court and visit with their families and friends. So now the court turned into a not enjoyable party, at which one was able to observe more closely certain personalities of the trial. There was Mrs. Brown, the widow of the murdered taxi driver, a spare, spectacled woman of the same austere type as the Hurds. She was dressed in heavy but smart mourning, with a veiled hat tipped sharply on one side, and she was chewing gum. So, too, was the professional bondsman who was the animating spirit of the committee that had raised funds for the defence of the defendants, a vast, blond, baldish man with the face of a brooding giant baby; but he was not genteel, as she was—he opened his mouth so wide at every chew that his gum became a matter of public interest. It had been noticeable during the trial that whenever the judge showed hostility to the introduction of race hatred into the proceedings, this man's chewing became particularly wide and vulpine. A judge from another local court, and various other Greenville citizens, drifted up to the press table and engaged the strangers in defensive conversation. The Southern inferiority complex took charge. They supposed that an English visitor would be shocked by the lynching, but it was impossible for anybody to understand who had always lived in a peaceable community where there was no race problem. They hoped it would be remembered that when coloured people were killed in race riots in the North nobody said anything about it, and that it was only when these things happened in the South that people made a fuss about them, because all Northern congressmen were voted for by black men. They added that anyway they were sure that our Northern friends had said very unkind things about the South. It was no use saying what was true: that lately Europe had not been really what any of us could call a peaceable community, and that its standards of violence were quite high, and that the lynching party did not seem very important as an outbreak of violence but that it was important as an indication of misery;

that the English had a very complex and massive race problem in South Africa, where one of the indubitably great men of the British Empire, General Smuts, professed views on the colour bar which would strike Greenville as fairly reactionary; and that our Northern friends, on hearing that we were going to the lynching trial, had remarked that while Southern lawlessness has a pardonable origin in a tragic past, Northern lawlessness has none and is therefore far more disgraceful. All this, however, brought no response. We might have been sitting each in a glass case built by history. Here was such a breach as divides England and Ireland.

I was glad when the common attention was distracted by Mr. Hurd. Everybody was now circulating freely in the court. Fat Joy seemed to be everywhere. Two of the attorneys and a friend had sat in the jury box for some time, but they had gone and two of the defendants had taken their place and were sitting with their feet up on the ledge. David Fredenthal, the *Life* artist, had been passing about the court making sketches from various points of view, and now he had come to ask Mr. Hurd, who was in his usual place, not far from the press table, if he would sit for him. Mr. Hurd became quite wooden with shyness, but his attorney and his father urged him to have his picture drawn. He came forward and sat stiffly in a chair within the bar of the court. It could be seen that he was really delighted. Mr. Hurd's father hovered about him, watching the artist with the greatest curiosity, but was too well mannered to come and look over his shoulder, as the hardier Mr. Culbertson and I were doing. Gradually people noticed that Mr. Hurd was being drawn, and several of the defendants came and stood beside us. They became quite silent. Mr. Fredenthal is a draftsman of the modern school, with the vagrant, caricaturing line of Feliks Topolski, and they were plain folks who like their art strictly representational. After the drawing was finished Mr. Hurd's father very politely asked if he might see it. When he was given it, he stood still and looked down on it for a minute. His son asked for it and he handed it to him without saying a word. This was probably one of the most acutely disappointing moments in their lives. He returned it to his father, who handed it back to the artist with a bow, forcing his features into a courteous smile. Then they rose and went away and sat down in their usual seats, staring in

105

front of them. The defendants who had been watching the artist then took up the drawing, seemingly to make sure that it really was as crazy as they had thought it from a distance, set it down with a murmur of thanks, and drifted away.

Edward Clark, the *Life* photographer, should have been a novelist; he detects the significant characters and episodes in the welter of experience as an Indian guide sees game in the forest. He said to me, "I want you to come and talk to one of the defendants and look at his hands." He took me over to a fair man in his early thirties, a plump and smiling person in his shirt-sleeves, who looked rather like Leon Errol. It was his wife who came daily to the court with five children. Clark introduced us and said, "Now show us what you have got on your hands." The man held them out proudly. On the four fingers of his left hand he had tattooed, just above the knuckles, the letters "L-O-V-E." And on the four fingers of his right hand he had the letters "H-A-T-E." Then he flipped up the thumbs. "T" was on the left thumb, "O" was on the right. "Love to hate," he read. He had done it himself, he said; he had a tattooing outfit. The more you washed the letters, the brighter they got. He had done it when he was seventeen, he said, and when I asked him why, he broke into laughter and said, "Lack of sense, I reckon, lack of sense. Leastways, that's what a lot of folks round here would tell you." This man had married a girl of thirteen ten years before. She had had a child every year, of which six were living. They lived in a street on the outskirts of Greenville which is counted one of its worst sections, though to the stranger's eye it looks pleasant enough, since the houses are set far apart in a pretty countryside. But the houses are old and poorly built and unsanitary, and the psychological climate is at once depressed and ferocious. The poor-white population lived there, but as prosperity waxed in the twenties they moved out to better quarters and the Negroes moved in. Then came the depression, and the whites lost their jobs or their pay was cut, and they were glad to get back to their old quarters whenever they could, even though it meant living beside the Negroes, whom they hated more than ever, because they now were anxious to do the menial jobs that till then had been left to the Negroes. This man had grown up during this horrible period when blacks and whites

106

snarled at each other like starved dogs fighting over a garbage can. There was no necessity to darken his world. But people who talked like Mr. Culbertson and Mr. Wofford had given him fears he need never have felt. "Don't take my picture," he said to Clark. "These days I drive a truck up North and I know what they would do to me if they knew I'd been in this."

A red-headed defendant was telling us that his old schoolteacher had sent him twenty dollars to help pay for his defence when it was announced that the judge was going out to dinner and would not be back until half-past nine. The defendants were taken to the jail to have their dinner; it was there discovered that during the courtroom party they had acquired several quarts of rye. The press went out after them, because it was obvious that the jury, even if they came to a decision, could not announce their verdict till the judge returned. At a little after half-past eight it was known that the jury had sounded its buzzer, which meant that they had made up their minds. This certainly meant that the accused persons had been acquitted of all charges. The jurymen had been out only five hours and a quarter, and they would have had to stay out much longer than that before all of them would have consented to a conviction; and they would have had to stay out much longer before they could have announced that they had failed to agree. This last, which would have led to the declaration of a mistrial, was what many people hoped for, since it would have meant that the defendants were not flattered by a proclamation of innocence, while at the same time there was no conviction, no risk of race riots, and no breach of tradition. But it was hardly any use hoping for this, since no juror who stood against an acquittal could be certain that some other juror would not betray him; and, as the fate of Mr. U. G. Fowler had shown, a juror would not be unduly pusillanimous if he let that consideration weigh with him. The press knew what the verdict was and knew there was still an hour till the judge would return. Yet we knew too that it is not what happens that matters so much as how it happens. Every event of any magnitude changes life unpredictably. There would by now be something happening in the court house that we could not have guessed would happen. So we got up from the table in the hotel dining room, where they were serving a beautiful meal that never was eaten, and ran into the street and through a heavy rain and up the court-house steps and along the corridor and up the staircase into the courtroom, and there it was, the thing we could not have guessed.

The place was given up to gloom. All the spectators who were not connected with the case had long since gone home to supper, and so had most of the defendants' friends, and those members of the defendants' families who had duties at their homes. The defendants had not yet been brought back from jail. So their wives and fathers and mothers had been sitting in the hall, now empty and full of shadows, looking at the press table, where there were no journalists; at the bench, where there was no judge; at the jury box, where there was no jury; and a fear of nothingness had come upon them. The wives were huddled in twos and threes, and most of these child-bearing children were weeping bitterly. The girl in green was sitting in the universal attitude of anguish, her head bent, the fingers of one hand spread along the hairline on her brow, the wrist brought down on the bridge of her nose. Mr. Hurd's father sat slowly turning his straw hat round and round on his knee, looking down his long nose at the floor. The windows showed us the sluices of the rain pouring between us and a night palpitating and dyed scarlet by an electric sign on the hotel. Up in the gallery thirteen Negroes were sitting in attitudes of fatigue and despair. Behind them three windows looked on a night white above the lights of Main Street.

This had been a miserable case for these Negroes. They had not even been able to have the same emotional release that would have been granted them if Willie Earle had been an innocent victim, a sainted martyr. It happened that the night Willie Earle had hired Brown to take him into Pickens County he went into a store in the Negro quarter, carrying a cheap cardboard suitcase. He accidentally dropped it on the floor at the feet of an older man, a university graduate who is one of the most influential figures in the Negro community of Greenville. The suitcase burst open and the contents were scattered all over the floor. The older man was surprised when Willie made no move to bend down and repack his suitcase, looked at him, saw that he was very drunk, so himself knelt down and did it for him. Hence the higher grades of coloured people, though referring to Earle with admirable charity and understanding as a maimed soul who acted without knowledge, made no issue of the case, as they would have done if the victim had been normal and blameless. It happened that the only constructive proposal concerning this morass of misery stretching out to infinity round this case that I heard during my stay at Greenville came from a Negro. That, oddly enough, was a plea for the extension of the Jim Crow system. "There is nothing I wish for more," he said, "than a law that would prohibit Negroes from riding in taxicabs driven by white men. They love to do it. We all love to do it. Can't you guess why? Because it is the only time we can pay a white man to act as a servant to us. And that does something to me, even though I can check up on myself and see what's happening. I say to myself, 'This is fine! I'm hiring this white man! He's doing a chore for me!' " He threw his head back and breathed deeply and patted his chest, to show how he felt. "If riding in a white taxicab does that to me, what do you think it does to Negroes who haven't been raised right or are full of liquor? Then queer things happen, mighty queer things. Killing is only one of them." It is apparently the practice in many other Southern towns, such as Savannah, that whites use only taxis with white drivers and Negroes use only taxis with Negro drivers.

No more Negroes went into the gallery. There were still only thirteen when the verdict was given. But the courtroom slowly filled up during the hour and a half that elapsed before the judge's return. The bondsman who had organized the defence fund came in and sat with a friend, who also resembled a giant baby; they whispered secrets in each other's ears, each screening his mouth with a huge hand while the other hand held, at arm's length, a tiny cigarette, as if a wreath of smoke could trouble their massiveness. The widow Brown ranged the aisles hungrily, evidently believing that an acquittal would ease her much more than it possibly could. The attorneys came in one by one and sat at their tables. Mr. Wofford was, as they say down there, happy as a skunk, flushed and gay and anecdotal. He and his group made a cheerful foreground to the benches where the wives of the defendants, fortified by their returning friends, wept less than before but still were weeping. As one of the Southern newspapermen looked about him at the scene, his face began to throb with a nervous twitch. At length the judge was seen standing at the open door of his chambers, and the defendants were brought into court. They were all very frightened. They bore themselves creditably, but their faces were pinched with fear. Mr. Hurd, though he was still confused, seemed to be asking himself if he had not been greatly deceived. Fat Joy was shifting along, wearing sadness as incongruously as fat men do. As they sat down their wives clasped them in their arms, and they clung together, melting in the weakness of their common fear. The judge came back to the bench and took some measures for the preservation of order in the court. He directed that all people should be cleared from the seats within the bar of the court unless they had a direct interest in the case or were of the press. The bondsman who had organized the defence committee was in such a seat and did not at first rise to go, but the court officials made him go. The people thus ejected stood round the walls of the room. Those by the windows turned to look at the downpour of the rain, which was now torrential. The judge ordered all the officers of the court to take up positions in the aisles and to be ready for anyone who started a demonstration. They stood there stiffly, and the defendants' wives, as if this were the first sign of a triumph for severity, trembled and hid their faces. The jury entered. One juror was smiling; one was looking desperately ashamed; the others looked stolid and secretive, as they had done all through the trial. They handed the slips on which they had recorded their verdicts to the clerk of the court, who handed them to the judge. He read them through to himself, and a flush spread over his face.

As soon as the clerk had read the verdicts aloud and the judge had left the bench and the courtroom, which he did without thanking the jury, the courtroom became, in a flash, something else. It might have been a honky-tonk, a tourist camp where they sold beer, to use Mr. Culbertson's comminatory phrase. The Greenville citizens who had come as spectators were filing out quietly and thoughtfully. Whatever their opinions were, they were not to recover their usual spirits for some days. As they went they looked over their shoulders at the knot of orgiastic joy that had instantly been formed by the defendants and their supporters. Mr. Hurd and his father did not give such spectacular signs of relief as the others. They gripped each other tightly for a moment, then shook hands stiffly, but in wide, benedictory movements, with the friends who gathered around them with the ardent feeling that among the defendants Mr. Hurd especially was to be congratulated. The father and son were smiling shyly, but in their eyes was a terrible light. They had been confirmed in their knowledge that they were the chosen vessels of the Lord. Later Mr. Hurd, asked for a statement, was to say, "Justice has been done . . . both ways." Meanwhile the other defendants were kissing and clasping their wives, their wives were laying their heads on their husbands' chests and nuzzling in an ecstasy of animal affection, while the laughing men stretched out their hands to their friends, who sawed them up and down. They shouted, they whistled, they laughed, they cried; above all, they shone with self-satisfaction. In fact, make no mistake, these people interpreted the verdict as a vote of confidence passed by the community. They interpreted it as a kind of election to authority.

They must have been enormously strengthened in this persuasion by the approval of Mr. Culbertson, who, as soon as the judge had left court, had leaped like a goat from chair to table and from table to chair, the sooner to wring the hands of his clients. Oddly, Mr. Ashmore, the prosecuting attorney, was also busy shaking hands with some defendants, with the rallying smile of a schoolmaster, and saying, "Now you must behave yourself," and "See you stay out of trouble." Clark had now produced his camera and flashbulb and was standing on a chair, taking photographs of the celebrations. The defendants were delighted and jumped up on chairs to pose for him, their friends standing below them and waving and smiling towards the camera, so that they could share in the glory. In these pictorial revels Mr. Culbertson was well to the fore. First he posed with the Hurds. Then he formed part of a group that neither Greenville nor the CIO could greatly enjoy if they should see it in *Life*. On a chair stood Fat Joy, bulging and swelling with pleasure, and on his right stood the bondsman and on his left Mr. Culbertson, baring their teeth in ice-cold geniality, and each laying one hard hand on the boy's soft bulk and raising the other as if to lead a cheer. It was unlikely that Mr. Culbertson was unaware of the cynical expression on Clark's face,

111

and he knew perfectly well what other members of the press were thinking of him. But he did not care. *Life* is a national weekly. Mr. Culbertson does not want to be a national figure. He means to be a highly successful local figure. My future, he was plainly saying to himself, is in Greenville, and this is good enough for Greenville, so let's go. It will be astonishing if he is right. At that, he was a more admirable figure than Mr. Wofford, however, because at least his credo had brought him out into the open, standing alongside the people whose fees he had taken and whose cause he had defended. But on hearing the verdict Mr. Wofford, who possibly has an intention of becoming a national figure, had vanished with the speed of light and was doubtless by this time at some convenient distance, wiping his mouth and saying, "Lord, I did not eat."

There could be no more pathetic scene than these taxi drivers and their wives, the deprived children of difficult history, who were rejoicing at a salvation that was actually a deliverance to danger. For an hour or two the trial had built up in them that sense of law which is as necessary to man as bread and water and a roof. They had known killing for what it is: a hideousness that begets hideousness. They had seen that the most generous impulse, not subjected to the law, may engender a shameful deed. For indeed they were sick at heart when what had happened at the slaughter pen was described in open court. But they had been saved from the electric chair and from prison by men who had conducted their defence without taking a minute off to state or imply that even if a man is a murderer one must not murder him and that murder is foul. These people had been plunged back into chaos. They had been given by men whom they naïvely trusted the most wildly false ideas of what conduct the community will tolerate. Not only had they, along with everyone else, been encouraged to use the knife and the gun in ways that may get them into trouble—for it is absurd to think Greenville is really a place whose tolerance of disorder is unlimited—but they had been exposed to a greater danger of having the knife and the gun used on them. The kind of assault by which Mr. Brown died was likely to be encouraged by the atmosphere that now hung over Greenville. It seemed that these wretched people had been utterly betrayed.

It was impossible to watch this scene of delirium, which had been conjured up by a mixture of clownishness, ambition, and sullen malice, without feeling a desire for action. Supposing that one lived in a town, decent but tragic, which had been trodden into the dust and had risen again, and that there were men in that town who threatened every force in that town which raised it up and encouraged every force which dragged it back into the dust; then lynching would be a joy. It would be, indeed, a very great delight to go through the night to the home of such a man, with a few loyal friends, and walk in so softly that he was surprised and say to him, "You meant to have your secret bands to steal in on your friends and take them out into the darkness, but it is not right that you should murder what we love without paying the price, and the law is not punishing you as it should." And when we had driven him to some place where we would not be disturbed, we would make him confess his treacheries and the ruses by which he had turned the people's misfortunes to his profit. It would be only right that he should purge himself of his sins. Then we would kill him, but not quickly, for there would be no reason that a man who had caused such pain should himself be allowed to flee quickly to the shelter of death. The program would have seemed superb had it not been for two decent Greenville people, a man and a woman, who stopped by the press desk as they went out of the courtroom and spoke, because they were so miserable that they had to speak to someone. "This is only the beginning," the man said. "It is like a fever," said the woman, tears standing in her eyes behind her glasses. "It spreads, it's an infection, it's just like a fever." They were in a sense right. For several odd things happened during the next few days. Irrational events breed irrational events. The next day a Negro porter at the parking place of a resort hotel near Greenville was seen to insult white guests as no white hotel employee would have dared. The news of the acquittal created a nervous tension which made the more sensitive Negroes not know what they were doing. For some weeks, all over the South, hysterical people, white and coloured, made trouble for themselves and each other by bizarre behaviour, showing abandonment to panic before imaginary provocation, by hallucinated aggression. But that man and woman were wrong. The lynching trial in

South Carolina and its sequels were a symptom of an abating disease. The history of the acquitted men during the following year shows how the germ was failing. Some of them were happy, and had no history; and Mr. John Marchant appears in the records only as serving the graces of life as an usher at two weddings. Six saw trouble. But it is worth while noting the kind of trouble it was. One was charged with transporting moonshine whisky. Two more were sent to a federal penitentiary for violating terms of probation. Another attacked a female friend and tried to cut his throat when he was arrested. Another was obliged to ask the police for permission to carry a gun because his life had been threatened. But only one was accused of an offence against coloured people. He had fired a gun into an automobile filled with Negroes. Nobody was hit, and it is possible that it was only a boorish joke, though the Negroes must have seen it in a different light. He was fined a hundred dollars, which in view of his particular circumstances was severe enough and probably less to his taste than a sentence of imprisonment. But he was cultivating an obsolescent interest. There was a strange and dramatic tempo to be felt at the Greenville trial; wickedness itself had been aware of the slowing of its pulse. The will of the South had made its decision, and by 1954 three years had gone by without a lynching in the United States.

Greenhouse with Cyclamens II

(1949)

GREENHOUSE WITH CYCLAMENS II

Often people said, "You must have met some very interesting people when you went to the Nuremberg trial." Yes indeed. There had been a man with one leg and a child of twelve, growing enormous cyclamens in a greenhouse, and miraculously selling them in a country where there was no trade save a dreary public victualage and barter of the soiled and worn. Since then they had taken over the whole of Western Germany. Even here in Hamburg, a city which had seemed dead as a gutted animal after the war, trade of a dogged kind was achieving a prodigious growth.

This was partly the work of the Allies: of the unacknowledged great, such as a mining engineer from Doncaster named Harry Collins, now Production Director on the Durham Division of the National Coal Board, who performed one of the great administrative feats in history by going into the ruined Ruhr and feeding the starving miners and improvising housing and putting the heart into them to get the coal out of the ground; of the officials who pushed through the currency reform of 1948, which was launched by the British and the Americans and the French with a true regard for German interests, in opposition to the Soviet Union. But the essential factor was the itch to industry, the lech for work, that forced the Germans to make things and sell them, that kept the one-legged man hobbling and twisting between his wood furnace and his greenhouse.

To visitors from abroad the spectacle of this renaissance was sometimes quite repellent. Their repulsion was almost entirely unjust, yet it was inevitable. Hamburg presented a deplorable spectacle from the altruistic point of view to which Great Britain was by

117

then deeply committed. Except for the fringe of houses round the harbour and the great lake of the Alster, the city was waste land. All round it was scar tissue, more repellent than similar damage in the City of London or Plymouth or Hull or Bristol, not only because the damage was greater here but because the area was desolate but not depopulated. It was teeming with tired and dusty people, raffish from lack of privacy, who were still living in cellars and air-raid shelters four years after the end of the war, and had plainly not yet got out of the war. They looked as if they had not heard that there yet is peace, because there was so much bad news round them that they had no time to listen to good news. Many of them looked hungry and were hungry. The meals that were eaten off old doors and packing cases in the air-raid shelters were pitiable. A number of them had not the money to buy even the rationed foods.

But if one stopped in the right street one could refresh oneself at a large tea shop, which was full of people, mostly women, and all Germans. Allied personnel were forbidden to enter a restaurant or a hotel or any place where they might eat German food and invite the accusation that the Allies were pillaging the German economy, though the Allies were actually living on a scale well below full nutrition. In this tea shop each of the fortunate Germans was drinking a cup of chocolate or coffee topped with a swirl of whipped cream, and was bending piously, as in performance of a rite, over a plate on which there were at least three cakes; say, a slice of chocolate layer cake and another of strawberry torte, both smothered in whipped cream, and a confection of meringue and chopped hazelnuts.

Germans questioned on this point often alleged that these debauchees would have no later meal that day. But in the evening several Hamburg restaurants, such as the Rathskeller, were filled with Germans who managed to consume and pay for such a light repast as a plate of hors d'œuvres, where smoked eel and rose-pink ham and slivers of Matjes herring lay in a circle of mayonnaise eggs, followed by a fish soup glistening with cream, a duck golden with the juices of its basting, and an ice-cream bombe masked with hot meringue.

Many Europeans have been shocked, some into lasting anti-

Americanism, by the amount American soldiers and tourists drink. Almost all non-Germans who visited Germany after the currency reform were as shocked by the amount the more prosperous Germans ate, and by the sympathy they received at a very high level.

German politicians meeting Dorothy Thompson, who had been as good a friend of anti-Nazi Germans as she was an enemy of the Nazis, and deserved well of them for opposing the Morgenthau Plan, did not find words to thank her, but at once attempted to enlist her support in a quarrel they were waging with the Allied Control Commission on the subject of pigs. To put it briefly: the Germans wanted to feed pigs on the grain sent them under the Marshall Plan, so that they might eat pork, while the Allied Control Commission desired them to consume the grain as grain, for the nutritional experts asserted that there was a considerable waste of food value in converting it into meat. It was plain that, in raising this matter rather than others with Miss Thompson, the politicians felt they were putting first things first.

It was indeed impossible not to feel shocked at the spectacle of people refusing to make the sacrifice which we were offering up in England by curbing our appetites that all might share alike. But this was largely nonsense. Let us leave on one side the painful consideration that at this date Germans of moderate means ate better than their English equivalents, simply because the English had not the art of making good cheap sausage. To begin with, the situation seemed more gross than it was, because the bad is more easily perceived than the good. A fresh lobster does not give such pleasure to the consumer as a stale one will give him pain. A beautiful woman living in chastity gives fewer indications of her state than a beautiful woman kept by a rich lover. Even so, the women in Hamburg who ate creamy cakes could be seen doing so by anybody who troubled to visit a certain confectioner's shop. But only old ties of friendship brought us together with a woman bearing a famous name in the city annals. An English official explained to us that we would find her very tired, because the homeless were still billeted on the lucky whose houses were intact, and while the conscienceless found ways of getting rid of them, this woman had accepted her responsibilities to the full. She let the authorities put a family in each of her rooms, and herself went

119

up to a cold attic, where her family portraits hung slanting on the gabled walls. But she was not only tired, her eyes were red with weeping. "But of course I remember visiting your mother-in-law in London. It was all so pleasant. She played Brahms so beautifully. No? Then perhaps it was a sister. No? Well a friend perhaps, and there was a beautiful Chinese shawl on the piano. And another day she took me to Ranelagh. It was all so very pleasant." But later she had to tell us the preoccupation. "I can tell you as you are strangers. A woman was billeted on me a short time ago, and it seems that she is really a bad woman. She pretends to me that she goes to bed and she shuts her door so that I hear it and says good night, and then she gets out of the window and goes down to the bomb sites, and dreadful things happen, you can imagine. And really, to have people getting out of the window, in the house where you were born. But she does it that way so that I should not complain and get her turned out, and I suppose I should, for there are young people in the house, and it is not right for them to be with her. But, oh dear, oh dear, a bad woman needs a roof over her head as much as anybody else, I do not like to do this."

She smiled brilliantly when we spoke of the cream cakes and said that good could come out of evil and great good had come out of these cream cakes. When the pastrycooks started making them again the news did not escape the attention of a body of women who had formed an organization called "Woman" as a result of listening to Dorothy Thompson's broadcasts from the United States during the war. They had formed a secret society which offered resistance to the Nazis by good works, by doing kindnesses to Jews and other persecuted people; and they were still working together now. "We thought it absurd that people should be eating cream cakes and torte when there was no ration of milk for the little children, so, just think, we marched on the Town Hall and demanded that this should be done. And they did it. They just had not thought, you know."

There were many such Germans who were sharing all they had in as handsome a spirit as ever was shown in England. But the truth was often just as the stranger saw it: there were many Germans who were brutally selfish and fought their way over their weaker brethren to the trough. Nevertheless, as one travelled through Germany in 1949, it emerged that many Germans fell into neither category. They believed that no good would come of deliberately sharing things, that even the person who was handed the unearned share would not benefit. They believed in free enterprise. They thought that if people did what they liked, ate what they liked, made what they liked, and sold what they liked, the laws of supply and demand would function so healthily that in the end every citizen would have a substantial slice of cake and there would be no reason for anybody to share anything with anybody else.

It was strange that they struck foreign visitors as inert, and that so many British and Americans abused their governments for having no policy in Germany; for the entire German people was formulating a policy with every breath, and that policy was to develop their industry in accordance with their laissez-faire economic theories and to refuse to be impressed by the welfare state and planned economy which was actually established in Great Britain and which existed in fantasy in the minds of American intellectuals. The degree to which they were not impressed was quite remarkable. The Germans had always been willing to be impressed by the British before; but at this moment, when they had most reason to respect them, they refused to make any sign of intellectual obeisance. But it would have been a historical impossibility that they should accept the idea of the welfare state and a planned economy. To begin with, the Nazi regime had claimed to be a welfare state and had certainly imposed a planned economy; and all that had worked out very badly. Also, the Allied Control Commission was itself imposing a planned economy on Germany, not without incident. "I do not know if this is very interesting reading for a lady," said a British official kindly, handing over the desk the Monthly Report of the Control Commission for Germany (British Element) for April 1949. The lady found it interesting enough. She opened it at page 84 and read in the Finance Report of the Bipartite Section the paragraph:

> One of the anomalies in the income tax law, as amended by Military Government Law 64, was that the aggregate amount of income and property taxes might—in the case of very wealthy taxpayers—exceed 100 per cent of their incomes. By making

Property Tax a deduction in computing income tax assessments, Economic Council Ordinance 95 removes this anomaly.

This is a use of the word "anomaly" without precedent, except in the mad scene in *Hamlet*, where, of course, Ophelia says, "Anomaly, that's for the Treasury," just before she remarks that the owl was a very wealthy taxpayer's daughter. This was no anomaly but an offence of the kind the modern state is forced by its own complexity to commit times without number against its unfortunate children. None of us who are the victims of such mistakes ever learn to like them when they are committed by our own kind. Try to think how much less we should like them if they were committed against us by our conquerors.

The Germans found it particularly irritating when the Allies not only tried to impose a planned economy on them, but tried to march them even farther left than they had gone themselves. In Düsseldorf two young men, one an American liberal journalist, the other an English University Fabian, were interviewing a German politician. "And what about land reform?" they asked with heavy suspicion, which was directed not against the Germans but against the Allies. "That's not getting on very fast, is it?" The German politician was something of an attitudinizer; he had been giving a Stadttheater performance of a patriot saving his country in its hour of need, but he cocked his eyebrows at them with a surprising shrewdness. It happens that at Yalta the Russians sold us a pup named Land Reform, by which we bound ourselves to break up the large landed estates in the British Zone, with the ostensible object of destroying the excessive political power of the landowners. We experienced considerable difficulty in carrying this out, because there were few large landed estates in the British Zone; and inspirational force was lacking because research showed the landowners in this region had exercised little political power. At this point the wise thing was to go home with one's hands in one's pockets, whistling, but Mr. Bevin and his familiars in the Foreign Office decided that no German farm, outside certain special categories, should be over two hundred and fifty acres. As this is not a very large acreage, considering the poor soil found in many parts of Western Germany, and as it raised some tedious problems of resettlement, the officials of the Allied Control Commission were obeying these instructions with a certain leisureliness which suited Germans of all parties. "And you gentlemen," said the German, "what steps are you taking to pass a law in your countries imposing a limit on the acreage of farms?"

Like words were spoken in an office on the Ruhr. "Oh, indeed? You gentlemen approved of the extent to which the workers have to be represented on factory management committees and would like the proportion to be increased still further? Well, I am not against that myself. But had you not better first make such a system compulsory in your own countries and see how it works?" On such occasions it became apparent that if an occupation were to be enjoyable the natives of the occupied territory should wear nose rings and not be able to read. The Germans spent far too much time with their unringed noses in British and American left-wing publications. They were too well aware that there was a British left-wing element with an eye on cooperation between the British Labour government and a German Social Democratic government, which would enable the British Labour government to go to the electorate with the claim that they had scotched German industrial competition by inducing the German government to impose trade-union restrictions of the British type. All over the British Zone, Germans suspected that though the British Control Commission officials might be decent fellows their compatriots at home were humbugs and halfwits; and in the Ruhr they were quite sure of it, because of the continuance of the dismantling policy. This, in 1949, was the sheerest tomfoolery. In 1945 and 1946 it had been reasonable, for that was not a time for reason. Then it was right for the Allies to go into Germany and say to the Germans, "You chose to live by the sword, and now we shall see to it that you forge no more swords," and to overturn their smithies and force them to make good the damage they had inflicted on the industries of other lands. But by 1949 all feasible restitution in kind had been effected and the penal aspect of dismantling had been annulled. Let us consider the case of a great factory, a noble factory, a true work of art, its black diagram of ingenuity visible for miles in the spacious industrial area of the

Ruhr, known to many Germans from their youth up, and to many of them a promise of employment. The Ruhr population had worked well under technicians like Harry Collins of Doncaster and had come to think of themselves and the Allies as joint conspirators in productiveness. If they suddenly found gangs of their fellow countrymen at work under Allied command tearing down this factory, they did not say, "Ah, we are now expiating our sin in waging that war—you remember, that one which ended four years ago." They simply felt that the occupation authorities, whom they had done their best to please and had come to like, had suddenly turned nasty and were destroying German property and putting them in danger of unemployment; and they could not imagine what motive could inspire this action except trade rivalry.

By 1949 the sole purpose of dismantling recognized by both sides was the reduction of Germany's war potential; and on that basis there was carried on a long and degrading argument in which nothing was said that could be believed by any sensible person. The German industrialists overdid their protestations that the works scheduled for demolition were unimportant as war potential; they were synthetic petrol plants, with fatty by-products, and that told its own story. They also exaggerated the beneficence of the part they played in the German peacetime economy, which obviously did not stand or fall by its synthetic petrol plants any more than the British or French peacetime economies stood or fell by theirs. The British opponents of dismantling were still more offensive than the Germans, for they based their case on the thesis that the Germans were a sinless people who can be trusted with any amount of war potential, that the Germans were essentially and unalterably pacifist.

But the case for the continuance of dismantling was just as imbecile. Though synthetic petrol plants were war potential, it was no use pretending that they were decisive war potential. Stress was laid on figures which showed that the works were carried on at a loss, but it seemed probable that the degree of the loss was largely due to an imposed obligation to work them to fifty per cent or less of their capacity while they still stood; and in any case it would not have been unnatural if the German government should have chosen to subsidize a process which yielded fatty by-products, especially since Lord Boyd Orr, that banshee of the nutritional world, was then prophesying a world shortage of fats. The propaganda for the continuance of dismantling made painful reading then and makes painful reading now, but it was the very best the case allowed. This policy was enormously dear to the Foreign Office, and to Mr. Ernest Bevin, the Foreign Secretary who has been most completely in the hands of his officials. The Foreign Office was unmoved by the fact that every British official worth his salt and the German trade-union movement in a body were opposed to dismantling.

This crusade left Germans with the poorest impression of British common sense. Many of them read with interest the Foreign Affairs debate in which Mr. Bevin justified his policy: a debate which then appalled and still appalls by its incoherence. They were told that France and the Soviet Union were hounding the Foreign Office and the State Department to implement the dismantling agreement to the bitter end. They knew that the Foreign Office and the State Department were not at all likely to run into trouble in order to please France, and they knew that the insistence of the Soviet Union was an impudence which demanded disregard. The Russians had long abandoned dismantling in the Eastern Zone and were permitting factories to work in their own zone of Germany which were the exact analogues of the factories they were hounding the Allies to pull down in Western Germany. In every country outside Germany, Communists were urging haste in dismantling and were declaring that the delay was due to fascist big business influences in Great Britain and America and Germany. British and American and French Communists and fellow travellers visited Germany and sent home articles which bolstered up this story. But the Communists inside Western Germany opposed dismantling so vigorously that, as a protest against the policy, the Works Council of a famous factory in the Ruhr for the first time elected three Communists to the three presidential chairs. Not only were the Communists of Western Germany parading in full propaganda fig in defence of the threatened plants, the Eastern Zone was pouring a continuous stream of letters and telegrams on the management and workers of these plants, congratulating them on their resistance and encouraging them to make an even bolder stand. They did not fail, in these letters and telegrams, to point out that the similar plants in the Eastern Zone were running "to benefit the German economy," and as a master stroke various provinces in the Eastern Zone adopted the staffs of these dismantled factories as American and British towns used to adopt the populations of war-damaged Continental towns. This nonsense went on and on until 1950, when, against the passionate resistance of the Foreign Office, the policy was abandoned.

The Germans liked the officials of the Allied Control Commission and thought them on the whole honest and conscientious and kind. Even those who looted and fiddled they did not greatly resent; that they could understand. But they did not respect the government of Great Britain. They were therefore won away from the idea of free enterprise, and it is not for democrats to deny their right to practise and preach any economic theory they chose. All the same, the altruistic impulse which made Britain wish to share and share alike was warming, and that warmth too it would have been agreeable to share. It is true too that it was largely a lack of social conscience and flighty industrial ambition which gave Hitler his chance. But if we are going to be moralists, we had better. Note what the Germans have done to lift a burden of moral guilt off the shoulders of the rest of us.

This moral guilt related to the persons present in Germany as displaced persons, expellees, and refugees. The blame for the presence of the displaced persons rested primarily on the Germans, for most of them had been brought in by the Nazis as slave labour; but they had remained in Germany because they were not Communists and Mr. Churchill and Presidents Roosevelt and Truman had imposed communism on their countries without consulting the inhabitants. Then there were the expellees, whose presence was entirely due to the Allies. They were the groups of German origin in East European countries which the Potsdam Conference had agreed to remove from the places where their ancestors had lived for centuries and sent to Germany. There were also the refugees from the Eastern Zone of Germany, who were fleeing from Russian inefficiency. In these categories there were about ten million people.

Many of the displaced persons had emigrated. The lot of those who had not was often terrible. Outside Munich there was an abandoned air station, wind-swept and waterlogged, where five thousand White Russians lived in hutments falling into ruin. This was high summer, but every hut was watered by a drip from the ceiling. In the winter the rain came through the broken roofs and soaked the insulated material, and it never got quite dry before the next winter came on. There were eight or ten people in every room, usually belonging to two families. They could hear everything that their neighbours were saying or doing in the rooms on either side. The roads from these huts to the canteens and ablution centres and social buildings were fissured with ruts. The cement floors of the kitchens and canteens were scuffed and splintered, and the inmates were always catching their heels in the cracks and falling when they were carrying food and drink. Anyway, they got sick of the canteen food and found it dear, and many used to cook in the rooms, but their stoves wore out and they were short of fuel, so they sat at their tables and ate cold food out of the paper from the delicatessen store. It was hard to know which were in worse case: those who went out to work and shared in the bustling life of reviving Germany and had to come back to this morgue at night, or those who had to stay there all day. "I could mend the roof," said the old man. "Look, I am strong, I was very strong once, I am still strong, but I can get no corrugated iron." They could have mended the cement floors too, and the stoves, and even the roads, but they had no material.

In that camp there was a large criminal society, vile and varied. There were dope pedlars and pimps and blackmailers, and every sort of thief. A woman flung out her arm as she passed a group of horrible young men whose hair came near meeting their eyebrows, broad-shouldered and crouching gorillas. She screamed at them and they jeered back. They were a gang who watched to see which of their fellows were earning good wages and buying new clothes and bedding and stoves, and then, under cover of night, threw midget bombs into the hut and, while the terrified occupants rushed out by the door, climbed in at the window and stole all that was valuable. They had stripped this woman and her husband of the first decent possessions they had had to call their own for thirteen years. There were many bloody assaults, and even murders. There was also a cold intellectual hell in this camp, an iceberg in which there was preserved every political faith which has emerged in Russia during the last hundred and thirty years, with the single exception of Stalinist bolshevism; everything from Decembrism to Eurasian fascism and Trotskyism, and even some deviations within Trotskyism. All these faiths had been frozen hard by the misery of those who held them, and they were now so chill that they burned. All these Russians loved Russia, and for that reason each party hated implacably all the rest, for having whored after strange political gods and brought the beloved country to ruin, and themselves to this wet and windy end of hope.

It mattered very much what happened to these people, for between these hot and cold hells a stable society had established itself. There were many people who astonished by their nobility. One family had achieved a miracle. The father had been an officer in Tsarist Russia and had escaped after the Revolution to Yugoslavia, where he had become a teacher. In middle life he had married the daughter of another White Russian, and they had one son. From the time the Germans had invaded Yugoslavia in 1941 the family had had the worst of both worlds, for the Germans persecuted them for their liberal opinions, and they later had to flee into Germany from Tito and the Russians. Never once, in all their wanderings, had the father and mother let a day pass without giving their son his lessons, and the boy had been so well taught that he had just been admitted to Munich University, after sitting for the entrance examination at the usual age. What was more remarkable, the boy was serene. He talked without rancour and without fear, and might have been brought up in some country magically left untouched by the two wars.

There were a number of young people in the camp who presented the same unscathed appearance. This was not the result of a happy accident but of ferocious efforts on the part of their elders, who had, to be sure, been given a church and a school by the authorities, but had added much to those gifts. An Orthodox church is nothing without its furnishings and its liturgy. The inmates had taken some old airplanes to pieces and had hammered out an iconostasis and great candlesticks, and had painted their own icons, and the services were performed with careful ardour. They had scraped together their pennies to pay such amongst them as were qualified to teach in school, and to buy lesson books, and they constantly impressed on their young that it would be dangerous to go out into the world without the protection of their people's culture. The ridiculous vanity of Pan-Slavism looked out of their eyes, changed to a homely remedy against evil.

With these people were three hundred Kalmucks, descendants of those Western Mongolians who went to South Russia in the eighteenth century. These belonged to a group that had fled to Belgrade after the Russian Revolution and taken over the cab-driving industry there between the wars. In Yugoslavia they had always looked very steadfast. "It is a delusion," a painter had told us there. "It is due to the epicanthic fold, which drapes the eye with a stern, straight curtain of flesh, and the austere moulding of the cheekbones. If I had these advantages, gipsy as I am in my nature, I could look a pillar, a stronghold." But here it was plain that they were in fact steadfast. They clung quietly to the customs of their people and were solicitous for their children, and in one of the huts had made a little tinselled Buddhist temple. The ritual calls for prostrations and genuflections in different parts of the temple, and the grave brown people trod out the prescribed movements round a number of tin baths set to catch the trickles from the ceiling.

The displaced persons were a diminishing group. The Kalmucks, for example, eventually went to Canada and the United States. But there were nearly four million expellees in Western Germany, and the number was stable. Some of them, chiefly mothers and children, were lodged in the great houses of the rich, and they were in a sense the luckiest. But our own British evacuees know the disadvantages of such quarters, and the great houses of Germany are even more isolated. From the casement of the medieval castle we could look down on the moat and see the little ex-

129

pellees playing on the grass marge between the water and the forest, while their mothers walked about knitting, tucking the ends of the needles under their armpits in the German way. "Is it usual to have cowbells in this district?" asked someone. "No. We put them on during the war because it was so terribly lonely." There was no village near the castle, the nearest town was ten miles away; the women had no means of transport at their disposal, and no money beyond a dole of a few shillings. Others lived in bombed houses. Half of them, indeed, were recorded as living in damaged houses. Many of them were living in camps vacated by displaced persons; and that means that they were living in hutments which had been occupied by the armed forces since 1939, or even earlier, until 1945, and during all that time had had almost nothing done to them in the way of repairs.

What happened to these camps was beyond the range of normal imagination. In Bavaria, where the expellees and refugees numbered a third of the population, a German official in the Ministry put his head down on his desk and wailed aloud at the close of a telephone conversation which had brought him tidings of a permanent camp to which he had intended to move some thousands of refugees that very day. It had previously been occupied by Jewish displaced persons, who had recently gone to Palestine. They had all been engaged in trade of some sort and had found themselves, when they had to leave, faced with the problem of moving their possessions, which they had all accumulated. With a resourcefulness for which nobody could blame them, they set about making packing cases out of every piece of wood they could detach from the buildings. When the German officials came to take over, they found the place a shell. The German official had therefore nothing to do but to move the refugees to another camp, which he did not himself consider fit for human habitation.

But doubtless the refugees were glad to go, for at least they left a transit camp, and few places were more horrible in 1949 than a transit camp. There men and women and children arrived dirty and bleary-eyed after a journey over the frontier that might have lasted for days. They had to be packed like sardines into huts until they could be screened and diagnosed for what they were.

That was one of the most horrid aspects of their situation. They had all to be treated at first as if they were guilty, for their own sakes. They might be honest refugees moved by hunger and terror, fleeing from the uranium mines, or from conscription into the military police, or from investigation by the MVD; they might be Soviet spies; they might be criminals; they might be lunatics who imagined they were being persecuted. Some of them might not have come from the Soviet Zone at all, they might be naughty children who had got into trouble with their families and thought they would pose as refugees and get a hiding place. As the flow over the border increased, the pipe got choked. They had to stay longer and longer in the transit camps.

Some had been more than six weeks in the transit camp in the pine woods of Schleswig-Holstein. There were two thousand of them there, living in Nissen huts put up by a British regiment that had meant them for its own temporary use and therefore put in no insulation; so they were icy in winter and stifling in summer. The refugees were sleeping seventy or so in the dormitory huts, which stank. That was not their fault. Though the Germans were eating cream cakes and drawing a bigger fat ration than the British at that time, there was very little soap. Some of these people were beginning to stink morally too. "My people," said the sea captain who was camp superintendent, and had learned his English at sea, "are bloody liars, but you must not blame them." And there he was right. They had no assets but their hard-luck stories; and as they were surrounded by people who had just as poignant stories they started to compete and learned to be, as he said, bloody liars. They learned other things as well. Every few days the police came round and the superintendent wearily helped them to search the camp for sacks full of poultry, and if to find what you seek is good luck, then they were lucky. "And the young girls, and the young blokes," said the sea captain, "what shall I do with the young things? All these woods, how should they not go into them?"

Old people hobbled about the clearing in the sunshine. There was nowhere for them to sit down and enjoy the warmth. It was forbidden to take chairs out into the open air, for too many chairs had been spirited away to be chopped up and used as firewood.

There was nothing for anybody to do. In the afternoon the women lay in their bunks and stared straight up at the ceiling. The matron was extravagantly grateful when Dorothy Thompson gave the camp a sewing machine. "But it seems silly to give only one to such a large camp," said Dorothy, and the matron answered, "Those who never get to use it will hope that someday they will be the lucky ones."

"What have they to look forward to?" we asked the official from the Schleswig-Holstein Ministry in charge of refugees. He explained that they hoped to be accepted as residents in Schleswig-Holstein, where they would look for work, but as there were nearly as many refugees in the district as natives, the prospect of finding it was uncertain. If they did not find work they drew an allowance of about a pound a week. If they did not pass the screening they would either have to go back to the Soviet Zone or live like outlaws, without even a ration card. It was hard to hear what this official said, he was so hoarse. He was a refugee himself, a lawyer with an anti-Nazi record, from an East German city, and he was very tired. He had to work in Kiel, where there was an acute housing shortage owing to the bomb damage, so he had to rent an expensive house in a seaside resort two hours away for his large family. This left him so short of money that he could eat only in the cheapest restaurants, and the food and service disgusted him, so he lived on coffee and sandwiches and never had a hot meal except when he was at home during the weekends.

But he was really very hoarse, even for a tired man. No, it was all right for him to talk, he always had a sore throat these days. Chronic hoarseness would make a sensible man in his forties consult a doctor, just to dismiss a certain suspicion. But it was easy to see why he had neglected this precaution. He could not take his mind off certain calculations. He could not see how the refugees could fail to bankrupt the district's treasury, or how, even if responsibility for the refugees was accepted by the Bonn Parliament as a federal burden, that too could lead to anything but bankruptcy, as about fourteen hundred people were coming over the frontier every day. Then he would be axed, and he would have to go on the refugee allowance, and he and his family would

132

sink to depths that even he, having seen so much, could not foresee; and it was even possible that the refugee allowance would no longer be paid. Then there would be—he raised his hands and dropped them, saying that there would be a *débâcle,* a *débâcle,* pronouncing the word in the stiff-jointed way that Germans pronounce French words. For the Western Germans would turn against the refugees and hate them, as the Nazis had hated the Jews, and the refugees would turn against the Western Germans . . . He gave a deep sigh, which his poor throat turned into a whistle.

That is precisely what would have happened had Germany not achieved her industrial resurrection. The sufferings of the displaced persons and expellees and refugees have been a terrible burden on the conscience of the Western Allies. We should not have allowed ourselves, in the course of fighting a just war, to have been transformed into the likeness of a torpid Attila, a slow-motion Tamerlane, a stuttering Ivan the Terrible. Of course there was a strong case for removing the German minority groups from the countries against which they had conspired treasonably with Hitler. But there was an unanswerable case against it. It was fatuously stipulated at the Potsdam Conference that the expulsions must be conducted "in a humane and orderly manner." But it must have been obvious to any sane persons that only in an inhumane and disorderly manner could some millions of people be set down (with no more property than they could carry) in a strange land where there was already a housing shortage and the social and economic system was in ruins. The Western democracies were therefore responsible for an amount of suffering which puts them on a level with those tyrants whose names, fifty years ago, stood for a wide and radiating cruelty believed to have passed for ever from the face of the earth. It is true that governments succeeded in cancelling much of that suffering; yet that waterlogged air station outside Munich, and the many hells like it, and the transit camps, were enough to make the salvation of the Western democracies a questionable matter. But we should have fallen to a still lower level, we should have been equal to Hitler, had Germany gone bankrupt and the parties to this dreadful relationship been brought to a common grave by famine and aimless revolution.

Because Germany did not go bankrupt but broke out into a passion of productivity, the waterlogged air station outside Munich was closed in the early fifties. German jails must certainly have received many of its inhabitants; but the rest found a place in German factories and workshops. The transit camps continued to stink, screening continued to take weeks. It is impossible to guess a period when there will not be weeks when over a thousand East Germans cross the frontiers every day. But in the early fifties the routine was injected with hope. There was nothing like full employment. There was enough unemployment to cause a considerable amount of suffering. But there was enough employment to keep the community solvent and stable. There were so many jobs going that a capable refugee had as much chance of getting one as a competent native West German. The refugees were well enough off not to have justified the fear of their political influence, which many had feared in 1946. At elections they voted neither for the extreme Right nor for the extreme Left, but for the same parties that were supported by the native community.

But it is hard to see how any but a speculative and uncurbed economy could have been flexible enough to assimilate the expellees and refugees and relieve the Allies of so much of their guilt. It is sobering to consider what would have happened in postwar Britain, which has about the same population as Western Germany, if ten million people had been dumped in the country (with no more property than they could carry) and a million and a half of these had immediately begun to draw unemployment benefits while the rest competed with Britons in the labour market. Yet it is not hypocrisy to pretend that the rigid British economy was framed in the idealistic hope that no man shall be in need if his brothers can help him; but it would be revolting hypocrisy to deny that the German devil-take-the-hindmost economy was merciful to those whom the British and Americans had abandoned. Here, as so often before, we see that history takes no care to point a moral.

❖❖ 3 ❖❖

The Germans served us by taking away the guilt of a grave sin against the refugees. But it was not clear what the Allied occupation did to help the Germans rid themselves of their sins. There were many Allied Control Commission officials who took their duties with extreme seriousness and sought to use the occupation as a means towards the betterment of the world. One, who was greatly beloved and highly efficient, was clearly understood by his friends. He was a practising Christian, and regarded the Germans as sinful, but felt no superiority to them, because the difference in degree of sinfulness between himself and the Nazis was as nothing compared to the contrast between the sinfulness of all human beings and the sinlessness of Christ. He believed that the Germans should be provided with the necessities for the body which enable the soul to start on its journey to salvation, and saw to it that they were given houses and food and schooling and work, while he joined with other Christians, whether German or not, to establish a relationship with God and his Church which would enable grace to be visited on the situation. At the other end of the scale were men who refrained from treating the Germans dishonestly or unkindly, even under extreme temptation, but could have given no reason for their abstention from such conduct, except, perhaps, that it was not sporting. Yet the occupation as a whole left a sense of insipidity. It was, to use a Scottish expression, a long drink of water.

The reason for this was best understood in the French Zone. This was an area ill spoken of elsewhere. In the British and the American Zones the French were never mentioned save as the stumbling block in the way of the regeneration of the Germans by exalted ethical methods; and their Zone was regarded as Old Testament country, where an eye for an eye and a tooth for a tooth was recognized administrative routine, and all was as if there had never been a star over Bethlehem. But it has to be remembered that there is a great deal to be said for the Old Testament. The French, instead of importing food into their Zone, according to the British and American practice, exported it to their own country, rapidly and in large quantities; and far from preventing their officials from living on the German economy, they encouraged them and their families to live well on it, and sent in parties of schoolchildren and convalescents and old people to have holidays off the country. They also brought with them the vast vituperative resources of their language. On their arrival they told the Germans in raucous tones that they were barbarians, had waged the most barbaric war in history, had asked for trouble by being defeated, and were going to get it. Officially German guilt was never left undenounced if an opportunity offered; and unofficially pigs and camels and excrement were frequently named in sentences animated by the rudest of verbs. Yet in the end the French were liked better than the British or the Americans, for the reason that many simple souls find the eye-for-an-eye and tooth-for-a-tooth morality a help to their simplicity as they go through this complex world. If a man has been seduced by a demagogue into committing and condoning acts which he knows to be wrong, and everything after that goes very badly, he may find it easier to fit this phase of his life into the pattern of a reasonable universe if at this point a representative of a number of his victims rushes at him and calls him a pig, a camel, an excrement and threatens to mutilate him in resourceful and imaginative ways should he offend again; and he may find it quite bewildering if instead there appears before him another representative of his enemies, offering to love him. There was an element of moral restfulness in the French Zone which could be disregarded only by the doctrinaire.

Moreover the French did not keep up their abusiveness. They got tired of it and got on to another phase in the relationship. A German doctor, long an anti-Nazi refugee, first in Paris and then in London, was at work in the French Zone; and he regarded instances of the aggressiveness of French language and deportment with the resentment which any self-respecting German was bound to feel, only to explain that he recognized that it was of no real consequence. His words were halting. "The French . . . they live with us." He told a story to clarify the point. One evening he had been called out by a German living in a village outside Baden, whose wife was in labour with her fourth child. As he hurried to the case it crossed his mind that when he had last visited the family six months before they had just had billeted on them a French official, a typical minor civil servant, who had struck him as thoroughly disagreeable and full of nationalist feeling; and it struck him that this uncongenial guest must be adding to the strain of the moment. But when they got to the house they found the French official giving the older children their supper, hearing their lessons as they ate their soup, and telling them quietly that they could help their mother best by being good and behaving as if nothing unusual were happening. When the baby was born the French official was called in to see it like the rest of the family. "Not all French officials are like this," said the German doctor, "but quite a number are." There were very few British and American officials who lived with the Germans in this sense. It could, of course, be described as living on the German economy, but it could also be described as fraternization with greater accuracy than the process known by that name in the British and American Zones, which often seemed to have nothing to do with the Latin word for brother.

Sometimes the French fell into the bog of mutual misunderstanding that was always waiting to engulf officials in every Zone. There was, for example, a row over a schoolbook which defied all attempts at explanation. The French put out schoolbooks for use in their Zone which were, on the whole, admirable; and they were quite certain that the history of Germany for intermediate pupils represented a real moral victory over their own chauvinism. They felt therefore that the Germans were merely being insincere propagandists when they denounced this book on the ground that among the illustrations was a caricature of Bismarck. In this they were wrong. The Germans are so deeply respectful to their rulers that strict laws, which the community supports, forbid any but the mildest ridicule of public figures; and the proper place for a caricature of Bismarck seemed to them a grossish comic paper, and not a schoolbook. But the French claw whom they crown, and by their standards the caricature of Bismarck was hardly a caricature at all. It was wholly lacking, they pointed out with pride, in any touch of obscenity.

But usually literacy oiled the wheels. In office after office in the administrative centres one found Frenchmen who could give to any question on their subject an answer which had a beginning, a middle, and an end, and who used words as precisely as mathematicians use numbers and symbols. It would be idle to pretend that the other zones afforded such treats. A strange historical nostalgia makes American parents like their young to talk as simply as if they were Huckleberry Finn and Tom Sawyer, and unsuccessful efforts in this direction make many American adults talk with a poverty of vocabulary and a sustained attack on the graces of syntax which would have disgusted Mark Twain himself. For this reason educated Germans often underestimated the quality of American officials; just as they (and British and American correspondents) also put down British officials as "stuffed shirts" who were in fact intelligent and sensitive and well informed, but who had been subjected to English public school and university education, which acts like a vacuum cleaner on the English language, drawing the richness out of it as if it were dirt. But the French were always masters of speech; they could give every German with a mind worth enlisting on their side the assurance that they too inhabited the world of thought.

Yet about all these Frenchmen, who were handling the task of occupation so well, there was a disquieting languor. A political officer would deliver a wise and learned disquisition on German public opinion far too slowly. He would speak as if he had all the time in the world and was not happy about it, as if he had been forced to retire before his time, and was being fobbed off with something less than real work. The same weariness could be detected in many of his most able colleagues, and it came from a common cause. They did not in fact believe that the occupation was worth while. They did not think it was doing anything to the German people. We all know that there are some events which become experience and others which do not: some events which give us information about the universe and ourselves, and some which tell us nothing. When Britain and America were obliged to occupy Germany they very creditably renounced all idea of revenging themselves on their defeated enemy and planned an occupation which would be a great and enlightening experience for the German people. This ambition was likely to be disappointed. No man is able to foretell when or where he himself or a man of his own kind will encounter an event which is also an experience, and he is much less likely to be a sound prophet if he tries to arrange a rendezvous with enlightenment for a man belonging to another people, shaped by a different history. But the moralist cannot bear to admit this, and the British and Americans are fundamentally moralists. The French, however, are fundamentally intellectuals, and nothing held them back from foretelling the failure and recognizing it when it occurred.

This was not cynicism, though it was often taken for that. Rather was it gravity. The truth was that Western Germany was a frightening place. British and Americans were not injecting the Germans with their philosophy, if they could be said to have one in common, and the Germans showed no signs of holding a faith of their own. The one-legged man who grew enormous cyclamens in the greenhouse at Nuremberg was becoming a nightmare figure. The greenhouse seemed likely to cover the whole of the country before long, changing its form for the production of things other than flowers: textiles, chemicals, motorcars, ships, steel. But the man's face had not changed. He had care for nothing but growing more and more cyclamens, better and better cyclamens. He was as indifferent to all but his own industry as if it were a stupefying drug, and his fellows knew the same obsession. But inevitably their industry would create a situation in which they would have to interest themselves in much else, for their productivity would engender wealth, which would engender power, to which they would have to give direction and a form. But above that greenhouse rose the Schloss built by the last generation which had attained wealth and power, and its lobster-claw turrets, its hobgoblin gables, had been the signs of surrender to fantasy too elemental and wild, which had let loose the forces of madness and death. There was no news of a faith that would bind German wealth and power to the service of sanity and life. There was indeed little evidence that anybody in Western Germany felt any need for such a faith.

It was no hardship to leave Western Germany for Berlin.

❖❖ 4 ❖❖

The blockade of Berlin still held. So the plane, packed tight with green vegetables and officials, went straight up into the air, as if it were a ball a giant child were throwing at the clouds. There was so much traffic on the Berlin run that a plane which was seven minutes late at its journey's end had lost its place in the queue at Gatow Airport and had to go back to its starting point and try its luck the next day. So the pilots dared not waste a second on those gentle spiral ascents which coddle the passenger off the ground in an ordinary commercial flight, and there was no nonsense about the descent either. The ground rushed up and stopped just in time, while ears popped and silted up with deafness. The passengers were whisked off the ground, for each plane had just fifty minutes at the Berlin airport to unload and fuel. This athletic miracle was performed not only by the slim and the straight and the young and the male. A great many women worked on the loading, and among them were some of the lusty old girls who three years before had been clearing up the rubble. Their eyes glittered among their wrinkles as they cawed together like crows and hurled the trolleys along. They had never missed a good fight in their neighbourhood yet, and this was the best of all.

It was odd to find oneself in prison in this loosest, least confined of capitals. Lakes and waterways run through it, and there is much wet and sandy ground on which it is not safe to build, so there are heaths and pine woods and birch woods and good alluvial fields well within the city limits. But now it was a prison, the largest prison ever known, with walls that rose to the sky and were as thick as the whole encircling Soviet Zone. Everybody in Berlin was a prisoner. None was free, not even those who claimed to be warders. The Berliners were prisoners because they were conquered. The Allies were prisoners because they were conquerors. The Americans could not leave lest the Soviet Union take their withdrawal as an admission that they were willing to surrender the whole world to it and stay at home in peace; and a Third World War might well have followed such a misunderstand-

140

ing. The British could not leave Berlin lest the United States and the Soviet Union take their withdrawal as an admission that they were a bankrupt people destitute of power: a misunderstanding which also might have hastened the outbreak of a Third World War. The French could not leave Berlin lest the world draw its conclusions from the state of serfdom into which they had fallen in 1940 and think them destitute of power.

The Russians also were prisoners; theirs was the deepest degree of captivity. They could not leave Berlin without abandoning what was then the sole Russian idea: that they could occupy any country into which they could send the Red Army to cooperate with the local Communist party, no matter how greatly the population loathed them, and that by imposing a police state they could then induce in such countries an appearance of satisfaction which would make it difficult for the Western democracies to gain moral support if it tried to drive them out. The Russians had therefore to stay in Berlin and pretend that they found it easy to administer their Sector, at the same time doing their best to drive out the Allies. For the inhabitants of their Sector obstinately voted against communism in their free elections, and this evidence of discontent could be suppressed if the Allies abandoned the quadripartite control of the city, and there need be no more free elections.

In the summer of 1949 they were working at the task of ousting the Allies with all that peculiar bitchery which was Stalin's stamp and seal. A year before the Russians had refused to cooperate with the British and the Americans and the French in the currency reform, though this was obviously necessary, since the official currency was still Hitler's Reichsmark, which for long before the defeat had been the parthenogenetic child of printing presses unmated with any gold reserve. They picked a series of petty quarrels over the new Deutschmark and proceeded to use the power which the Potsdam Conference had given them when it embedded Berlin in the heart of the Soviet Zone. In June 1948 they had closed all land communications between Western Germany and Berlin. Their hope was that this would inflict such privations on the Sectors controlled by the Western Allies, which relied for their important export trade on Western Germany, that the Berliners would not want them to stay. This threat was met by that great act of genius, the airlift, which supplied the city's essential needs at a cost of a hundred thousand pounds a day, and by a ban on the export of all goods from Western Germany to the Soviet Zone in East Germany. In May 1949 this ban had reduced Eastern Germany to the verge of economic collapse, and the Russians, with a great fanfare on the radio and in the newsreels, let the trains and the automobiles and the canal barges go through their Zone to Berlin.

But as soon as the Russians got the goods they needed and were saved from administrative disaster they began to cheat. It happened that a large number of railway workers in the Soviet Zone went on strike, an event which genuinely amazed the Red Army and the commissars, since strikes are not permitted in the Soviet Union. But they turned it to their own purpose and refused to settle it, for so long as it went on no goods could be carried to or from Berlin, and the Soviet authorities could plead that they were not imposing a blockade, it was the German Railway Workers' Union that was responsible for the hold-up. This ruse was peculiarly Stalinist. It explained why Lenin, and the party as a whole, had never thought much of Stalin in the early days, for it was incomplete. It left the automobiles and the canal boats unaccounted for, and they had to be turned back by Soviet guards who demanded documents of which nobody had previously heard, and this revealed to the simplest minds that there was a disingenuous element at work.

So, in the summer of 1949, the little blockade was on. In the sky over Berlin the airlift hummed perpetually, though on the ground it was very easy to find parts of the city which seemed remote from strife, and even from life. The bogus classical villas round the lakes of Dahlem were now truly classical, and as graceful and elegiac as the willows which drooped silver over the waters. In the past their pompous colonnades had shut out light much needed in a northern climate, and they had been dumpy with darkness. Now these colonnades were doubly irradiated, by the light that shone on them from without, and the light that poured down into their rooms through the shattered roofs. The gardens were now more tame and more wild: the lawns and parterres were covered with neat rows of vegetables, the un-pruned rambler roses hung in great curtains, billowing in the wind, from porches and balconies. Bullet-pocked shutters made easy a burglar's entrance to a house that was intact. Built into a colossal mantelpiece, a huge marble female head, crowned with faintly green laurels on its faintly gilded hair, looked over the dusty parquet floors of the empty salon and was reflected in the cracked and sallowed mirrors, set in nouveau art frames repre-senting twined water lilies. It seemed a good house to explore, but the handle of the door had been taken off and put on again at an odd angle. To open that door might be very unhealthy, and, in-deed, if an intact house in this district lacked inhabitants it usually meant that it had been mined by German troops in their last stand against the Russians and had not yet been cleaned. That door handle had been noticed so nearly at the last moment that it seemed good to go outside and sit on a bench in the garden and breathe the air with a proper appreciation.

On the other side of the lake was a great white mansion, flying the Union Jack; and on its lawn, between two taller visitors, walked a trim man with a white moustache. This was Sir Cecil Weir, the president of the Economic Sub-Commission of the Al-lied Control Commission for Western Germany, a Glasgow manu-facturer who had been one of the chief planners of British in-dustry during the war and had reorganized French industry after the liberation. He was the perfect bourgeois whom Marx had denounced in the Communist Manifesto one hundred and one years before, with double inconsistency, since he was a determin-ist, and the bourgeois was a natural product of the capitalism which he had certified as an inevitable and temporarily beneficial historic phase: the perfect *boorjoo,* whom the Russians were still denouncing with the same inconsistency. But me imperturbe, Sir Cecil might have said with Whitman, for within himself he was adventurous and serene. He and Harry Collins, who had brought the coal out of the ground in the Ruhr, belonged to the same type of thinkers who dealt with concrete things in an abstract way. Harry Collins believed in bringing coal out of the ground, no matter whether the ground was British or American or French or German, because coal is a good thing for human beings to have about the place. Sir Cecil believed in trade as the foundation of civilization. Wherever raw materials flowed into a factory and manufactured goods flowed out and the product was satisfactory and the accounting honest, houses and schools and hospitals were built, and men became cleaner and wiser and kinder. Hence he was as profoundly shocked by the blockade of Berlin as he would have been at a blockade of Glasgow.

This impersonal effort was often to be recognized among Allied officials. It had its bearing on the moral issue raised by the people, mostly English, who arrived in Germany with the avowed intention of loving the Germans and claimed to be inspired by Christ's injunction that we should love our neighbours as we love ourselves. But they had surely mistaken a difficult injunction for an easy one. Christ did not tell us to love our neighbours as we love our lovers or our kin, which is not a hard task for people with a certain vacancy of nature; every woman tried for murder receives a number of proposals from total strangers. He did tell us to love our neighbours as ourselves, and that is a cool and intellectual love. Few of us take joy in ourselves. Were it possible for us to wait for ourselves to come into the room, not many of us would find our hearts breaking into flower as we heard the door handle turn. But we fight for our rights, we will not let anybody take our breath away from us, and we resist all attempts to prevent us from using our wills. It is our duty to fight as eagerly for the rights of others, to admit the unique and sacred character of their souls and their wills, and here in Germany that duty was often faithfully observed. No parachutist dropped on the Ruhr could have guessed that Harry Collins was not wrestling for his own people; and Sir Cecil Weir might have been managing factories that belonged not only to his own nation but to his own firm. It is true that even in those days some objected because the ultimate result of such services to Germany must be her reappearance as Great Britain's most formidable competitor in world markets; but that is a dilemma which the cited injunction disregards.

But it was rarely a civilian official caught the eye in Berlin. The city belonged to the armed forces. The blockade was a state of war without the horror of death and wounds, and so the air was brilliant, for war is in fact an exhilarating sport, and it was sweetened by the comradeship which springs up among those living under a threat. For of course there was an overhanging threat, the worst of threats. There was also a great demonstration of panache, particularly among the Air Forces. They were superb and they knew it; there had in cold fact never been any feat like the airlift since the world began. On these preservers the Berliners fondly directed a gaze which often seemed so fond as to be frivolous. They talked of the generals as if they were film stars, praising their handsomeness, their look of health, their disciplined bearing, their good manners, the neatness of their uniforms. But that showed only that people in dread of extinction recognize the qualities which make for survival. It is written in the Book of Judges that the Lord bade Gideon send his ten thousand men down to the fountain of Harad, and dismiss to their homes all those that knelt down on the shore and bent their mouths to the water, and to keep with him all those who lapped the water from their hands, for with such men he could conquer the hosts of Midian; and though he found but three hundred of such men among ten thousand, they brought him victory. The Berliners were seeking for like evidence of deliberation and delicacy.

The lot of the generals was often such that it was hard for them to present the imperturbability proper to idols. The American commandant of the city was one General Howley, an advertising man from Philadelphia, a robust character given to horseback-riding, with a fine record in show jumping. His quality can be deduced from a passage in the reports of the Kommandatura proceedings for July 1, 1948. Colonel Kalinin, the Soviet Chief of Staff, told the representatives of the Allies that the Soviet Union would take no further part in the meetings, at any level, of the Kommandatura. He gave two reasons, one of which was the Western Allies' introduction into Berlin of the new Western currency, and the other was the behaviour of General Howley at the previous meeting. This was really startling. The British authorities coldly stated that they could not accept a verbal announcement by a Soviet staff officer as terminating the quadripartite government of Berlin. Search in the Minutes shows what

145

it was that Colonel Howley had done to cause a Soviet staff officer to blaspheme against the name of Potsdam. It appeared that after the Russians had dragged out a discussion on administrative details for some hours, as was their wont, General Howley had risen and stated that his deputy would take over, as he was leaving because he was tired. At that the whole Soviet delegation had rushed out of the hall in a rage, and that was natural enough. One had only to look at General Howley to see that he had never felt tired in his life. The Russians had every reason to resent an attempt to make them believe any statement so palpably false.

One morning this hearty soul sat in his office and described to some visitors how, a few days before, he had settled the railway strike. This was indeed a feather in his cap. It could have been no easy triumph. Once the strike was ended the Russians would have no excuse for stopping the trains on the line between Western Germany and Berlin, so the blockade would be broken; and the settlement had involved negotiations on the delicate matter of currency. The Soviet Union had refused to cooperate with the Allies in the new currency reform, because they liked having a depreciated mark in their own Zone and in their Berlin Sector, as it meant a cheap market where they could buy for Russia. They were also aggrieved because the currency reform had dismantled a financial structure from which they derived extraordinary benefits, owing to certain fantastic arrangements made by the United States Treasury at the end of the war. They were now paying all the Berliners who worked in their sector in their depreciated mark, which was worth something like a quarter of the new reformed mark. But many of these workers lived in the Allies' Sector and had to pay out Western marks for their rent and all goods except those they could carry home from the Soviet Sector. This cut down their real wages to something between a quarter and three-quarters of their nominal wages. This was the real reason why the railway workers struck, though rebellion was manifestly dangerous, since over three thousand Berliners were known to have been kidnapped by the Russians. They had even surged into the Tempelhof Station and attacked

146

General Kvashnin, the transport chief, which made the Soviet authorities very angry indeed.

But General Howley, who was the kind of man who greets the seen with a cheer, whatever it may be, had advanced on this tangled situation and set it to rights. After hours of negotiation with General Kvashnin he had got him to accept the compromise plan which gave the railway workers sixty per cent of their wages in Western currency and promised them freedom from victimization. The Allies had put these terms to the strikers, making no secret of their eagerness that they should accept the terms and go back to work and end the blockade, and there was to be a ballot the next day. General Howley told us comfortably that he knew how the railway workers would be voting, and yawned. He had risen early for a ride and was now pleasantly relaxed, and he began to talk of horses, and how he had competed against the Russians in jumping events, and what decent fellows they were when they got a chance to be themselves and were not jerking about at the end of a string that stretched to Moscow. The telephone buzzed, and he put the receiver to his ear, and it was proved that when people are astonished they really do open their mouths and forget to shut them. "Why, no," he presently told the man on the line, "I don't have any confirmation in writing. I guess I just accepted his word as an officer." The Soviet-licensed news agency had issued a denial that there had been any negotiations of an official character and that the Soviet Military Government had made any specific promises of the sort on which General Howley had based his appeal to the railway strikers to return to work. Already the railway union was sending out a whip to instruct their members to vote for a continuance of the strike.

A man who has been the victim of such a trick feels that he looks a fool, and General Howley obviously felt just that. But he need have nourished no such fear. All his visitors thought he took the blow stoutly, and the two Britons among them were enthralled at seeing a moment of historic drama, which they had seen performed once before, now re-enacted by a different player. On March 17, 1938, they had turned on the radio and heard Neville Chamberlain shrilling and choking with anger because he had had news that Hitler had broken faith with him and sent his troops into Czechoslovakia. The Chamberlains were typical of the industrial bourgeoisie that had risen to political power during the nineteenth century, and he had brought to the office of Prime Minister the outlook of a respectable businessman accustomed to deal with businessmen of the same order. When a managing director finds that his firm is being inconvenienced by the operations of another firm, he and his colleagues will think it natural for him to meet his opposite number in the other firm and work out a compromise with him, giving way on some points and claiming concessions of at least equal value. If both firms are of good standing there is no reason to fear that the bargain will not be kept, for both have every reason to wish that their reputations should shine unblemished before their customers, their suppliers, and their banks, and indeed the whole community, since the credit system makes it advisable to leave a favourable impression on as many people as possible. So there was not a thing to worry about after such a meeting, except that one would not like to forget to send a box of cigars or a case of sherry as a Christmas gift. The Nazi rape of Czechoslovakia horrified Neville Chamberlain, not because he felt any tenderness towards the Czechs, whose representatives he continued to treat with the same coldness and discourtesy he had always shown them, but because he found that the world had changed around him, and he had been doing business with people who did not keep their word, because they did not mind whether they were thought honourable or not, and could not be made to suffer for it, since they were living outside the credit system. He raged at the destruction of his world.

So too did this younger man in his Berlin office. It must be granted that he was an advertising man, and copywriting is often metaphysical; it celebrates not the imperfect article that actually exists and is being vended, but the *universalium ante rem,* the article as it was in the mind of God before it existed. But an advertising firm of repute must keep faith with its clients, its staff, its stockholders, its bank. The general looked like a bewildered boy as it dawned on him that there were men he knew, men against whom he competed in the show ring, men who were his opposite numbers in the highest ranks of an imposing military hierarchy organized to meet a vital historic moment, who did not keep faith. It also was breaking on him, as it had broken on Neville Chamberlain, that the ground was not solid beneath his feet, that it is impossible for society to survive if the mass of men cannot be trusted to abide by their word. He must have known this with his mind for quite some time, but as he sat there, grasping the telephone and taking in its odious message, he was realizing it with his veins and his pulse and his sweat glands.

But he turned back to his work, and the Western commandants were soon hurrying about Berlin, trying to get the Soviet authorities to withdraw their repudiation of the settlement terms and issuing appeals to the German railway workers to vote for a return to work under a guarantee that the Western Allies would get them some form of satisfactory settlement. General Howley made a statement in which there was manifested brth handsomeness of spirit and shrewdness: he gave it as his opinion that had matters been left to his brother-officer General Kvashnin, the settlement he had arranged with him would have stood, and implied that it was Moscow that had upset it.

And, indeed, it had been upset. The result of the ballot was as had been foreseen. Two thousand of the railwaymen voted for a return to work, twelve thousand were against it. The British commandant, General Bourne, had then to take over the negotiations, and these dragged on for weeks, because even after the Russians agreed to a settlement they kept on failing to implement it. But terms of that settlement were very much the same as those proposed by General Howley. Moscow gained nothing by cheating him of his triumph except a delay, which forced the City of Berlin to go on and on paying out unemployment benefit till it could see the bottom of the treasury till. But this financial victimization could not greatly impress the Berliners, who knew from the airlift that the Western Allies were willing to spend unlimited money on them. What was needed to further Soviet interests in the city at that moment was an act of generosity, not an irritating infliction of an unjust fine; for a common resentment against such ill-natured futilities drew together the representatives of the Western Allies in Berlin. But it is doubtful if it drew together their countries. A large majority of the British high command in the city were professional soldiers, who were to stay in the army for years to come; but the proportion was much lower among their American comrades, who were therefore likely to go home and become civilians at any moment. Hence it was soon true that there were a number of civilians in the United States, all free to engage in political activity, who on a basis of personal experience disliked and distrusted the Soviet government, while Englishmen who had suffered the same experience formed a small and detached group, who were expressly forbidden to take part in politics, and who probably continued to serve abroad. This is one among the elements which, from time to time, have produced divergencies in American and British public opinion.

◆◆ 5 ◆◆

Never has an occupying force had a higher regard for the people of the territory it occupied. The Western Allies realized quite well that it was not for them to perform the feat which Napoleon described as the one thing an army could not do; they were not sitting on their bayonets. They were sitting on the ballot boxes, which, at the last election, Berliners had stuffed with votes against communism and for social democracy. They admired this action as all human beings admire the actions of others which promote their interests; but they felt another form of admiration which was less facile and more idealistic than this. They were soldiers in an age of war, and, as they had had to run the risk of being killed much more often than they liked, they were aware how attractive life seems when there is a risk of losing it. They therefore deeply respected their former enemies for making this declaration of independence when they were wholly encircled by Soviet territory. They knew quite well that the prime motive of Berlin's resistance was self-interest: that the Berliners knew that the first results of surrender to the Soviet Union would be an apocalyptic purge, the imprisonment and disappearance of thousands, and perhaps hundreds of thousands, and then a long descent into the depreciated existence, compact of lower feeding and underclothing and drabness and fear of arrest and deportation, which the Eastern Zone and the satellite states had all suffered and were still suffering. But this self-interest was taking such risks that it was hardly possible to call it by that name any more. Had Berlin fallen into the hands of the Russians, every day of its resistance would have been counted a reason for the infliction of further punishment. Every Berliner was staking his personal fate on the safety of the city, and was day by day, if he were an active and conspicuous person, sending his sentence up from three years to seven years, to ten years, to life, to capital punishment; and were he obscure he was sending down his bread ration. And the Berliners were not gambling on a certainty. To them the victory of the Western Allies seemed far less assured than was believed in London or New York.

They had grave reason for doubting the power of their defenders to defend them. They thought the French *kaput,* because they themselves had defeated them. The French flag was flying from the Victory column in the middle of the Tiergarten only because Great Britain and the United States had brought in a beaten foe to crow over them; and they were sure that the United States had had most say in that matter, for they suspected that the British were on their way down to join the French in the dusk where great powers outlive their greatness. A chief cause of this suspicion was the shameful parsimony shown by the British government in regulating the expenditure of the British members of the Allied Control Commission and the occupying forces. In Berlin and Western Germany alike, the Germans saw all but the highest British officials far worse clothed and fed than any German who had scrambled out of the abyss after the currency reform, and they knew quite well that the weaker vessels among them were trading on the black market. But there were even more eccentric forms of cheese paring. At a time when there was no blockade and consequently no great strain on the air service, a British general was summoned from Berlin to an investiture at Buckingham Palace to receive a decoration from the King. The Treasury would not allow him to use an RAF plane to make a special flight from Berlin to London and back. He was obliged to travel as an ordinary passenger by BEA; and since there was no return flight on the day of the investiture this meant that he had to miss a very important meeting with the Russians concerning a problem on which he was the British specialist. Every office in Berlin was a whispering gallery, and the news of this skinflint decision was all over the city in a couple of days.

The Berliners had grounds for regarding the French and the British as bankrupts whose discharge lay among the remoter probabilities of the future. They had as good grounds for thinking the Americans a little silly. It is insufficiently appreciated how curious the Germans found the reiterated statement by the American generals that their chief reason for letting the Russians take Berlin and occupy Prague, after Vlassov had taken it, was their own dedication to the pursuit of the Nazi leaders and the German Army, which they believed to be about to carry out an "Operation Redoubt" and retreat into the mountains of South Germany and Austria. An educated and informed Berliner, such as the mayor, Ernst Reuter, must have found this excuse quite terrifying. It is difficult to know how any general could have believed that the German Army could use the road system leading to the mountains except at a pace which would condemn it to destruction from the air, or how it would be able to feed itself if it succeeded in gaining the heights. The educated and informed Berliner would be forced to suspect that that faith in "Operation Redoubt" was a pretext which dispensed American generals and their government from the need to confess that, at a time when victory was still incomplete, they had used their troops not for the military purpose of defeating the Nazis, but for a political purpose—and that the relationship between the United States and the Soviet in 1949 proved this purpose to have been ridiculous.

The Berliners had reason to think the Americans silly because they had given the Russians the prestige of taking Berlin, and reason to think all the Allies very silly for their treatment of the Russians now they were all shut up in Berlin together. In 1949 the protocol of the Westerners laid down that Soviet rudeness was answered by politeness, Soviet delay by unlimited patience, Soviet greed by concession; for there was a theory afloat among the Allies that all Russians were rude, unpunctual, and greedy problem children, whose better nature would be released only if Nanny were kind and firm. Berlin was full of people who had good reason to consider this protocol and that theory quite comically mistaken. For it was a city of Social Democrats, most of whom, and nearly all those above a certain age, knew the history of Continental socialism. They realized that Moscow insulted its Allies, kept them waiting till the small hours for messages that could have been delivered during the working day, and asked for twice as much of everything as it had any right to get, because Moscow was Stalin, and Stalin was Lenin's pupil, and had seen him gain control of the Russian Socialist party by rudeness, procrastination, and exorbitant demands. Lenin brought into being the Bolshevik party as an irresistible power at the London-Brussels Conference by prolonging it and inspissating it with intrigue and by keeping ice-cold, while his simpler enemies grew hot and confused in rage at the waste of the precious time and the precious party funds, and at the besmirchment of the shining cause by trickery; and again and again he created a nightmare of tedium and ill feeling round his opponents, and let them break out of it only when they conceded him part of his demands, which naturally he made as gross as possible. Stalin sat and watched him, and as Lenin went up in the world went with him. A German like Ernst Reuter, who had gone out of social democracy into communism and come out of it again, must have watched in amazement while Stalin exercised this old conference technique on the Allies, and they succumbed to it as if they had been Menshevik innocents of fifty years before.

It is a technique which can be successful only as long as it be not recognized and imitated by the other side. The deadlock in Berlin would have been ended as soon as it began had the Western Allies politely matched tiresomeness by tiresomeness. When the Soviet representative insisted on delivering a memorandum at the awkward hour of midnight he should have got his answer at two in the morning; when the Soviet representative put up a proposition he obviously knew to be ridiculous, the Americans and the British and the French should have put up propositions which they obviously knew to be more ridiculous; and the Foreign Office and the State Department and the Quai d'Orsay should have used their resources, which in this respect are not inconsiderable, to produce bores who would have maddened the Russians till they too, like General Howley, rose and said that they were tired and must go home. The only deductions that Stalin and his army could draw from the Allies' failure were unlikely to restrain them from aggression; they could only put down the Allies as masochists who liked being treated rough and who would enjoy being conquered. Possibly some Berliners guessed that the Allied policy was as it was because there were not half a dozen men in the Allied military governments who knew anything whatsoever about the early history of the Bolshevik party, and their home governments were as uninstructed; but this was hardly a reason to give them confidence in the Allies.

A Jew, one of the ablest who fled from Hitler, one of the first to settle down in Germany after the defeat, gave an explanation of the Berliners' choice which did not at first hearing ring true. He said, "The Berliners are for the Allies and democracy, because at last they learn from the Russian Sector what totalitarianism is." "At last?" we asked sceptically. "At last," he reaffirmed. "You see, under the Nazies, strangers did not come by night and take you away unless you were a Jew or an important Social Democrat or an important liberal or a party member who had got in wrong with the high-ups. If you were not a Jew or a conspicuous politician or a party member, and were an unimaginative person as well, you did not realize what this meant, and perhaps persuaded yourself that it did not really happen. And if you were a sufficiently unimportant German, who only knew the people next door and had no Jewish friends, and never joined the party, then you might very well never get any intimation that it did really happen. But now any German in the Russian Sector, whatever his race or politics or degree of distinction, may hear a knock on his door at night and know that he is to be taken away and may never come back. And in the other sectors anybody may be kidnapped. So now the Berliners have learned, all of them, what totalitarianism is."

It was impossible not to say, coldly, "They ought to have learned that long ago. There was a stinking pile of evidence which should have taught the deaf and the blind." But the truth lay thereabouts. It manifested itself most clearly if one followed the clue given by the analysis of the Berlin polls: eighty per cent of the electors voted against communism, and of those anti-Communists sixty-five per cent were women. Women are notoriously idiotic in the prime sense of the world, they like to be private persons and are apt to be indifferent to public affairs; and these women had private business of an urgent sort. There was a great deal of man's work which they had to do because the men who should have done it were not there. The figures of war casualties computed by the German General Staff have never been published, and the figures issued by the Bonn Information Service are arrived at by political rather than by arithmetical calculation. But the truth can be gathered obliquely. In many German cities the majority of the breadwinners were women. In Berlin the proportion was fifty-two per cent. These women went to the polls to record a defiant decision. They looked like rocks, Neumann and Reuter, the men who led the resistance of the city, but they would have been as sand had it not been for these tired women, who were feeling something strongly. It was hard to know what until one had met them face to face, then it was plain.

There were twenty women of that kind sitting round the table in the conference room of UGO (Unabhangige Gewerckshafts Organization), a new federation of nineteen trade unions which had had to be started because the old federation was in the Russian Sector and became a Russian instrument. All of them were very tired. They were all employed women with homes, and it is always penal servitude to do a day's work in a factory and then do another day's work cleaning and cooking. But these women had much more to bear than that. They had come through a bad winter: as all fuel had come in on the airlift there had been very drastic electricity cuts. Each district had only two hours of electricity in the day and two in the night, at times which varied from week to week. This meant that all women employed in factories near their homes had to go to their work in the two-hour period which fell by day and had to do their cooking and washing in the period which fell by night, though this might be between two and four in the morning. Now power was less strictly rationed, as it was summer and the fuel went further, but they still lived in great discomfort, for few had a pane of glass left in their windows. They were drawing pathetic satisfaction from a recent decision of the British authorities that the old Berlin custom by which a tenant was responsible for the repair of windows was abrogated and that the landlord must shoulder the responsibility. They considered that a great advance, for they still thought it a law of nature that landlords have more money than tenants. But whether the landlord could pay or not, these women certainly could not afford glass, for a square yard of the stuff cost a fifth of their weekly wage. They were tired, and they were poor. Between a quarter and a third of that weekly wage had to go out in rent and rationed food, "and that," said the two young women who represented the Railway Workers in UGO, "is why we are striking. Think of those of us who work in the Eastern Sector and live in the Western Sector—we have to pay Western prices in rotten Eastern marks." That quarter or third became the greater part of their wage.

Need the Russians have tried to make their hard lives harder? "They never fight fair," the women sighed, "they always lie. They spoke of the seventeen strikers who had been arrested and the two who had been kidnapped; they spoke too of the strikebreakers, who were for the most part members of the East German Police Force. These boys had been brought by train from Magdeburg and Thüringen, having been told that there had been a Nazi putsch in Berlin and that they must defend their country against civil war. It is said that many of these boys had deserted, and with the pardonable egotism of martyrs, these women assumed that their motive was sympathy with the strikes, though it was as likely as not that they were sick of the poor food in the Eastern Zone. But not for long did the women speak of the strike, for that was not really one of their troubles, it was an exercise of courage, and courage brings its own intoxication. They were tired, they were poor, they were brave; and, like all the brave, they were cowards. They feared unemployment.

They would sooner have been dead than without work. They spoke of a Third World War with less apprehension. This fear was urgent, because the factories in Berlin were essentially plants where half-worked goods were finished for the market, and these, of course, were bulkier than raw materials, so the airlift could not carry the full load necessary to keep the machines working, and there was no knowing how long the blockade would last, or what it would do. "Look," they said, "you would think that farming would always be the same. But look . . ." So laced with country-side is the city of Berlin that there are two thousand farm workers and foresters and market gardeners working within its limits, and of these the market gardeners had been hit in a way that they had never expected. The previous winter, when the blockade was at its tightest, and little space could be spared in the airlift for fresh vegetables, the nurserymen had spent a lot of money on buying seeds and coke on the black market from the Eastern Zone. They had had to buy many seeds, for the quality had been undependable since the war, but now fresh vegetables were coming in by air and from the Eastern Zone, and these were dirt cheap, because of the rotten Eastmark. It was therefore not worth while for the market gardeners to plant out their seedlings. "It is not that we are not well paid," said the young war widow with professional pride, "but we are working only three days a week, and that is unheard of, we could not have guarded against it." To be a hard-working woman and have an impish misfortune, an economic poltergeist, twitch the work out of one's hand, it was not fair.

They were tired, poor, brave, and afraid; and they had also a solemn and delicate grief in common. It is not true, by the way, that eels get used to being skinned. There were two robust old parties representing the building trades, one a specialist in the repairing of roofs in the blasted and burned-out houses, a job rather like rick-covering, and the other was forewoman of a squad that cleared up rubble and sorted out what was usable for re-building. They were proud of doing such heavy and such valuable work, but for all that a wistfulness fell on them, and they sighed that till now it had not been done by women, and perhaps it was not suitable for them. No, they decided suddenly, looking abashed, it was not at all suitable.

Supposing, they said, there was a little girl. A nice little German girl. It would be terrible to look at her and think that when she grew up she would have to do all that pushing and pulling and climbing, and handle all that dirty stuff, and be out in all weathers. The young woman who was a woodworker nodded her sympathy. Women were definitely at a disadvantage in her trade, but they liked it. They could not manage the heavy machines and had to fiddle round with odd jobs, often splitting up among several of them a piece of work which could easily be done by one man. "But we can keep clean," she said, and all the women sitting round the table, the battered, weather-beaten women, murmured, "Ah, very nice that," and, "Yes, indeed, that is a good kind of job." Each of them, when it came to her turn to describe her work, discussed hesitantly how far it took her from the traditional sphere of woman, which, thanks to Hitler, she would not have a chance to re-enter before the grave took her. They had been robbed of their birthright, and they were not reconciled to the loss. But they were not bitter, simply they murmured when they heard of an occupation in which a woman need not get filthy, "Ah, very nice that," and "Yes, indeed, that's a good kind of job."

How many Berlin women were in the building trade? About four thousand, against sixteen thousand men; or so they thought. But all their figures were very uncertain, for when the federated unions fled from their offices in the Russian Sector they had had to leave all their papers behind, even to the membership records. They had had to rebuild the whole organization from the ground up. Fiercely they spoke of the innumerable inconveniences of like sort which they had suffered at the hands of the Russians, nothing to do with ideology, just infernal nuisances. As they regretted the love which had been driven out of their lives *manu militari*, so they were always regretting the law which they had lost.

It was not the kidnappings that made them grieve for their vanished order. Then the intoxication of courage lifted them up, for they but put themselves under a spotlight by joining UGO, and they might yet be among the kidnapped. It was the everyday violations of civil rights in the Russian Sector which enraged them. "In every block of flats there is a spy installed, just as there was in the Nazi times," one said, and another added, "And sometimes it is the very same spy that worked for the Nazis." "And our letters are opened," another said; "if I want to write to Western Germany and keep what I say my own affair, I go and post my letter in the Western Sector." They stirred on their chairs, they tapped the table with their fists, they uttered phrases echoing verse that German children learn at school and inscriptions written on monuments, phrases more conventional and less personal than their ordinary language, although they used them to indicate that what they were then saying was more intrepid and more personal than what they ordinarily said. They were declaring that they would never submit to communism and the Russians because they believed in democracy and liberty. Through the open windows came the roar of the airlift, defying the laws of historical gravity, because of the fuel of these women's preferences.

To say in this room, "I was at the Nuremberg trial," would have meant nothing to any of these women, and, indeed, it would have presented them with an argument less developed than their own. There men had made a formal attack on the police state. But here these women had incarnated the argument. They were discussing the matter with their bodies as well as their minds. Because it would not do if the wrong people read the letter to brother Hans in Cologne, the tired legs had to trudge down the tenement steps and up the street and over to the Western Sector and back, the old shoes letting in the water and rubbing the corns. Because the man from the Eastern Zone with a message from Grandmama in Magdeburg could not come to the granddaughter's home, lest the spy in the tenement should see him, she had to go a long way to meet him in a café where she was not known, and the fare and the price of the coffee left her short of what would have bought sausages for supper.

By tired feet and leaking shoes, and by the watering of mouths over missed meals, these women had learned with their whole being that justice gives a better climate than hate. Aching, they saw a vision of a state that should think each citizen so precious that it would give him full liberty to be himself, provided only that he did not infringe the liberties of others to be themselves; a government that would love the individual. This is the democratic faith, and it was to this they had learned allegiance. Because the learning had come to them through their whole beings, in the course of their daily lives, their children would grow up with it in their blood. Mother had fair hair. She cooked good liver dumplings. She was a garment worker. She kept us when we were little. She found freedom a necessity. As she got older she got slightly deaf. She died at seventy. So a tradition is established.

For these women, for all the men of their kind, the occupation of Berlin had been an event which was also an experience. The Nuremberg trials had not changed the Germans; the occupation of Western Germany had not changed the Western Germans; but Berliners were changed by the occupation of the city. The value of an experience does not depend on the number of people who are affected by it. If a man stranded on a desert island should become a saint under the coconut palm but is never rescued, it should not be pretended that what happened to him is of no importance; for if that be conceded, then nothing is important, since humanity is stranded on this desert world and will certainly never be rescued. Had Berlin made its revelation only to Berliners, it would still have had an absolute value. But it cannot have been so limited in its scope. It must also have changed the Russians. It touched them in their special area of wonder. For they were what Lenin and Stalin had made them, and those two had not prepared their charges for all the surprises that were to meet them in Berlin. It was the distinguishing mark of the Bolshevik party in its early days that it repudiated gallantry. That was why it so profoundly shocked Continental Socialists. True, it accumulated the huge funds, which gave it an advantage over all other parties, by the bank hold-ups and highway robberies of the "expropriations"; and it was only showing its good sense (as Cavour had argued long before) in preferring intrigue to fighting on the barricades. When it came to taking the Russian Revolution out of the hands of the Mensheviks who had made it, the Bolsheviks showed daring enough; though the fire that made the civil war came out of the belly of Trotsky, who had been a Menshevik. But once the party had come to power there was no place for courage in the Soviet Union. There was no field in which it could be exercised. No internal force survived which could be resisted without treachery to the state. Obedience was called for, and industry, and fortitude, but not courage. The tracts of course prescribed it, but the words lay dead on the didactic page; and, indeed, the purges that began in 1934 made it dangerous to present the appearance of potential bravery.

But when Hitler attacked the Soviet Union the Russians found that courage was the primal necessity and that they possessed immense stores of this treasure. It must now have astonished them to recognize it in the Berliners. They cannot have expected to find courage in the vanquished, for they knew better than did them credit what reason such people have to speak softly and do as they are bidden: the rapidity with which their houses might change from homes to smoking ruins, themselves from the quick to the dead. The Russian higher command must have been constantly amazed because Ernst Reuter defied them from his mayoral chair. They knew, and they knew that he knew, what would happen to him, a lapsed Communist, if the Western Allies were driven out of Berlin. But eminent men, as all Soviet officials must recognize acutely, are often prevented from obeying the instinct of self-preservation. It must have been amazing to them that obscure Berliners who could have chosen to lie low coolly went into disciplined action against them and looked at them, not in fear, but in anger. They must have asked, "Why are these people putting their names on the priority list for the firing squad? Why are they inviting the flames to revisit their city?"

They had received answers, not in words; such answers as had been given by these twenty women in their lives. The resistance of Berlin began as a soliloquy, but it must end as a dialogue. It would spread into a debate. In the Eastern Zone and in the satellite states the people were not openly rebellious, but the strikes and demonstrations made it plain what fire lay under the sullen smoke elsewhere. There was enough to make the Russians ask, "Why do these people hate us? What is it that all who are not us feel we have taken away from them?" The crucial political argument of our time will not be carried on in books, it will be lived. Perhaps the debate may continue for decades, for centuries, during which the West and the East may flag and fade, their lifeblood flowing away in armaments. But in the end the obscure millions must establish a truth, by discovering what is necessary for them.

Mr. Setty and Mr. Hume

MR. SETTY AND MR. HUME

❖❖ 1 ❖❖

The murder of Mr. Setty was important, because he was so unlike the man who found his headless and legless body. It was news, after the pattern which was established when the Wise Men came out of the East and questioned their way to the stable where the King of the Jews had been born; for they were of course neither kings nor philosophers, as has often been pretended, but newspapermen, and they had seen no star, but had received the call not heard by the ear but felt by the nerves, which announces that somewhere there is news. For news is always an incarnation. Interest comes when people start to act out an idea, to show what a thought is worth when it is worked out in flesh and blood; and both Mr. Stanley Setty and his discoverer, Mr. Tiffen, were engaged in such dramatization.

Mr. Setty had no apparent connection with ideas. He was one of those cases of abnormally unlucky precocity followed by abnormally lucky maturity, which, though the good luck adds up to nothing impressive, nevertheless present modern England with a disquieting problem. He was born Sulman Seti in Baghdad in 1903. He was brought to England by his parents when he was four, and at fourteen was working in a Manchester cotton mill, as the law then permitted. Two years later he and his brother set up in business as shipping merchants with a registered capital of something like three thousand pounds. After two years a receiving order was granted against the little lads, who owed about twenty-five thousand pounds and had only five pounds' assets. As Mr. Setty was still only eighteen he could not be made a bankrupt, a status reserved for adults. Four years later, in 1926, he had saved five hundred pounds and started up in business again, calling himself a shipping merchant, but dealing in every kind of merchandise on which he could lay his hands. A year later he had run up twelve hundred pounds' debts, and he ran away with two hundred pounds he had abstracted from the till to Italy, where his father lived, in hope of getting help from him. But blood ran thinner than water, and he was back in Manchester in the following spring without a penny. He rapidly tried to mend his fortunes by gambling on horses and dogs, but soon acquired another three thousand pounds of debts.

Meanwhile a receiving order had been made against him, and in August 1928, at the age of twenty-four, he was sentenced by a Manchester court to eighteen months' imprisonment, having pleaded guilty to twenty-three offences against the Debtors' and Bankruptcy Acts, such as having kept no proper accounts, left his place of business with the intention of defeating or delaying his creditors, and having used the two hundred pounds with which he went to Italy for his own purposes instead of handing them over to his creditors. His counsel made a moving plea for Mr. Setty, putting the blame for his misadventures on the community, which should never have allowed him to be a master or employer—he had "evidently not the mentality to deal with sums of money or large quantities of goods."

Ten years later, in 1938, just before the war, he appeared before another court, still, according to his own account, a shabby and woeful figure. He applied for his discharge from bankruptcy, explaining that he was working as a dealer on commission and that his earnings were pitiful, amounting to two or three pounds a week, and that he wanted to raise some capital and start up in business again. This ambition he could, of course, not gratify until he got his discharge, since as an undischarged bankrupt he could not have a banking account and could not obtain goods on credit without disclosing that he was an undischarged bankrupt. Now it is not difficult for an English bankrupt to get his discharge. He has to submit to an inquisition concerning his means and his character, which he is likely to remember with a smart of shame for the rest of his life, but the findings of the inquisitors are not unmerciful. If a man seems to have failed through ill luck or a local or historical crisis, or if he has worked really hard to pay off his creditors, he can usually get his discharge long before he has paid his debts in full. A percentage of thirty to sixty is often accepted. But the judge to whom Mr. Setty made his application evidently found reason to harden his heart beyond the habit of his kind. He gave him a blank refusal, remarking grimly that Mr. Setty appeared to be planning to set up business "in a way which might or might not be for the benefit of the business community."

It would be interesting to learn the present income of the counsel who pleaded that Mr. Setty had "evidently not the mentality to deal with sums of money or large quantities of goods," or of the judge who refused him his discharge. There is not a chance in the world that the judge, anyway, could enjoy anything but a fraction of the lordly income which, when the clouds of war cleared away, Mr. Setty was seen to be enjoying. His address was now impressive. He was not so grand in this respect as his brother, Mr. Max Setty, owner of the most fashionable night club in London, The Orchid Room, who lived in an apartment close to the American Embassy in Grosvenor Square, which, fifty years ago, was inhabited exclusively by peers of the realm and bankers. There was perhaps more restraint in his choice of the apartment, which Mr. Setty shared with his sister and her husband, Mr. Ali Ouri, who is one of the wealthiest Arab landowners in Israel. It is soberly distant from the West End, in the grey stucco district north of Hyde Park. He did nothing to disturb the sedate atmosphere. He did not drink, he gave few parties, he dressed quietly but expensively. He could afford it. He never carried less than one thousand pounds on him, and it was known that, if he was given an hour or two of notice, he could produce five times that sum.

But he still had no banking account. He was still an undischarged bankrupt. He still had no office. Because his ostensible business was dealing in second-hand automobiles, he had a garage in Cambridge Terrace mews, a dead end of old coach houses converted into garages, hidden away behind the stately houses that look on Regents Park. But chiefly he carried on his trade on the pavements and in the public houses and snack bars of Warren Street, that warm, active, robust, morally unfastidious area which has a smack of Dickens' London. This meant, of course, that he was hard to tax. The Inland Revenue must have found it very hard to find out what his profits were and assess him; which meant that the assessment of all other British subjects had to go up. But it meant more than that. This is the centre of the second-hand automobile market, and there, at that time, flourished a curious medley of the legitimate and the illegitimate. Countless automobiles were bought and sold here without blame in the sight of God and man; but there was also a trade in English automobiles designed for export and banned in the home market, in foreign automobiles which had been illegally imported, in new automobiles which were not allowed to be resold under the twelve months' covenant, in stolen automobiles, and in petrol which was drastically rationed.

Mr. Setty was active in the purely legitimate trade, but even there something strange was suggested. He was said, by those who knew him only as an automobile dealer, to do business on a scale suggesting that he had capital to the amount of about fifty thousand pounds. He bought many cars, and he often paid large prices for automobiles which used a high amount of petrol at times when the ration of petrol was still small, and would have to keep them for a considerable time before he could resell them. Yet, in 1938, when he had asked for his discharge from bankruptcy, he had represented that he was earning from two to three pounds a week, and a court which was scrutinizing his affairs with a hostile eye made no suggestion that it disbelieved this story and that he could afford to pay out a dividend to his creditors. It is hard to imagine how in the intervening eleven years he could have accumulated fifty thousand pounds' capital. Taxation alone would have made that impossible, no matter what gifts he might have developed in the meantime. But there was no registered company behind him, and he seemed to have no associates.

He was also a curbside banker. Anybody who wanted to cash a cheque without passing it through a bank came to him and he gave them money for it with a discount, which he never made unreasonable, and passed it on to an associate who had a banking account. Here again is a field where the legitimate and the illegitimate are mingled. The most honest of undischarged bankrupts may like to have some means of cashing the cheques he receives in the way of business other than by explaining his state over the counter of his customer's bank; and we also have a legacy handed down from Tsardom. Up till the first five years of this century Great Britain took in countless immigrants from Russia and Poland, and many of these, partly from the inferiority complex the alien feels before the native, and partly from a peasant fear of being swindled by lettered men, never learned to use a bank. Survivors of that generation, and even some of their children, go on cashing their cheques with the man who has never let them down yet and is always to be found outside the Three Feathers between five and seven, even when those cheques run into thousands of pounds. But after the Second World War the curbside banker was used more and more by people who wanted to evade taxes or cover up illegal transactions, such as currency frauds or payments for illegal imports slipped in on false invoices. Nobody can tell now what branches of the profession were cultivated by Mr. Setty, since he had no papers. The figures were all in his head, which is perhaps why in the end it was cut off. But certainly every day he handled thousands of pounds.

It could be taken for granted till now that the English racketeer has been less well acquainted with violence than his American counterpart. He and his friends exchange endless cruelties, they cheat one another and squeeze one another in blackmail and railroad one another into prison, but they rarely draw a gun. A beating-up is the furthest most of them ever go, and that is not common nor drastic. But Mr. Setty had all that summer been showing signs of acute apprehension. Nothing would induce him to get into any automobile but his own, which is an unusual form of shyness in an automobile dealer, and he went less and less to his own garage; and, indeed, Cambridge Terrace mews at certain hours might feel uncommonly like a mousetrap to a nervous man. His garage lay across the dead end of the mews, and, going in or out of it, he could be covered by a single enemy. He would not go into a strange garage, or go upstairs into an office or warehouse. His clients had to seek him where he stood in the open street or in a public house. All the same, on October 4, he disappeared. He told his family that he was going to look at an automobile in Watford and drove off in his Citroën, which later was found abandoned near his garage.

His family were quick to take alarm. Very soon they offered a thousand pounds reward to anybody who could find him for them. Remoter relatives, including a sister named Mrs. Sadie Spectreman, converged on the apartment house, the other tenants of which were startled by their new knowledge of their neighbour. A Miss Constance Palfreyman told the reporters that no, a day had never been actually fixed for the wedding, but they had hoped it would be soon. While this group mourned and wondered, the police remained quite calm. Three days after Mr. Setty's disappearance his sister and her husband reported a bizarre circumstance: they went out for the afternoon, after turning the key in two mortice locks in the front door, and came back to find it swinging wide open. Coldly the police issued a notice to the effect that they had found no indication that the apartment had been entered. There was as cold a tone about all their announcements. Indeed, they inspired an announcement which was bound to leave any reader suspecting that they thought that Mr. Setty had come to no harm and had left home for his own purposes.

Then, suddenly, part of Mr. Setty appeared. Off the Essex coast, some distance north of the Thames estuary, there is a marsh, a curious springy cushion of mud and grasses, patterned with a net of rivulets, and frequented by a great many duck and widgeon. On October 22, Mr. Sidney Tiffen, a farm worker who was taking a week's holiday but not leaving home for it, went out in his punt to get some game. He saw something grey being lifted off the hummocks by the tide and thought it was a drogue, the target, not unlike the windsock of an airfield, which a training plane trails behind it in fighting exercises. As he had earned five shillings often enough by picking up these drogues and taking them back to the RAF station not far away, he paddled over to it. When he got there he found that it was not a target but a grey bundle tied up in a thick piece of felt, like the carpet of an automobile. It was so carefully secured with such stout rope that he deduced the packers must have thought it valuable, and wondered if this was flotsam from a wreck. As it was too heavy and unwieldy to take in his punt, he cut it open and found himself looking on a body, swaddled in a cream silk shirt and pale blue silk shorts, from which the head and legs had been hacked away. He drove a stake into the mud and tied the torso to it, then paddled ashore and went two miles over the marshes to fetch the local policeman. Eventually the body was carried ashore and its fingerprints were taken. The murderer who hopes to commit the perfect crime should exchange references with his victim. Mr. Setty's enemy had not known that he had ever been convicted, so he had not cut off his hands. Thus Scotland Yard was able to identify his body in a few hours. Seven days later a man of twenty-nine named Brian Donald Hume, owner of a radio shop in a London suburb and managing director of a small factory producing gadgets for domestic and workshop use, was arrested and charged with the murder of Mr. Setty. In court he was accused of having dropped the body on the marshes from an airplane.

Very soon the experienced newspaper reader began to suspect that Mr. Tiffen was, in some way, an exceptional person. The legal restrictions on crime-reporting in Great Britain are far beyond American conception. They are admirable, and it should be our pride to obey them, for they go far towards preventing trial by prejudiced juries. If a gentleman were arrested carrying a lady's severed head in his arms and wearing her large intestine as a garland round his neck and crying aloud that he and he alone had been responsible for her reduction from a whole to parts, it would still be an offence for any newspaper to suggest that he might have had any connection with her demise until he had been convicted of this offence by a jury and sentenced by a judge. Therefore the veins swell up and pulse on the foreheads of reporters and sub-editors, and somehow their passion seeps into the newsprint and devises occult means by which the truth becomes known. The experienced newspaper reader can run his eye over the columns of newspapers which are paralysed by fear of committing contempt of court (and this fear has justification—only the other day the editor of an English tabloid was sentenced to three months in jail for stating, quite truly, that a man had confessed to a murder for which he was afterwards hanged, and served every day of it), and can learn with absolute certainty, from something too subtle even to be termed a turn of phrase, which person involved in a case is suspected by the police of complicity and which is thought innocent. It was at once apparent that Mr. Tiffen was regarded by the police as guiltless of any part in Mr. Setty's murder, although his story was precisely that which would have been told by an accessory after the fact who had been paid to take Mr. Setty's body out to sink on the flooded marshes, had found it more difficult to do than he had anticipated, and had in panic resolved to try to clear himself of suspicion. There was also discernible to the eye of any newspaper writer the sort of block round Mr. Tiffen's name which comes when a reporter would like to write more fully about a person or an event but is stopped by some consideration, most probably lack of space, but sometimes a matter of emotion.

A friend had a legitimate reason for visiting Mr. Tiffen, so one evening, after a fifty-mile drive from London, we came to a little town on the east coast just north of the Thames estuary and got out in the high street. In a tower a big clock, pale orange like a harvest moon, bright above the low mist, told us that it was too late to look for Mr. Tiffen at his home some miles away. We found a hotel and dinner, and then went out to find a public house where Mr. Tiffen might go, for it was Saturday night and not impossible that he might have come in from his village for a glass of beer and a game of darts.

We found the public house which was Mr. Tiffen's favourite port of call, but he was not there. A man can be judged by his public house, and we left thinking well of Mr. Tiffen. We had settled down to watch a game of darts, and only gradually realized that we had strayed into a private room, reserved by custom for the use of some friends who met there every Saturday night. But the people saw that we did not know and made us welcome; and they were pleasant too to a girl who belonged to that wistful company who love playing games and are duffers at them all. Each time she lifted her hand to throw a dart her eyes shone like a begging dog's; and each time it fell somewhere out of the scoring areas, often right off the board into the wall behind. They were just right for her, not so sorry for her that they rubbed in how bad she was, but sorry enough to dispel any suspicion that

172

they were knocked speechless by her ineptitude. By such signs a gentlemanly society reveals itself, and it looked as if Mr. Tiffen might be a gentleman. We went back to our beds, and the next morning showed us the river like grey glass, with a hundred or so little boats lying in the harbour basin. On the opposite bank the sea walls which kept the estuary from doing harm were darker grey, the trees rising above them were black and flat like so many aces of clubs, and some barns were red. Yachtsmen and yachtswomen came down and breakfasted, glossy with content because they were presently to get into their boats and sail off into the shining water, as if taking refuge in a mirror. We drove away through the little town, at the very moment when the lie-abed leisure of Sunday morning changes to the churchgoing bustle, into a countryside that was the simplest arrangement of soil conceivable. It was featureless as the flats of Holland and Belgium it was facing across the North Sea. Some force had patted this piece of it into rising ground, but not very hard; the plateau was quite low. It was cut up by hedges into green pastures and fields of fat black earth. There were a few trees, some farms and cottages, no great houses. It could be seen that a ragged and muddy coastline had kept the railways out of this corner of England, and the sea winds and heavy soil had limited the size of the settlements. Here society had been kept simple; and what simplicity can do if left to itself was shown to us when we halted at a cottage to ask the way, and a woman, young but quite toothless, with several tubby children at her tubby skirts, stared at us without answering, without ill will, without good will, neutral as dough. I wondered whether the reporters' pencils had halted on Mr. Tiffen's name because he belonged to this recessive phase of the bucolic, and it had struck them as painful that the worst of town life, in this murdered body, should in its finding have come in contact with the worst of country life.

Before long we found his village. We passed a prim edifice with "The Peculiar People" painted across its stucco forehead, towards which some lean and straight-backed men and women were walking with an air of conscious and narrow and splendid pride. That strange faith which has no creed and no church organization but believes simply in miracle, in the perpetual re-

173

creation of the universe by prayer, is about a hundred and ten years old. Each death which has occurred during that period is a defeat for it, since all sickness should be prayed into health by the faithful, but these people walked away from us with the bearing of victors. People were streaming towards the church too. We stopped a boy of twelve or so, who must have been a choirboy, for he was carrying a surplice, and asked him the way to Mr. Tiffen's house. He smiled at us; the little frown between his eyebrows registered not ill nature but his sense of a conflict between duties. He had to hurry if he was to be in time for church; but one had to be polite to strangers. So he paused to give us full directions, detailed enough to bring us to the housing estate where Mr. Tiffen lived. A few houses built of yellow wood stood among others built of alternate slabs of concrete and breese on land which had obviously been a field till about five minutes before.

The door was opened by a young woman. She was at the opposite end of the scale of rural society from the family made of dough. Completely articulate, she explained that she was Mr. Tiffen's married daughter, and kept house for him, and was sorry, Dad had gone to see Gran, he always did on Sundays. We asked where Gran lived, suggesting that we might follow him, and, though she was careful not to discourage us, lest she should be implying that Dad would not find our company agreeable, her gaze softened with pity. She did not think we could follow him. Gran lived four miles away in the old coast-guard's cottage. Well, that was all right, we had an automobile and four miles was nothing. Yes, but the cottage was on the sea wall. Two miles was as far as we could go by road, after that the way was across the drained marshes, muddy and hard to find. Oh, but we went anywhere. And how long ago had Mr. Tiffen started? Half an hour? Was he driving as far as the road went, or did he ride a bicycle? Oh no, he walked. We reflected on the remarkable filial piety of Mr. Tiffen, who walked eight miles every Sunday to see Gran, and hurried off, saying that we would catch him up.

But we never did. He was not on the road, and he was not in sight when we left the car among the hayricks in a farmyard on the edge of the marshes. We could see Gran's house in the distance, a small coal-black square under the sharp pie-crust edge of the sea wall which bounded the landscape, and there seemed to be no living thing between us and it. This was, of course, an illusion. The air was alive with the cries of countless marsh birds. All here was lively. To town dwellers winter is a season of death, but here it was a brisk cleansing process. The earth was being tilted so that the heat which had collected during the summer drained away, freshness was flowing in. Growth had not stopped. Through the black fatness of some fields the winter wheat and oats were sending up green blades bright as paint, the ploughed fields lay cut up into dark shining bricks as obviously nourishing as butter. On that nutrient material we slid and skipped and fell as we worked our way across the flatlands to the sea wall by the sides of the deep irrigation ditches. We kept at it hard, pausing only once when we came on a dead fox, which looked less pathetic than would seem possible for a dead animal, because it was still a trim and barbered wise guy. We crossed an irrigation ditch, jumping from one slope of dark butter to another, and got to the sea wall, and clambered up through the long wet grasses that clothed it.

The tide was out. So far as the eye could see there stretched the matted bents of the mudflats: a soft monotony blended of grey and green and blue and purple. It had a quilted look, for the thousands of rivulets which cast a network over it followed the same course day in, day out, and had worn down the mud into channels between the hummocks some feet deep. To the small creatures which lived here this must have been a most fantastic landscape. At the bottom of these deep channels the tiny streams, only a few inches wide, had their established, deeply graven waterfalls, their rapids which tested to the utmost the gallantry of straws, and lakes with bays and beaches; and on the islands grass roots found purchase on the mud by gripping it and one another so that they grew into cushions of jungle, one plant rising on another like minute vegetable pagodas. The scene was incised and overstuffed with profligate ingenuity; and it was odd to think of all this elaboration being wiped out twice in every twenty-four hours, the rivulets losing their identities in the rough inundation of the tide, the springing grasses, so obstinate in their intention

175

of making dry land out of mud, becoming the bottom of the sea. There was the same spendthrift and impermanent fabrication going on at ground level as there was over our heads, where great clouds, momentarily like castles, temples, mountains, and giant birds, were blown by the cleansing winter wind to the edges of the sky, here not clipped away by hills or streets and astonishingly far apart. There could not have been a more generous scene, nor one which was less suited to receive the remains of Mr. Setty, who from infancy had been so deeply involved in calculation, and so unhappily, who had tried keeping figures outside his head and got sent to prison for it, and had kept them inside his head and got killed for it.

Gran's cottage lay about a quarter of a mile away on the landward side of the sea wall, not small, containing at least eight rooms, but nonetheless a deplorable habitation. It was built of brick covered with tarred weatherboard, which was falling away in splinters, and the windows of one half of it were broken. The only approach to it was by a couple of planks laid across an irrigation ditch. It seemed unlikely that Mr. Tiffen would allow Gran to live there, or that she would consent to do so, unless they were sunk so deeply in poverty that they had forgotten how to make demands. The young woman who had received us at Mr. Tiffen's home was perhaps a sport from a rough stock; or, just as probably, we had mistaken for gentleness what was really the inanition of anæmia. We fumbled at a door, but of course it led only into a woodshed, for it was on the seaward side, and here the front door would have to face landwards, or on many days it would be impossible to open and shut it against the gales. As it was, so strong a gust blew on us as we knocked at the right door that we were pulled inside, and thus were suddenly confronted with the character of the Tiffen family, and gaped. It did not matter. They were expert in all forms of courtesy, and knew how to receive guests, and how to give them time to recover themselves if they had lost their self-possession.

They were sitting in a room which was surprisingly warm. The house was much better than we had thought; it kept out the weather, this room had a pleasing and individual shape, the fire was drawing well in the grate. There were four of them, sitting round a table, drinking cups of tea and eating mince pies, and they were obviously an elect race. If they were not eminent it was because generation after generation had chosen not to be, having the sense to know that they would have more fun and do as good a job by remaining obscure. Gran, who was eighty-four, had been a beauty. She was still pleasing to the eye, with abundant white hair and a very white skin, and a plumpness which seemed an accumulation of satisfactions. Her daughter sat beside her, red-cheeked and blunt-featured like a Brueghel peasant, but aristocratic and artistic by reason of her unusual powers of perception. Beside the fire, next to me, sat her husband, and it could be seen that she had taken to herself a man who might have been outside the tribe but was one of the same kind. He had a good head and body, he bore himself with dignity, he made sensible remarks in beautiful English. It was to be noted that on the walls there hung two religious prints, one of them a copy of Leonardo da Vinci's "Last Supper," and numerous photographs of weddings, in which both brides and bridegrooms looked thoroughly pleasant human beings. Obviously the Tiffens, whom I realized had been looking after my interests in many ways which I had never suspected, had been carrying on successful experiments in eugenics on quite a large scale. There remained Mr. Tiffen, who was sitting over in the window, instantly affording a complete answer to the problem of why the reporters' pencils had checked for a moment when they came to write of him. He was a small man, with dark hair which was tousled because he constantly ran his hands through it in wonder. It could be seen that he was not a rich man, because his spectacles were the cheapest kind that are made; but he needed nothing, he could get everything he wanted out of what he had, save certain things which the nature of things denied him. But he was thinking of that denial in a way which made it something other than a frustration.

Our friend settled with Mr. Tiffen the matter which was the cause of our visit, and Mr. Tiffen thanked him, and told us all was going well, and set about making our visit a pleasant social occasion. We spoke of the agreeable warmth of the house, and it turned out that Gran's tenancy of it was quite a story. She had gone there as a young woman because her husband had been a coast guard, a member of a marine police force recruited from time-expired naval men, which used to be quartered at regular intervals along the British coastline, but has been superseded since the advent of the combustion engine by smaller mobile forces operating from the harbour. In the old days there had been a row of these houses, and she had had plenty of company; there may have been a dozen adults set down here on the marshes. When the coast guards were disbanded the pensioned men and the widows were allowed to stay on, and as they died off the houses were pulled down. "And quite right too," the women agreed, their voices rising. They were not archaic. They were part of the modern England which was building itself anew. "No woman," they said, "ought to be asked to live like this. There's no water here except the rainwater in the cisterns on the roof."

Now the family who had lived in the other half of this house had gone; that was why the windows had not been mended after having been broken by the winter gales. So Gran was the last one to linger here, and a mercy it was she had held her ground and not gone up to the village when she could have, before the war, for now her son-in-law and daughter were living with her, and glad they were to have a roof over their heads, for they had lost their home while he was serving in the Navy during the war. Of course it was very hard on the son-in-law to be down here on the sea wall, for he was a builder and never worked nearer than the village and sometimes farther away, so in the winter he had to do the two-mile walk across the marshes in the darkness of early morning and late afternoon. But goodness knows what they would have done if Gran had not been able to take them in; and she could do that only because of the trouble that had fallen on Mr. Tiffen.

Sorrow ran through the group like wind through the branches of a tree. It was because of that trouble that Mr. Tiffen had been so upset when he found Mr. Setty's body. He could not get over it, although it had happened some years ago. He had had a wife, the mother of the girl we had seen in the village and of some sons. She was forty-two years old and had hardly had a day's illness in her life except for childish troubles. She and Mr. Tiffen and the children had all lived along of Gran, and all had gone well, none of them had a care in the world. One day she had gone shopping in the village and seemed full of unusual happiness. "I've never seen you looking so well," the grocer had said, and she had answered, "I don't know what's the matter with me, I feel on top of the world." He was not the only one; everybody she met that morning remembered how she had laughed and joked. Then she turned homewards across the marshes. Gran and the children were at the windows, waiting for her; and they saw her pause as she stepped off the plank over the ditch and fall to the ground. They found her lying among the parcels spilled from her shopping bag, dead of heart failure. The faces of these four people asked why there should be all this fuss about murder when death is the real wonder. Think of it, a body is in the state in which all living bodies are, and shows no signs of alteration; it is loved; many people wish it to go on just as it is. Suddenly it is dead; it becomes necessary for those who love it to let the undertakers take it away and bury it. This is much more difficult to understand than somebody dying because they have been stabbed or shot or poisoned by somebody that hates them. Natural death seems far less natural than unnatural death.

After Mr. Tiffen's wife died he could not bear to stay in this house. He saw her everywhere in it. So he moved into the council house in the village which we had visited that morning. He had had to pay a great price for it, for council houses are given only to farm labourers; they have priority. He was a fisherman and a fowler, and had been so all his days and loved that life, and he hated agricultural work. But to get one of these council houses he left the water and took a job with a nearby farmer. It irked the family that had he got over his feeling about the haunting of Gran's house and had wanted to come back there, he still could not have exchanged quarters with his brother-in-law and handed his council house over to him, who would have found it most convenient for his building work. The regulation which gave these houses to farm labourers could not have been set aside, and this is reasonable enough, for there is a much greater dearth of farm labourers than of builders; but it is hard for people of independent character, as fishermen tend to be, to accept gladly something that so overrides their wills. That, however, did not vex Mr.

Tiffen himself; he still missed his wife so much that he could not have borne to go on living in this house.

It was because of his thoughts about death that he had turned so squeamish over this body, and had not been the same man since he had had to touch it. He had been in two minds about taking any notice of it, but it was such a great parcel that someone might have set store by it; it wasn't just a thing you could let go, and once he had seen what it was he had to do his duty by it, though nobody likes handling that sort of thing, really. It was not easy to handle either. He had got the stake into the mud easy enough to tie it to, but he had tried to get the rope between the arm and the body, it made a neater job that way, but then the arm had dropped off and to keep it he had had to put the rope round both arm and body, and that was quite a business. Then he paddled the punt back to the sea wall, about a hundred yards it was, and he went the two miles over the marshes to the police station, and he found a constable there, about midday it was, and he brought him down to look at it. They sat in the punt together and looked at the great thing held up above the grey waters by the stake, and the constable said to Mr. Tiffen, "There's something wrong here," and Mr. Tiffen answered, "Yes, I think there's something wrong here." Then the constable said, "It's my opinion this is a murdered body," and Mr. Tiffen said, "Yes, I do think it is a murdered body."

These comments on a torso which had been found wrapped in felt and tied up with rope might seem comically obvious; but they were said for a purpose. The constable and Mr. Tiffen saw the remains of a human being who had been dispatched without mercy, and they had neither of them ever seen such a thing before, and they knew that if too many of such things happened it would be the doom of their kind. They were deeply moved and had a sound instinct to find words to express their feelings, so that they would commemorate their emotion and make it more powerful. Doubtless they fumbled in their minds among the texts from the Bible and verses from the Church Hymnal and tags from Shakespeare they carried in their minds. But murder is so rare an event that there is no widely known formula for expressing the feeling it arouses, and so they had to do what they could for themselves. They did it well enough, for as Mr. Tiffen solemnly repeated what they said, their holy loathing of murder was manifest, and as we listened we were moved back several stages nearer the first and appropriate shock caused by Cain. His talk told then of the fatigue and tedium which follows catastrophe. The constable had said it was not for him to handle the body and that he must telephone headquarters, and then there was much running backwards and forwards that went through that day into the next. For darkness had fallen by the time the great ones were all assembled and ready to take Mr. Setty ashore, and they could not find him, and had to wait till he showed up across the flats on his stake through the morning light.

Mr. Tiffen acted as guide, made a statement to a Scotland Yard Inspector, learned who the dead man was and that he had reason to expect a thousand pounds' reward, and went home feeling deadly tired and nauseated by the thought of the parcel, though believing that a sleep would get him over that. But it did not; and the next night a chill came on him. He shivered and piled on the bedclothes, and his son-in-law brought him his army greatcoat to lay on top of him, and there is real warmth in those army greatcoats, but still Mr. Tiffen shivered so that the bed rattled. In the morning his son-in-law brought him a cup of tea, and he said he did not want it. His son-in-law said, "Go on, try it, Dad, you must have something," but he only brought it up. He was like that for a week, and all that time he was away from work; it was as if he had a real chill, but it was not that, it was the shock of handling the body. Of course he had brought in bodies before. In the war he had found several RAF men and a couple of German sailors out on the marshes, but that was helping them to Christian burial, you didn't think anything of it. But this was different. Mr. Tiffen's brother-in-law agreed that it was different, something apart. He had brought in a suicide, a woman that had drownded herself (they all four used the old form of the past participle), and had thought nothing of it, but he would not have done what Mr. Tiffen did, not for anything. "Come to think of it," said Mr. Tiffen's sister, "Have you seen anything in the papers about them burying the body? I haven't." "They ought to lay it at rest," said Gran. "Well, I suppose it's awkward for them having only the one part of it," said the sister. "It'd be better if they got the whole of it. I go up all the time to Mum's room with the binoculars, to look if I can see another parcel coming in, but I never see anythng." "You never will," said Mr. Tiffen, "all the rest is at the bottom of the sea. And it is awkward for the family. Nice people, they seemed, too. They were at Bow Street when I went up to give evidence. Mr. Setty's sister's husband came right across the room to shake hands and thank me for the trouble I'd taken, very civil."

Death was a sacred mystery to these people and a loathsome obscenity; but also it had sometimes to be inflicted, and the risk of it suffered, in the way of duty. Gran had brought in cups of fresh hot tea, and for a minute or two we all drank and were silent. My eyes went to two photographs of destroyers on the walls, and Mr. Tiffen's brother-in-law said, "My ships in the war. We're all in the Navy here." "All in the Navy," nodded Gran, and sure enough all the bridegrooms in the wedding groups wore naval uniform. So death was not altogether terrible here, for it was part of a familiar and accepted and enjoyed discipline. Indeed, they had subjugated death still further, for though it was solemnly realized, it was also domesticated, a part of household economy, not taken too seriously, carelessly dispensed to the birds and beasts and fishes, along with love.

"It came of being my holiday then that I came on this thing," grieved Mr. Tiffen, "for, it being my holiday, of course I went down on the marshes and got out in my punt; that's what I like to do, have a bit of shooting in my punt." "He is a proper wonder in his punt," said his brother-in-law; "nobody can do more with a punt gun than he can." "Only time," said Mr. Tiffen sadly, "that I ever had anything to do with the police before all this fuss and bother was to go to the police station and get a license for my gun. Duck we can get," he said more happily, "and widgeon. There's many like widgeon better than duck, it's richer. It's a nice kind of sport too. It's not like other shooting, you know. You don't wait for the birds to rise. You paddle along, quiet as you can, lying down in the boat, facing forward, till you see a nice lot of birds settled on the water, and you get to the right distance, so that the shot splays out amongst them, and you get the lot." "Twenty or thirty he gets at a time," rejoiced his brother-in-law. "We take what we want," said Mr. Tiffen, "and we get rid of the rest easy enough. I don't even have to send them to market; I just take them home to the village and sell them up and down the street. People are glad to have them to make up the meat ration." "He has his fun and makes good money out of it," said the brother-in-law. Mr. Tiffen's glasses shone with satisfaction. The times had got him with his back to the wall; they had made him a farm worker when he was a fisherman and a fowler, but he had found the only loophole, he had an exceptional gift, and, in his several ways, he was enjoying exceptional rewards.

We asked him questions about this gun which brought down twenty and thirty birds at a time, and they were foolish questions, since neither of us had ever shot from a punt. We were worried about the kick of such a wonder-working gun, because we thought it must be fired from the shoulder, like other guns. "No, no," said Mr. Tiffen patiently, "you haven't got this right. The boat takes the kick, not my shoulder. It isn't near my shoulder, it's lying on the floor of the punt. There's a couple of ropes like a cradle at the back of it like, to take the kick. It's got no sights, I just look along the barrel, and when I get it lined up on the birds I ship a paddle and pull the hammer-trigger with my hand. But you come out and see for yourselves the way it is." "Yes, you ought to have a look at that punt and that gun," said the brother-in-law, "you won't see better." "I never saw better," said Mr. Tiffen. "I don't know who made them. They belonged to an old man used to live round here. I bought them when he died. I was young myself then. Come and have a look at them. It's just a step along the sea wall."

Outside the warm house the air came cold through our clothes to our skins; it was as if we had dropped into a swimming pool, we shivered and said "Brrr," but liked it. We walked in single file along the top of the sea wall, Mr. Tiffen going first. His feet were very small, and he put them down lightly and firmly as if he were a ballet dancer. Like us, he had come over two miles of drained marsh, and he had explained that we had not overtaken him on the road because he had come by a short cut of his own across the fields. But though we were muddied to the knees there was hardly a speck of dirt on his neat brown boots. We stopped to look over the blue-green mudflats and listen to the cry of the seabirds. It was as if the still air were striped vertically with the pure, thin, ascendant notes. "The teuks those are," said Mr. Tiffen. "Some call them red shanks."

Staring out to the sea, which was now just visible as a dark shining line on the horizon, he ran his hand through his hair and said, "An unnoticing man he must have been, a most unnoticing man. This Hume, the man they said had done the murder. You see how it happened that the body was laying about so that I found it? He dropped it from the plane where he saw deep water. That is why I say he must be a most unnoticing man, for they tell me he was round here during the war with the RAF. He should have noticed that all round the coast here there's places where it's deep water just twice in the month, when there's a full moon and a new moon, and all the rest of the time there's shallow water. When he dropped this parcel here the sea was flooding over the flats; it was near to the top of the sea wall, I grant you that. But the water runs away, after that there's only a foot or two of water even at high tide; that parcel was bound to lie about on the mud when it was low tide, same as it was doing when I found it. You'd think a man would know more about tides and such than to do a thing like that, wouldn't you, especially when he's been in the neighbourhood, like?" The face he turned on us was deeply lined by the strain of acute observation carried on all his life long, of a constant conversion of the knowledge he thus gained into wisdom. But for once he was inquiring into something which would remain for ever unknown to him. It was not for him to understand the peculiar bargain this age had driven with some of his fellow men: teaching them to perform one enormously complicated operation, such as flying a plane, but in exchange taking away their knowledge of certain very simple things, such as the pull of the moon on the sea, and the unlikelihood that a man can kill another man without being found out, or even the nature of murder.

The punt was lying in one of the channels, and we went out to it over the mud, again appreciating how neat Mr. Tiffen was on his feet. If we followed his trail exactly, treading on the tufts

184

of grass where he had trod, we remained dry-shod; if we strayed, we slid on stuff like toothpaste. For a little we hung over the punt and made clucking noises as if it were a baby. It had that mysterious secondary colour, apart from its paint, which very old boats have, and it looked too fragile to carry its gun, which looked like a drainpipe. "Do you ever capsize?" we asked. "Well, I did when I was very young," said Mr. Tiffen, and laughed as if he remembered a story against himself.

Just then the clouds broke. Circles of amber brightness travelled towards us over the mudflats and broadened out, and we were suddenly in full sunshine, and quite warm. We were surprised, but Mr. Tiffen told us, "It often gets hot like this down here, even in the wintertime; the coastline runs all twisted here, and the way this bay lies the sea wall shelters you from the east wind. Why, it wasn't long ago, we were right into November, that I came down here and found a great seal sunning himself in that channel over there. The punt was here, and he was over there, sitting up against the bank as if it was his own armchair. I said to myself, 'Well, I've never shot a seal and now I'm going to get one,' and I had my shotgun lying down here at the foot of the wall, and I came back and fetched it, and I was creeping up on him when he looked round at me and started shaking his head. You know, moved it from side to side, the way old people do when they're just sitting and are comfortable. Like this." Mr. Tiffen made a movement which brought before the mind's eye all the seals in zoos and circuses that look like old gentlemen, all the old gentlemen that look like seals. "After that I couldn't shoot him. I hadn't the heart to take his life. Not after he'd looked round at me and shook his head that way. I lowered my gun and let him be." His face deeply creased with smiling tenderness, Mr. Tiffen looked round at his marshes, his sky. "It was a nice day, just like this," he said.

❖❖ 2 ❖❖

The person accused of the murder of Mr. Setty, Brian Donald Hume, was twenty-nine years old. It was alleged that he had invited Mr. Setty to his flat in Golders Green and stabbed him to death, on the night of October 4, and cut him up into several pieces and packaged them on the afternoon of October 5; and that later that day he had taken some of these packages up in a plane and dropped them in the North Sea off the east coast, and that the next day he had dropped some more. He was a middle-sized young man, with an abundance of black hair, a face much fatter than his body, a mouth like a woman's, and deep-set dark eyes burning with eagerness. Whatever it might be that was going to happen next, he would greet it eagerly just because it was an event. He had a much greater lust for life than most people who get into the dock. He looked foreign; he might have been a Turk or an Arab.

The first sight of him suggested that he was a spiv. He wore the checked sports jacket, the pullover, the flannel trousers, all chosen to look raffish, which was then the uniform of the spiv, and he had the air of self-conscious impudence which is the spiv's hallmark. That in itself made it surprising that he was charged with murder. Spivs were then busy dealing on the black market in automobiles and petrol, meat and poultry and sugar, foreign currency and building materials. Though they broke the law in handling these goods, and some of them got involved in ware-house robberies and automobile thefts, most of them would keep their hands clean of murder. We still get most of our murderers and hang most of those we catch. It would have been surprising if Hume had been one of the spivs who disregarded this reason for caution, for though it was apparent that he wanted to live, it was apparent that he had suffered some head-on collisions with life in which he had come off badly. He was brassy but wistful.

The court was filled by the relatives and friends of Mr. Setty, who were not wistful. Rumour said that they were kin to the two great Shashoua brothers, who had built a flamboyant opulence for themselves in England during the first forty years of this century. They were no fools. Ben was an automobile dealer in the early days when it took real intelligence to find out what makers were worth following. Abraham was in the textile trade and kept going in that legitimate business until the great textile slump of the early twenties. Ben, who was the more picturesque, was in the end deported. This was not because any criminal proceedings were ever brought against him. It was simply felt that England and he were working at cross-purposes. He revelled in litigation; in the last twenty years of his residence in England he brought twenty-four actions in the court, and must have been an ill-used man, for he won fifteen. The other brother, Abraham, went bankrupt for a hundred and fifty thousand pounds and paid his creditors a half-penny in the pound. He greatly enjoyed all the technicalities of the proceedings and ranks as a very great concert bankrupt. At one point he raised his creditors' spirits by returning to his birthplace in Mesopotamia to realize some property he owned there, spending three years on the task, surely in courts and gardens where fountains plashed, and returned with the proceeds of the sale, which amounted to thirty-five thousand rupees, but presented an expense account for forty thousand rupees. When he had lived fifty fantastic years an automobile ran over him in a country lane; and a year afterwards his widow, Iris Shashoua, gently and ceremoniously killed herself because she could no longer bear to live without her beloved husband.

The relatives of the Shashouas who were in court belonged to a later and less adventurous generation, which never got its names in the papers; but they had kept the Baghdad quality. Mr. Setty's sister, Mrs. Ouri, was no longer a young woman, and she had wept the flesh loose from the bones on her face; but she had the arched eyebrows and oval face and bland symmetry which Arabian romancers would have ascribed to a girl lying on a mother-of-pearl bed, fanned by a Negro eunuch, behind the latticed windows of a palace. Like most other women in London, New York, and Paris at that date, she wore a black Persian lamb coat and a hat like a coronet; but it might have been the mourning wear prescribed by ancient custom for women of rank in some walled town on the bare rocks above an Asiatic plain. What the men of her rank in that same city wore at such a time seemed to be shown by her cousin, though he was actually wearing a camel's hair coat; but his skin was amber, his black hair was crimped like the long tresses and beards of the men sculptured on the monuments of dead civilizations, his features were heavy, not coarse or stupid, but weighty, as if his maker had determined to keep him in scale with retinues of elephants, and masonry built massively, as can be done where there is a multitude of slaves. These two told how last they had seen Mr. Setty. As his sister had walked in a street in the quarter where the automobile market is carried on, she had seen him drive by in his resplendent automobile, a yellow Citröen limousine with scarlet upholstery, some time between five and half-past on October 4. His cousin had seen him driving by, a little later, as he stood waiting for a bus. This seemed an improbable statement when he made it, for he should obviously have travelled either by elephant or by a limousine as spectacular as his cousin's; but indeed he could be seen every afternoon going home from the Old Bailey on the bus, which he made, by the mere act of boarding it, the rickety and ill-proportioned contrivance of an immature civilization. These two family witnesses were followed by two young automobile dealers, who told how Mr. Setty had visited their office later that evening, and how they had introduced Hume to Mr. Setty some time before. These young men were in the same line of picturesqueness as the Shashoua kin. Their clothes also reversed the drabness of the West and sent the mind back to the valleys of the Euphrates and the Tigris. One of them was solid and sleek, and was dressed in such richly coloured and finely woven stuffs that it seemed hard to believe that he did not keep his automobiles in a cave guarded by a jinni; the slenderness of his partner was so treated by his tailor that it came back to the mind that slim young men were often likened to the crescent moon in the Arabian Nights. Yet for all this gorgeousness of apparel they were not Shashouas.

The Setty relatives looked as if their interior lives matched their exteriors to some degree in picturesqueness, as if they intensely experienced love and hate and joy and grief, and could find words to express how these fires burned. These younger people's tongues were dead in their mouths. They gave their evidence in tired jargon. They could not say "no," they had to say "definitely no"; they could not use the word "about," they had to put in its place "approximately." They painted no pictures for their listeners, and their faces were never lit up by their minds.

These young men had had legal troubles of a complex kind which the Shashouas would have rolled over their tongues with the ecstasy of connoisseurs, and were quite unworthy of them. Shortly after the war, when it became obvious that the bulk of British automobiles must go abroad and only a few could be kept for the home market, the British Motor Traders' Association made a rule that none of its members should sell a new automobile without making the purchaser sign a covenant binding himself not to resell it for twelve months. This was a sensible enough provision, for it might well have happened that the auto trade passed out of the hands of the legitimate traders and became a matter of private sales at huge profiteering prices, which would encourage auto-stealing and the passing off of stolen autos as new ones.

Some dealers, however, had contended that the covenant was an illegal restraint of trade and refused to observe it; and these two young men were among their number. They therefore had been defendants in an action brought in the civil courts by the British Motor Traders' Association, a case which lasted a month and was remarkable for the number and brilliance of the attorneys involved. It would have been as good as a vintage claret to the brothers Shashoua. These young men showed in the witness box that they had never understood what had happened in court and blundered over the simplest legal terms.

Their ingenuousness went deep. When Mr. Setty's cousin and sister were in the box they looked at Hume with sombre courtesy. They and he were walking along the same road, and it had led them into the Valley of Skulls, which was no place for brawling. But when these two young men spoke of Hume it was as if the three of them were hobbledehoys quarrelling in a school playground. They knew him quite well, and it was through them that Hume had met Mr. Setty. Hume had put his name down on the waiting list of an automobile manufacturer, and when he got his new automobile sold it to these dealers, who afterwards introduced him to Mr. Setty as a possible scout for used automobiles. As a result of this contact these dealers had formed a poor opinion of Hume, and from the deals of his which were traced they seem to have been right: he once bought a new car and sold it shortly afterwards at a loss of thirty per cent, which was something of an achievement in those days. But they expressed their opinion with a curious infantilism. They were the big strong popular boys who were good at games, and Hume was the little odd-come-short who sometimes tried to suck up to the gods of the school but only got jeers and cuffs as a reminder that he must keep his place. When the sleeker of the two told how Hume had tried to borrow a couple of shillings from him so that he could make up a pound to buy a postal order to send off with his weekly football-pool coupon, he might have been saying that everything about the wretched little beast was paltry, he never even had enough pocket money. But if they showed no respect for Hume's danger, they also showed none of the resentment towards him which might have been expected, considering that in his statement he had suggested that Mr. Setty had been murdered by associates of this pair. Thus he must have brought on them hours of questioning in a most disagreeable connection; but, like many people who come into the law courts, they had the virtues as well as the defects of childhood.

It was Hume's story, unsupported by any other evidence, that he had come into possession of Mr. Setty's body through his meeting with three men, who, he said, were well known to these two young dealers: a tall fair man in his thirties named Mac or Max, who wore a single-stone ring which he was always polishing, a younger man wearing steel-rimmed spectacles who was called The Boy, and a Greek or Cypriot in a green suit who was called Green or Greenie or G. They had asked him to take up in a plane some hot presses, with which they had been printing forged petrol coupons, and drop them in the sea. Hume declared it was natural that they should make such an inquiry of him, since he was known for making illicit air trips to the Continent, some in connection with the purchase of planes and munitions for the Middle East. He consented to do the job for about four hundred dollars, and the three called at his flat with two parcels on the afternoon of October 5, the day after Mr. Setty disappeared. These parcels were supposed to have contained the head and legs of Mr. Setty, but, according to Hume, he never doubted that they were presses, and he went to his flying club and got rid of them in the sea just beyond the Thames estuary. He then went home, and found the three men waiting in the street below his apartment with a third parcel, which he took up the next day and dropped in the same area. He admitted that he had suspected that this third parcel contained part of a corpse, but he pleaded that he had been too frightened to go to the police, either then or when it was announced in the newspapers that the parcel had been found and what it was.

Certainly something extraordinary had happened in Hume's flat on those days, though it was not a place which most criminals would have chosen for a dangerous operation. It was a duplex flat in a line of houses, with shops underneath, that hugs one angle of a busy crossroads. The spot is well known to all connoisseurs of Victorian thrillers; for it was here that, in the first chapter of Wilkie Collins' *The Woman in White,* the drawing master, Walter Hartwright, met the escaped lunatic walking through the night in her dressing gown. Then hedges divided it from fields. Now it is the heart of a suburban shopping centre. The intersection is dominated by Golders Green Station, and Golders Green Theatre stands beside it. At the end of the line of houses where Hume lived there is a cinema. A line of streetcars links this spot with the farther suburbs, many bus routes run through it; it sees more than suburban traffic in the way of automobiles, for this is a short cut between West London and the Great North Road. There was a bus stop right opposite Hume's front door, and an electric standard that pours brightness on it when daylight has gone. The shops round about serve a wide district, in which German is heard as often as English, for many refugees from Hitler's Germany have settled there, and perhaps for this reason it keeps later hours than most London suburbs. At all times a policeman on point duty stands fifty yards or so away. The back entrance to the premises can be reached only by a narrow road behind the line of houses which runs past a garage and is overlooked by a number of flats. The neighbours would take note if any automobile used it late at night.

Even inside his home Hume had less privacy than many. He lived in the upper of two duplex apartments over a greengrocer's shop, and the structure was as insubstantial as cheap suburban architecture usually was fifty years ago. A dark, steep, and narrow wooden staircase with a murderous turn to it led past the front door of the lower duplex flat, which was inhabited by a schoolmaster and his wife, up to Hume's own front door, which opened on a slit of lobby. To the left was a living room, looking over the street; to the right was a smaller dining room, long and narrow, with a pantry beyond it, and beyond that again, an attic kitchenette, with the slant of the roof coming fairly low. None of these rooms was large. The living room was perhaps fifteen feet by eleven, and the dining room fifteen feet by eight.

Another steep and narrow and perilous stairway led up to a bedroom, a nursery, and a bathroom. The rooms were sparsely furnished, which meant nothing, for furniture was the last painful shortage in Britain, and only a very well-to-do young couple could then set up a brand-new comfortable home. But the place had been furnished according to the memory of a pattern established by the educated and fairly prosperous middle class. Somebody living here had been brought up in the kind of home where they took in *Punch*. The convention of interior decoration on that level of culture is simple and airy, so there were no nailed-down carpets and linoleum, no heavy curtains. The cheap wood floors, which were insufficiently caulked between the widely spaced boards, might as well have been gratings. If anybody shouted or screamed in any room in this apartment, or if anything heavy fell on the floor, it would have been audible in all the other rooms, and almost certainly in the apartment below, and probably in the houses to the right or the left.

There were three people living in this apartment: this nearly handsome, faintly raffish young ex-pilot, as his intimates considered him, Brian Donald Hume; his wife Cynthia; and their baby daughter, who was just over two months old. Cynthia Hume had an unusual and very strong personality. She was twenty-nine and looked six or seven years younger. She had soft dark hair, gentle eyes, a finely cut and very childish mouth, and an exceptionally beautiful creamy complexion. Her fault was that she appeared colourless. If she had been more definite in appearance she might have had the chiselled dignity of a Du Maurier drawing, of Mimsie in *Peter Ibbetson,* but she was too shadowy for that. In compensation she had a low-pitched and very lovely voice, and a charm that, had she been a mermaid, would have drawn all navies down into the deep water, man by man. Nobody could talk with her for more than ten minutes without feeling that she was infinitely kind and tender and simple and helpless, and that to succour her would be bliss. The only unfavourable suspicion she ever aroused was a doubt as to whether her look of childishness might not spring from a lack of adult intelligence. The doubt was unfounded. She was not intellectual but she was shrewd. Perhaps she was too languid to use her shrewdness to avert catastrophe; but she could survive catastrophe.

Her father was the chief examiner in a Midland Savings Bank which had four hundred branches, her mother was a woman of strong character and abounding affections. After she had been at a provincial university for a term or two she went into the Women's Auxiliary Air Force, at the age of nineteen; and life in the women's services did its curious trick of making a girl into a woman before her time and at the same time keeping her for ever a little schoolgirlish. She made an unsuccessful marriage, which took her into the night clubs and restaurants of the West End of London. She got a divorce, which neither she nor her family took lightly. She was secretary in a fashionable restaurant when, late in 1948, she married Brian Donald Hume. Ten months afterwards she had a baby, suffering a difficult and dangerous confinement. Now she was breast-feeding the baby, as well as looking after it herself, and doing all its laundry. She also did all the housework with no help except a weekly visit from a domestic worker. If she had a pretty air of sleepy remoteness it was not because she had assumed it in order to seem voluptuous and exciting. It was because she was tired, and by nature turned all things to favour and prettiness, even fatigue.

Nothing is known of what happened in this apartment on the night of October 4. Hume said he was at home, though at first he put up a false alibi; and Mrs. Hume said that that night was to her like any other evening. She could bring back to her mind nothing about it, until she looked at an old copy of the *Radio Times* and recognized one of the programmes as one she had listened to when she sat in the living room after supper, waiting to go upstairs to give her baby its ten o'clock feed. It was, in obedience to the sinister pattern of this murder case, an account of the trial of Landru. For the rest it was, as she kept on repeating, just like any other evening. She and Hume slept in a double bed, and he had come to bed as usual. At no time did she wake up and find him gone. And when she rose at six in the morning to give the baby its first feed, he was still there.

But if we know nothing about the night of October 4, we know a great deal about October 5. That day was built up all over again, as solid as when it was first lived, when it had seemed buried for months deep in the past. A procession of people passed through the witness box and showed what it is that the virtuous apprentice receives as his reward. They toiled and they spun and they were in no way like the lilies of the field; a bank manager, the manageress of a dyeing and cleaning establishment, a charwoman, a house painter, a taxi driver, and so on. Not for them tailoring that recalled the dyes of Tyre, the weavers of Arabia. Drab they dressed and drab they lived, but somehow their tongues were alive in their mouths. They said "no" and "about" instead of "definitely no" and "approximately." Because of their simple and economical use of language they achieved magic. It was as if all sorts of objects came floating over the housetops from Golders Green to the Old Bailey to build up that day anew; a trail of five-pound notes, a carpet, a prescription, a carving knife, a cup of tea, a piece of rope. But the magic was mischievous. Reconstructed, the day suited no one's convenience.

Hume had started the morning, it appeared, between ten and eleven by going to the local branch of the Midland Bank and paying seventy pounds in five-pound notes into his account, which was about two hundred and fifteen pounds overdrawn. Then he went home, and sometime that morning the family doctor called and looked at the baby, whose stomach was out of order, and prescribed some medicine for it and advised Mrs. Hume to take it to the Children's Hospital in Great Ormond Street. Hume listened to his instructions as to how he was to get his wife and child there, and asked for a prescription for sleeping tablets. Then he went out and had these two prescriptions made up at a drugstore. Later, not long before one o'clock, he went to the dyeing and cleaning establishment, which was a few doors away from his apartment, presided over by Mrs. Linda Hearnden. This was a middle-aged woman with a delightful smile, unfussed over good looks, and perfect manners. She had a peculiar horror of the crime which had been committed, and had never become used to the thought of it, as most witnesses do during the preliminary proceedings in the lower court. She was still taut with disgust, but she took time to be fair to Hume. She told how he had come in and asked if she could accept a carpet for cleaning and dyeing, and how, when she said she could, he had brought down the light carpet from his sitting room, rolled up and tied with rope, and asked her to get it dyed a darker green, and how she gave an estimate without having it unrolled; and she would not accept the prosecution's suggestion that she had judged this by guesswork because he had not wanted to unroll it. The prosecution was hoping to prove that he had tried to prevent her from seeing a stain on the carpet which had, since the carpet was cleaned, been identified as the result of a flow of some human secretion, probably blood. But she would not have it so. If the carpet was not unrolled, it was a matter of her unwillingness to have it spread out over the shop, not of Hume's reluctance.

After he had handed over the carpet he went upstairs again and soon came down with a carving knife, which he took to a garage round the corner and handed to one of the mechanics, asking him to sharpen it. The mechanic had the impression that he said to him, "The joint is on the table, and I want to get back quickly." But he did not give the mechanic time to sharpen it properly. He took it away as soon as the mechanic had given it a rough edge and would not let him finish it on the oilstone. This irritated the mechanic, and when Hume offered him half a crown he would not take it, saying he had not been allowed to make a thorough job of it. He was a proud and tetchy man, and was extremely annoyed by the process of cross-examination, refusing to play, and regarding it as he might have regarded an attack by any stranger on his truthfulness. He stood crossly answering questions about times and Hume's words and manner, knitting his brows in peevish concentration, while without his knowledge his hands calmly played with the carving knife, noting its properties, bending back the blade, testing the edge, feeling how it lay in

the handle, balancing it to see if the proportion of blade to handle
was right. Matter was having a highly intelligent conversation
with matter, while his and the lawyers' minds were having a much
less brilliant exchange. But he got it plain that he felt sure that
Hume had spoken of a joint on the table; and for all he knew
this might not have been an exceptional occurrence, for though
Hume had never asked him to sharpen a carving knife he might
have asked other mechanics at the garage to do it; and that if
there was an urgency in Hume's manner it was nothing more than
his habit. "It's his nature," he said, in a phrase which sounded
sinister when used of a man on trial for his life, "that he's here
today and gone tomorrow."

Hume went back to his apartment, and he and his wife ate
lunch and washed up the dishes. Then, a few minutes before two
o'clock, there arrived Mrs. Ethel Stride, the charwoman. Under a
little round hat she had the prim small face of a kindly cat, and
she looked ahead of her with the still integrity, the dedication to
exact vision, that shines in the eyes of a cat. She knew the truth,
and she told it. Why? Because she had sworn to tell the truth,
the whole truth, and nothing but the truth, and she believed in
keeping oaths; but even if she had taken no oath she would still
have told the truth, because she believed that to lie was wrong.
Simply she told the truth.

When she entered the apartment, a few minutes before her
regular time, Hume met her and asked her to go out and buy a
floor cloth because he had ruined one by trying to wash a stained
carpet. Casting an eye round the apartment, she saw that the
carpet was missing, and also a floral rug in the lobby. He also
talked to her about the floor round the carpet, saying that he was
going to have it stained again. He then gave her the money for
the floor cloth, and she went down the street to buy it, and then
remembered that the shop which kept the best kitchen articles was
still shut for the lunch hour. So she turned about and went back
to the apartment. Again Hume met her, for Mrs. Hume was upstairs feeding the baby before she took it out for the afternoon,
and he told Mrs. Stride that she was to go up and work there,
because he wanted to tidy up a cupboard in the kitchen to make
room for coal to be stored in the winter, and he said that he did

not want to be disturbed while he was doing it, "on no account and in no circumstances." If the telephone rang she was to answer it and say that he was not at home.

So Mrs. Stride went upstairs and cleaned the Humes' bedroom and the nursery and the bathroom. Presently Mrs. Hume went out with the baby, and Mrs. Stride went on with her work, using the vacuum cleaner from time to time but listening for the telephone bell. She never heard it. After Hume had been in the kitchen for about an hour he came out and asked her to make some tea for him. She brewed it in the scullery, and at the same time went into the kitchen, which she found quite orderly. Then Hume went out of the flat, carrying two parcels, one under each arm. One was square, a cube with sides of about eighteen inches, and this is presumed to have been Mr. Setty's head; the other, which was a long, bent shape and considerably larger, is presumed to have contained his legs. Mrs. Stride had seen no joint of meat in the apartment that needed carving, not in the refrigerator nor in any cupboard. Nor had she seen anything unusual in the flat, no sign of a man's body with the head and legs cut off, no blood. Nor had she heard any sounds like the sawing of bones. Nor had she smelled anything that might have been blood or a corpse.

Mrs. Stride told the truth; and she was very intelligent, she had keen perceptions, she had sound powers of deduction, and she handled her memory well. When she was asked whether she would have heard Hume if he had been sawing bones, she said that she thought she could, but it was so quiet that she almost thought Mr. Hume had gone out. When she was asked if she thought that she could have heard the doorbell ring when she was working upstairs, although she was using the vacuum cleaner, she deliberated and said that she believed she could, because the vacuum cleaner was a Hoover. Had it been an Electrolux, which made a different kind of noise, she might not have been able to hear a bell while it was working, but she could hear most things through the noise made by a Hoover.

When Mrs. Stride had left the witness box she had, by her measured and conscientious evidence, performed one of the most spectacular acts which have ever amazed a law court. She had, on the first day of the trial, wholly destroyed both the case for the prosecution (whose witness she was) and the case for the defence. For the prosecution claimed that Hume had enticed Setty into his apartment and had there stabbed him and cut up his body, and the prosecuting counsel laid stress on the fact that Hume went to the garage at lunchtime on that day and asked a mechanic to sharpen a carving knife, saying, "It may be that he had already blunted it by cutting up a body and maybe he wanted it to be sharpened for more cutting." But it was abundantly clear from Mrs. Stride's evidence that he had done nothing, in that eggshell of an apartment, of the hauling and pitching and dragging which would have been necessary if he were cutting up the body of a man weighing over a hundred and eighty pounds, and that he had certainly not been sawing through a spine and through thigh bones. If he had cut up anybody there the night before, there would have been some blood somewhere, which Mrs. Stride, who performed her duties with fervour, would certainly have noticed.

Another significant matter which was fatal to the prosecution was established when she was in the witness box. Hume was no fool, and he knew just what Mrs. Stride was. His face showed that he was following her evidence with the utmost appreciation of her character; and it was confirmed by his friends that he was in fact extremely fond of her and had often had long conversations with her about serious problems of conduct. He knew that she was intelligent and observant and honest, and he would certainly not have allowed her to come into the apartment had there been a body lying there still to be dismembered or only just dismembered. He would have met her at the door and made some excuse why she should not enter. One is glad to welcome a domestic worker arriving, but not so glad as all that.

But when the mind turned back towards Hume's account of the three men who had come to his apartment and left parcels on him which they said and he believed were presses, it was evident that Mrs. Stride had killed that story too. She had heard nobody come to the flat. It was a Hoover, not an Electrolux; the apartment had been so quiet that she thought Mr. Hume had gone out; and Hume had declared in his statement that the men had come at the time when she was in his apartment.

MR. SETTY AND MR. HUME

They drank their cups of tea together, these two, and Hume went down the stairs with Mr. Setty's head under one arm and Mr. Setty's legs under the other, and his pet dog, Tony, a mongrel Alsatian, at his heels. He packed the parcels into the back seat of an automobile hired from the nearby garage where he had had the knife sharpened at lunchtime, and with the dog beside him he drove off to Elstree Airfield, the headquarters of his flying club, about eight miles away. That morning he had telephoned to ask for an Auster plane to be kept ready for him, and he and a groundsman took the parcels out of the automobile and put them in the plane, the head in the co-pilot's seat, the legs in the passenger seat behind. Before he went up he paid the cashier of the flying club twenty pounds in payment of an outstanding account, in five-pound notes.

He took off from the airfield about half-past four and flew east, leaving London on his right and heading for the Thames estuary and the North Sea. He says that at a thousand feet up and four or five miles out to sea he opened the door, holding the controls with his knees, and threw both the parcels out of the plane into the water below. Then he came down at Southend Airfield, a mile or two inland from the Thames estuary, at half-past six. He could not take the plane back to Elstree because it was getting dark and he had no night-flying certificate, and he tried to get a member of his flying club whom he met on the airfield to fly him back, without success, since this man was staying down there with his family. As a result of this meeting the man had a good look at the plane and was able to give evidence that it was empty, that the parcels were not there.

As Hume could get nobody to fly him back to Elstree, he took a taxi back to London and paid the driver with a five-pound note. This turned out to be one of those which had been handed over to Setty by a friend named Isidore Rosenthal, an automobile dealer, who had got a cheque for a thousand pounds cashed for him on the morning of October 4. It was Hume's story that when he got back the three men were waiting for him, and that they handed over a third parcel to him, promising to pay him more money if he would drop it into the sea from the plane as he had done the first, and after some haggling and coaxing he agreed.

199

Nothing is known as to what happened that night in Hume's apartment. To Mrs. Hume it was, again, like any other night. But though October 5 must have been a very long day for Hume, he was out quite early on October 6. By nine o'clock he was being driven in another hired automobile to fetch the one he had left the previous day at Elstree, with the dog in it. The driver who took him there said that he had other parcels with him, which he moved into the automobile already at Elstree. This he denied, but the theory of the prosecution was that these contained the dagger with which Mr. Setty had been killed, the saw with which his bones had been cut up, the suit which Hume had worn during the murder and the butcher's work, and such oddments. Hume drove back to his apartment and was in good time to send his wife and his baby off to their appointment at the Children's Hospital.

Later he concerned himself again with interior decoration. He went to a painter who worked in the neighbouring garage and asked him to stain some boards in the living room and in the lobby, and this the man did in the lunch hour. When he had finished the job Hume asked him to lend him a hand with a parcel he had to carry down to his automobile, and produced what was in fact Mr. Setty's torso, tied up in felt with rope. It was very heavy, and the painter could not lift it by himself. He was trying to make it an easier job by putting his hands underneath it, but Hume stopped him and told him to carry it by the rope, because it was valuable property. This was plainly nonsense, since it is safer to hug a parcel to one's body than carry it by the rope which binds it. Holding the parcel up between them, the two men staggered down the staircase. At the awkward turn Hume lost his footing, and the two men slithered down the last few steps, with the parcel bumping about on top of them. It was at this point that Hume, according to his statement, heard a gurgling noise from the parcel and began to suspect that it might be part of a corpse, and even of Mr. Setty's corpse. By this admission he convicted himself out of his own mouth of being an accessory after the fact of murder, a crime which can be punished by life imprisonment; for as soon as he formed this suspicion it became his duty to report it to the police. But he drove the parcel off to the airfield at Southend, where, with the aid of a groundsman, he manœuvred the gross package into the plane he had abandoned there on the previous evening. Again he took it over the coast, and over a patch of water, which he believed to be deep sea but which was actually a mudflat flooded by the strong tide of the new moon, he prepared to tip out the torso. This time things went wrong when he opened the door, and the plane went into a vertical dive, during which the parcel fell out into the sea. He made a disorderly landing in a playing-field south of the river, in Kent, and though he went up again he did not succeed in getting back to his home airfield at Elstree but had to come down, still on the wrong side of the river, at Gravesend, at about a quarter to six. It was noted that he had brought nothing in his plane. He then crossed the Thames and got somehow to Southend Airfield, where he reclaimed the hired automobile, and got back to Golders Green the next morning. He must have been very tired. During the previous forty-eight hours he had made two flights, amounting to at least three hours, in bad weather and failing light, driven a hundred and fifty miles, attended to a large number of small commissions, and done more than many a father would in the way of aiding his little daughter to overcome her stomach ache.

There was no doubt that Hume was in grave danger. Though Mrs. Stride had made it almost impossible to believe that the prosecution could prove that Hume, singlehanded, had stabbed and dismembered Setty in his apartment, the jury might well be persuaded to believe that it had an alternative proof in the assumption that Hume would hardly have taken so much trouble to dispose of a corpse unless he had had something to do with the murder. This was the more likely because Hume's story of the financial inducements which had led him to take on the responsibility for the parcels was quite incredible. He said that the three men had promised him a hundred pounds on their first visit, which they had raised by fifty pounds when they left the third parcel; that is, about four hundred and twenty dollars in all. Of that he must have spent more than a third on the hire of automobiles and the plane, to say nothing of tips to attendants and the cost of dyeing the carpet and staining the floor. But Setty had had a thousand and five pounds on him, mostly in five-pound notes, of which two were traced back to Hume. One he had given to the taxidriver who brought him back from Southend, the other he had paid across the counter of the Stationery Department in Fortnum and Mason's for an address book. None of the other notes were traced, but those two were enough.

So they were saying gravely, the policemen and the reporters and the people in the streets, "He'll be topped, he'll be topped right enough"; and during that day the thought of death began to fill the court. It is strange how a man looks when that threat overhangs him. His life withdraws from the skin, leaving it blue, and seeks the concentrated shelter of the heart, so that the strong fluttering of the pulses disturbs the calmness of his hands and makes his head shift from side to side on the uncomfortable pillar of the throat. His eyes were fixed on the court in something more than attention, as if he were thinking that what he saw had a new and ultimate value, because it might be the last thing he would ever see. But his grasp of experience failed as the hours went by. Presently it was plain that he wanted the day to end with an exhaustion that had the intensity of appetite, that was as painful as hunger and thirst. It was a relief to all of us when four o'clock came, and he rose from his carved chair and gathered his red robe about him and, clutching the black cap which the judge must carry when he tries a murder case, walked out past the bowing aldermen. For the man we had been watching as death threatened him was Mr. Justice Lewis, not the man whom he was trying on a capital charge. A serious operation was performed on him a few hours after he left the court, and another was performed a week or two later. He died about the time that Hume would have been hanged had he been convicted and his appeal disallowed. This murder trial, which was doing nothing in order, which had the air of a morality play in its presentation of contrasting types of good and evil, was directing attention to the cruelty, not of capital punishment, but of natural death.

❖❖ 3 ❖❖

Because Mr. Justice Lewis had been taken with a fatal illness during the first day of the Hume trial a new judge had to take the case. Instead of Sir Wilfrid Lewis, sixty-eight years old, a Fellow of Eton College and of University College, Oxford, a passionate Churchman, slender and refined, like the statue of a bishop in a French cathedral, we now had Sir Frederick Sellers, fifty-seven years of age, a Northcountryman, educated at a grammar school and Liverpool University, a fine soldier in the First World War, with the unusual distinction of two bars to his Military Cross, a Liberal politician, handsome and hearty. That, of course, made a difference to Hume's fate. In the English system the tone of a trial is set by the judge, no matter how brilliant the advocates be. To let Mr. Justice Sellers get the reins in his hand, most of the witnesses who had given evidence on the first day were required to repeat their evidence. This was a great hardship to them. Mr. Setty's sister was still perfectly dressed, but the smoothness of her face was dishevelled. The manageress of the dyeing and cleaning establishment was still smiling and moving at a leisurely pace that was a kind of courtesy towards time; she would let every moment have its chance, would do nothing to push it out of the present into the past sooner than need be. But it would not have been surprising if she had wept. The person most likely to resent this lengthy recapitulation, Hume himself, showed no displeasure. He sat in the dock showing the heartiest appetite for events, this repetitive event, any event at all.

But soon an incident occurred which would have diverted anybody. There was suddenly a fluttering conference between Hume's solicitor and his counsel, into which the prosecuting counsel was drawn. Then Hume's counsel, Mr. Levy, rose and complained to the judge that Hume's solicitor had intercepted a telegram addressed to Mrs. Hume by the representative of a national newspaper which showed that he was trying to prevent her from giving evidence for her husband. At this a shudder ran through the court. The lawyers were genuinely shocked, and the newspapermen and women thought that one of their craft must have temporarily gone out of his senses. To interfere with a witness is a misdemeanour in English Common Law and carries such heavy penalties that, in fact, it is rarer in England than in other countries for witnesses, even in the gangster world, to be spirited away and intimidated. It is contempt of court of the worst kind, and the judge in the case can, if he be so minded, stretch forth his hand and say to the offender, "Here you go to jail, now," and he goes to jail there and then, and stays there until the judge decides he has purged his contempt or he makes a successful application against the judge's decision under the Habeas Corpus Act. Mr. Justice Sellers read the telegram, looked astonished, and told the officers of the court to go and find the writer and bring him to the court forthwith. In imagination one saw a surprised man taking off his eyeshade in a room of clattering typewriters, and one's heart bled for him.

The tide of recapitulated evidence flowed on, and then Mr. Levy rose again and said that a further communication from the same representative of a national newspaper had arrived in the form of a letter addressed to Mrs. Hume, care of Mrs. Hume's solicitors, and that they had got her permission to open it and had found that it was a letter on the same lines as the telegram. The judge read it, and looked more astonished, and directed that the sender of the letter and the telegram, who had meanwhile been brought from his office to the Old Bailey and was standing under guard outside in the corridor, should be brought into court. There then appeared, to the wonder of all the press, the crime reporter of a sensational but serious-minded Sunday newspaper, which likes torsos but supports labour.

This crime reporter was a man in his thirties who was supremely good at his job. He had been in the Navy during the war and found himself in command of a small boat that was continually attacked from the surface of the water and the depths of the water and the sky above, and had to attack as continually other craft and bring trouble on itself. He has a feeling that some criminals, and the relatives of accused persons, are much in the same position. Consequently he appears among the cast of every criminal drama not wholly damnable, proffering sympathy and doing odd chores. He gets news for his paper out of his process, but that is only because he is a loquacious man and has to express himself by speaking or writing; and if he were a millionaire and never wrote another line he would still be found getting the best out of the National Health Service for the murderers' baby, running errands for the corpse's grandmother. But he had a respect for the law. It seemed impossible that he could have interfered with a witness in a case under trial.

The judge remarked tremendously that there was such a thing as the Common Law of England, and Mr. Webb explained politely that he knew Mrs. Hume apart from this case, having met her a year before. He had often seen her since the arrest of Hume and had promised her mother to be her escort if she came down to the Old Bailey to give evidence, but he had understood that she was not going to do so. The letter and the telegram, however, had nothing to do with that. They had been sent in order to dissuade her from writing an article a certain newspaper had wanted from her, which was to be called "I Was a Murderer's Wife."

At this point the judge said, "Perhaps you had better not say too much about that." Everybody in court knew that a Sunday newspaper was paying the expenses of Hume's defence. It might or might not be the newspaper which had tried to commission this article from Mrs. Hume. The situation obviously had its delicacies. The judge then read the letter and the telegram again and said, "On that explanation I will say nothing more about this; but you should be reminded that to interfere with a witness is a Common Law misdemeanour." This was manifestly not quite logical. If Mr. Webb's explanation was accepted, then it was unnecessary to warn him of the danger of committing a misdemeanour which, according to that explanation, he had never had the slightest intention of committing. But the step the judge had taken was better than logical; it was eminently sensible. It would be disagreeable to have a discussion before a man on trial for his life concerning an invitation to his wife to write an article which would plainly be useless unless he were hanged, particularly if it might distress him to know who had made the offer. Moreover, the whole business of having a murderer's defence paid for by a newspaper which wants the inside story of the murder in order to increase its circulation, matter of established custom though it be, cannot well be presented in a way which adds to the dignity of the legal profession. Best to pass over the incident as smoothly as possible, while giving the defence lawyers no chance to feel aggrieved and raise these delicate points again. Nobody can say that these thoughts passed through the judge's mind. But they passed through a number of other people's minds, and the situation suddenly and beautifully disappeared. We found ourselves out in the street, looking for lunch.

In the afternoon the stream of witnesses went on. The twenty-fifth was Mr. Tiffen, the fowler and fisherman from the Essex marshes who had found Mr. Setty's torso. He had difficulty over taking the oath. The clerk gave him the printed card which he handed to all witnesses to read from, but he returned it to him; after some whispering the clerk spoke the oath and he repeated it after him. This man whose good manners and good sense and store of information were the wonder of everyone connected with this case could not read. Forty years ago, when he was a child living eight miles out of a village on the marshes, no education authority worried its head about him. It made one proud that in modern England such a child would be under no handicap at all. They would get it to school all right. If we can teach his kind, without spoiling its simplicity, we are safe. He gave evidence in language as strong and bare as the Bible. Met afterwards in the corridors, he was behaving much as if he were in church, but happiness was sparkling on his glasses, for he had just before Christmas been paid the thousand-pound reward which Mr. Setty's relatives had offered for news of him. He had given, he said, a hundred pounds to his two grandsons, Peter Perrin, who was getting on for eighteen months, and Robert John Warner, who was six months. Then, with the tenderness of a lover speaking of the planned honeymoon, he spoke of a fishing boat. It wasn't any use getting it now. To get one of the houses built by the rural district council he had had to become a farm labourer, but when he was fifty they wouldn't bother him no more; at that age this controlled labour business had to let you go. Then he would go back to fishing. He had been out with the boats since he was eight. It would be two and a half years till he was fifty, but that was none too long to think about buying a boat. You had to turn it over well in your mind. As for the rest of the money, he would keep it to help anybody in the family that was in trouble and to look after himself when he got old. He spoke of age with prudence but without terror; nothing, it appeared, could really touch a man who was about to buy himself the perfect boat. Now he was going to visit his sister who lived down by the docks. A bus went from the corner and he would go straight there, and tomorrow he would be back in Essex.

There followed the expert witnesses for the prosecution, the chief of the Scotland Yard laboratory and a pathologist, who proved conclusively that a murder had been committed in a way which was completely impossible. On the living-room carpet there was a large stain caused by some human secretion, most probably blood, which they had talked about earlier; there were traces of blood on the linoleum in the lobby; and in the dining room there was human blood on the floorboards and on the lath and plaster ceiling below; and there were traces of blood, though it was not proved to be human, on the stairs leading to the upper floor. These stains evoked a perfect picture of Mr. Setty being stabbed in the chest with a dagger five times, as we knew he had been, while he sat or stood in the living room, and then staggering out of the room into the lobby, where he went through a door which he might have thought led out to the stairs and safety, but which in fact led into the dining room, where he slumped and died face downward on the boards. These bloodstains showed that a considerable amount had been spilled, perhaps a fifth of all the blood a man of Mr. Setty's size might have in his body. Where it was proved to be human, it belonged to O group; and that was Mr. Setty's group. This was not conclusive, for O is the largest blood group and includes about forty-two per cent of the population; but it would have been nicer for Hume if there had not been this coincidence.

The case was all sewed up, except that the murder could not have possibly been committed in this way. It is not to be believed that Mr. Setty, when someone began to stab him, refrained from uttering a loud cry; and that, when he had been stabbed five times in the chest, he would have refrained from putting his hand to the wound, or that, as he walked across the room with the faltering step of a dying man and crossed the lobby and went into another room, he would also have refrained from supporting himself by leaning on the furniture or against the walls. But there was not a single fingerprint of Mr. Setty's to be found in the whole flat, nor any sign of blood on the furniture or on the walls, though these were of a substance which would have soaked up the stain and retained it indefinitely. But even if Mr. Setty had remained taciturn and erect while being murdered, Hume could not have counted beforehand on this unusual behaviour; and a single cry, a single lurch, might have been enough noise to be remembered and to hang him. If the noise had been loud enough it might have brought an inquiring policeman in at that very minute. But once Hume had taken these risks, why did he let a dying man, who could have been easily restrained, stagger from room to room, leaving a trail of blood behind him?

It might have been, of course, that Mr. Setty did not grasp the knife (and his unscarred fingers showed that he had made no attempt to do so) and had left no fingerprints on the wall and the furniture because he was unconscious when he was killed. He might first have been hit on the head with a cosh; but that is most unlikely, for murderers rarely change instruments in the middle of a murder. Or he might have been drunk; there was a good deal of alcohol found in his stomach. But in that case his assailant would hardly have stabbed him five times when once would have done; and as his stab wounds were all in the front of his body, if he had been unconscious and therefore presumably lying flat or leaning back, the blood would have run back into his chest cavity, and no doctor spoke of this having happened. Nor would a murderer, having an unconscious man at his mercy, have stabbed him where his blood was likely to fall on a carpet or have carried him into another room without wrapping him in a blanket or some absorbent material. It was impossible to believe that Hume had murdered Mr. Setty in this apartment singlehanded, and it was even more impossible to believe that he had murdered him with the aid of accomplices, for in that case it was even less likely that the dying man would have been allowed to stagger from one room to another, or that his corpse should have been borne unwrapped to drop a trail of blood. It was also impossible to believe that Hume had, alone or with help, dismembered the body in the apartment. The bones had been severed with a saw, and one of the pathologists assured the court that that must have been a very noisy proceeding, adding, "It is quite impossible to go on dictating to one's secretary if human bones are being sawed through in the vicinity." There was no table in the whole apartment long enough to lay Mr. Setty's body on during the dissection, and if such dissecting had been done on the floor it would surely have left bloodstains of a more diffuse, sprayed sort than any which were actually found.

It is certain that in essence Hume's own story was true, and that Mr. Setty's corpse had been left at his apartment already dismembered and packaged; and that he was not the murderer but only an accessory after the fact. This would do away with all the difficulties inherent in the theory of the prosecution; it did not ask us to believe that Mr. Setty, who had been noted for a timidity so extreme that he never would travel in any automobile but his own, would visit the apartment of a man in whom he had no reason to feel confidence. It suggested an explanation of the patches of bloodstain all over the apartment. Supposing that Hume had opened the door to some visitors and invited them to come into the living room, they may have brought all or any of the packages and dumped them on the floor. Hume may not have known at first or indeed for some time what the packages contained, but may simply have noticed that they were exuding a sticky fluid and suggested that they might be moved to the kitchen and put in the sink or the coal cupboard, if it had been proposed that he was to keep them and dispose of them. But unfortunately for Hume the details of his story annulled all benefit the outline of it might bring him. For he said that the three men who had come and left the first two packages had come between two and three on the afternoon of October 5; but he had sent the bloodstained carpet to the dyer that morning before lunch, the floral rug in the bloodstained hall had disappeared by the time Mrs. Stride had arrived a few minutes before two, and he had spoken of his intention to have the floorboards revarnished soon after her arrival. These circumstances, and Mrs. Stride's firm assertion that there were no callers at the apartment during the whole afternoon, knocked Hume's defence to pieces. For that reason this murder seems likely to rank as one of the great unsolved mysteries. The possibility that Hume murdered Mr. Setty can definitely be excluded. But who murdered Mr. Setty, and how, and where, is known to nobody except the murderer. Not for lack of evidence. That is piled sky-high. There is so much that whatever theory the mind may base on that evidence, there exists some fact which disproves it.

The case was the stranger because the prosecution was so curiously conducted by Mr. Christmas Humphreys, who had just become the senior prosecuting counsel for the government. He is the son of a very famous old judge, who presides over trials with a merciless, humorous, savage, solemn kind of common sense, often shocking to everybody in court except the prisoner, who, out on a limb where at last he knows what's what, can see what the old man is driving at. His son, who is getting on for sixty, looks as if he would be the conventionalist of all time, and would enjoy few activities outside the law except going back to his old college and having dinner with the dons at the High Table in Hall. He is in fact a passionate joiner of the wilder type. He starts near the centre by being chairman of the Ballet Guild and of a group that reads poetry aloud, then gets off to the left with osteopathy and psychoanalysis, then the Bates system of curing eye defects without spectacles lures him, and he runs along into herbalism and the movement against the use of artificial fertilizers. His top note is Buddhism. He is probably the only English-born Buddhist at the Bar. Conversions of any kind are uncommon among lawyers, who rarely want to become anything except judges.

This was the first case he had conducted as senior prosecuting counsel for the government, and it was therefore watched with interest. This turned to dismay. On rising to cross-examine this man who had been accused of the appalling crime of stabbing and cutting up Mr. Setty, Mr. Christmas Humphreys asked him, in accents cold, with a loathing which suggested that he had detected him doing something far, far worse, whether he had not taken a blond girl called Teresa out to a night club and paid the bill with a rubber check. It was of course pleasant to think of him doing anything so relatively innocuous, but Mr. Humphreys suggested that this was the kind of thing that stabbing and cutting up people led to if done too often. He also alluded with horror to the fact that Hume had an overdraft at his bank, though British banks indulge, to an extent which Americans find astonishing, in the amiable habit of letting their clients run into debt with them, if they either deposit security, or get a solvent friend to give a personal guarantee, or exhibit symptoms of future solvency. Such is the economic disorder of England today that probably at least half the people in this court were living on overdrafts. There were many faces which failed to light up as Mr. Humphreys suggested that Hume had been so distressed at having an overdraft that Mr. Setty's notes had offered him an irresistible temptation. Other suggestions of his brought forward as a reason for the butchery included even more common signs of indigence. He made much of the fact that Hume had pawned a suit. Yet it is part of the curious economics of pawnbroking that there are many objects for which pawnbrokers give much more than their second-hand value; and a large section of the population pawns things all its life, and a still larger section pawns things quite a lot when it is young, and yet neither habitually engages in murder. He cut an even wider swathe when he mentioned portentously that Hume had often been some days late in paying the rent. By this time the court was looking on Mr. Humphreys with awe as a financial virgin, who felt as strongly about his state as the Lady in Comus felt about hers and would have claimed at any moment that So dear to Heav'n is Saintly solvency That when a soul is found sincerely so, a thousand liveried Angels lackey her.

Rage rang in his voice, and it was very odd to remember his last book. He is quite an accomplished writer. His book on *The Great Pearl Robbery of 1913* is one of the classics of criminal literature; it conveys the peculiarly cosy character of British crime as it was before the First World War far better than any detective novel. He has also published several works on Buddhism, the chief of which is *Concentration and Meditation*. The last, *Via Tokyo,* is the record of his trip to Japan as a junior counsel for the British government in the International War Trial. It contains little about his legal mission, for he is preoccupied by his awed delight in the stillness and formality of the East, as they were exhibited in the Buddhist shrines and schools of dancing which he visited in Japan and the countries through which he travelled.

The emotional climax of his journey was his surrender to the Zen sect of Buddhism. This is a rarefied form of the faith, in which stupidity is regarded as the first enemy, to be overcome by the intellect, which, when it has been trained to its highest capacity, becomes the second enemy, to be overcome by the development of a higher faculty of wisdom. The means by which the intellect is transcended includes the asking of *koan,* refined conundrums for which there is no logical answer, and the practice of *mondo,* dialogues between master and pupil which sound like nonsense because they are carried on above the plane where sense holds good. As the pupil progresses he is rewarded with flashes of *satori,* immediate understanding, and his ultimate aim is to stop thinking and have no need for thought, because as soon as he becomes aware of a problem he himself becomes its solution. He enters into it by intuition, as he can enter into all things in the universe, without effort, by tranquil acceptance. *Via Tokyo* shows that its author is in love with tranquillity. In one of the poems which are scattered through the volume he writes of his regret that he must leave "the golden cool serene" of his room in a Japanese house; and his pages are covered with his desire to discard all hot emotions and intellectual superfluities and make himself an empty chalice to receive the wine of mysticism.

Yet the Old Bailey has not for many years witnessed anything like Mr. Christmas Humphreys' cross-examination of Hume. It was Hume's intention to be gaily impudent, and he soon found a way of mentioning that an escaped criminal lunatic called the Mad Parson, for whom all the police forces of England were searching, had lived for months unmolested in lodgings directly opposite the London police station where he himself had been detained and examined. But nobody can be funny for long when he is being tried for such a crime; there is something in everybody which forbids it. Soon Hume began to bicker and yelp and snarl, and nothing was said to him which might have exorcised him. Mr. Humphreys had several times described Hume as an inveterate romancer, so it happened that when he said to Hume,

"I suggest that you stabbed Setty in the sitting room and that he died in the dining room," Hume snapped back, "Now you're romancing," and when Mr. Humphreys went on, "And that you cut him up that night," Hume pouted out his lips in insolence and sneered, "Absolute baloney." The horrid subject matter was being discussed in too appropriate a style. From Mr. Humphreys' book it had appeared that one of the most intense pleasures he had experienced on his journey to the East, indeed, perhaps in all his life, was his stay in a Zen monastery, the Temple of Full Enlightenment, founded seven hundred years ago, a place of mellowed wood and grey-green tiles, set among flowering trees below a sandstone cliff. There was a Great Bell there, older than the Temple, at the top of a rising venue of worn grey steps. In this home of pure mysticism, purged of formality, nobody minded the bell being sounded at any time by anybody who was moved to sound it. So he used to go up the long steep stairs to the bell whenever he had time to take refuge in this Temple, and strike it to announce his coming, fusing himself with its ancient, harmonious voice.

There was a war of philosophical principles here. Mr. Humphreys is a fastidious person who is displeased with what man has made of the earth, and has therefore always distrusted the common practises of mankind and has put his faith in any alternative which has been less generally adopted. Ballet is not ordinary motion, therefore he adored it; prose is more habitually used than poetry, therefore he wrote poetry and read it aloud; he would not be satisfied by any rationalist view of the mind, he enjoyed the psychoanalytic reinstatement of the primitive; he rejected the findings of orthodox medicine for osteopathy and herbalism; he waved away modern agriculture; he would have nothing to do with the Christianity which lay at his hand shaped for the use of his Western personality, he insisted on going out of Europe into Asia to find a religion hardly modified by the spirit of recent centuries, which treated as insignificant that pampered darling of the West, the self.

But Hume had nothing against the self. He showed this when the cross-examination became such a bitter wrangle that the judge had to check it, and reminded him that he must not answer counsel violently, telling him that the purpose of the trial was to make a necessary investigation and that there was nothing personal behind the questions put to him by his cross-examiner and therefore no occasion for heat. To this Hume replied, "But my life is a personal matter to me." This was not only a very sensible remark, which the judge did not reject, it was a proclamation made with immense Byronic pride. Yet he made no claim that the life he wished to preserve showed any merit. No man ever went into a witness box to defend himself against a capital charge and took such trouble to convince the jury that he was of bad character. When he was asked whether he would call himself an honest man, he answered that perhaps it would be better to call him a semi-honest man; and his grin gave a deep nastiness to the phrase. He was announcing that he would not be good but he would not be bad either; he was presenting them with a problem of confusion and defied them to solve it. He had a deep love of chaos, and he was for the self because it can carry such a load of the stuff. It was his intention to revolt all who have tried to establish order, and to torment them by declaring that let the ballet be what it may, there would still be cripples who cannot dance and louts that will not, there will be blindness which cannot be cured by exercises, sickness which will not yield to herbal iodine and sickness which resists psychoanalysis, fields which will be barren for all the dung that is spread on them, and souls which refuse the gift of peace from Christianity or any other faith. Hume spoke with the voice of the spirit that denies.

It seemed odd that a person so strong in dissent should have lived the ordinary existence of which we had been told. He had been an RAF officer who had done well in the war, having won a decoration in the Battle of Britain, and had been invalided out of the service. Since then he had made a living in various ways, some of which were quite ordinary jobs of electrical engineering, and others of which, such as dealing in planes for the Near East, were more unusual and probably dovetailed with more dubious ones. He had had bad luck; he had started a factory in Wales to make plastic switches and it had been destroyed by two fires. He had his gay side and was seen about in night clubs, often with notably good-looking girls. But he was making a good living by acting as a commercial pilot. It was a very ordinary story. What made it extraordinary was that, though everybody who knew him, including his wife, to whom he was a devoted husband, believed it, not one word of it was true.

There had been some strange circumstance connected with his birth. His mother was a schoolmistress and called herself his aunt, and when he was three he was sent to some sort of institution which he always described as an orphanage, at which he stayed until he was ten. He interpreted this to mean that he was illegitimate and that he had been sent to this institution because his mother hated him and wished to cast him off. But there are reasons for disbelieving that the story was as simple or as sinister. His mother, an intelligent woman, sister of a well-known scientist, was married at the time of his birth, and it is possible that she may have concealed her relationship to him in order that both of them should escape the shadow of some curious calamity; and certainly many women have sent their young children away to boarding school not because they wanted to but because their circumstances prevented them from looking after them at home. In the village where she lived at the time of the trial she was liked and respected, and as in his childhood she took Hume back from his boarding school to make his home with her, and as she makes a later appearance in his story as conferring with somebody who wanted to be his benefactor, it seems unlikely that she behaved badly to him. Apparently the psychoanalysts are right, and the mind of a child cannot stand any prolonged separation from its mother during the first five years. In any case he continually spoke with rage of his mother, and went on and on through the years about her cruelty in leaving him in the orphanage. He once had a long conversation on the subject with Mrs. Stride, the daily help who gave evidence at his trial, and she gravely told him not to wear himself out by making a fuss over it, and said that she had a right to tell him that, because her father had died young and her mother had had to let her go away for a time, and she knew what it was to have that happen to you when you were a child. But you just had to forget it and get on with life.

He was a clever boy. He won a scholarship that might have taken him through a secondary school and given him a good chance of going to the university; but in a frenzy he rushed out into the world and earned his living as a kitchen boy in various hotels. It is strange that wherever this boy went, who was bitter because he believed his mother had failed to love him, the earth opened and there appeared people who were willing to give him deep and disinterested affection. One winter's day in 1934, when he was fourteen, he was seen by a motorist walking across a common in the suburbs of London, dragging a heavy suitcase and weeping. The motorist stopped and gave him a lift and asked him what his trouble was. Hume told him that he was running away from a job as a houseboy in a hotel where they had ill-treated him, and was going to the docks to find a ship that would take him. The motorist, who was a builder, offered him a job in his own business, bought him a suit of clothes, and got one of his own foremen to take the boy in as a lodger. This was amazing good luck, for the foreman's wife, an elderly woman named Mary Clare, immediately became his loving and beloved mother.

There began what should have been a happy life for him. By day he learned with some aptitude the craft of electrician; and in the evening he sat with his new mother in the kitchen and enchanted her and was enchanted by her. For a time he became a Communist and had a contented time planning revolution, but politics had hardly any chance with him because of his obsession with planes. When he was working on the wiring of a new house they could always tell where he had been, because he had scribbled drawings of planes on the plastered walls. It was this passion for planes which made him leave that business and take a job in an aircraft factory, and later another one in a Metal Engraving Company which had some connection with aeronautics. At the same time he joined the RAF Volunteer Reserve, and when war came he enlisted in the Royal Air Force.

Very soon he had a serious accident when flying. Probably he cared too much about it. Shortly afterwards he had an attack of cerebro-spinal meningitis, and he was declared unfit for flying duty and put on the ground staff. Eighteen months after he had volunteered he was declared unfit for any sort of duty in the RAF and was invalided out. Then he took a job as one of the spotters who sat on the roofs of factories and offices and gave

216

warning when a German plane was actually in the neighbourhood, so that the workers need not break off and go down to the shelter when the sirens sounded, which might announce the arrival of a plane anywhere within a hundred miles. At the same time he was trying to get back into the RAF through other avenues, and once got a call to an Aviation Selection Board, but was turned down. It happened about this time that Mary Clare, who had again given him a home, took in her own daughter and her husband, who were homeless owing to the war, and the girl had a baby. Hume became bitterly jealous and complained that Mrs. Clare gave the baby too much of her attention and that it cried so much that he got pains in his head. He became such a plague that she was forced to ask him to leave the house.

Shortly afterwards he revisited his benefactor, who had picked him up on the common six years before. He was in sergeant-pilot's uniform and told a story of having played a gallant part in the Battle of Britain. He gave his benefactor and some of the workmen souvenirs, parts of planes he had shot down and a German machine gun. Later he turned up again in officer's uniform, wearing the ribbon of the Distinguished Flying Medal; and in this rigout he went to the Metal Engraving Company works, where the firm gave him a substantial cheque in appreciation of what he had done for the country. Then his benefactor received a visit from the police, who told him that Hume had been using his name in the town to recommend himself to people on whom he played the confidence trick; and shortly afterwards he was arrested for masquerading as an RAF officer. He had for some time been carrying on a peculiar fraud, which required great talent and resourcefulness. After Mrs. Clare had asked him to go he had lodged with an ex-officer of the RAF, and had bought his uniform from him and had borrowed an RAF identity card. Thereafter he had travelled from one airfield to another all over the country, living in the messes, getting pilots to take him up for flights, and finally cashing worthless cheques and going on his way to another airfield. He even consulted an RAF medical officer and got him to certify him as unfit for duty, so that he had a certificate to convince any military policeman or anybody else who questioned him that he was on sick leave.

So ingenious was this plan of campaign that the police at first thought that Hume must be a spy. But they found out that the story was a simple one of imposture, and he was bound over to come up for judgment after being kept in prison for some time under medical treatment. While he was jailed he wrote to Mrs. Clare, who sent him sweets and food. But when he came out he did not go to see her. He cut himself off from his second chance of a contented home life because it was more important to him that he should be able to go on pretending to be a pilot. His marriage was a supreme episode in that impersonation; and there are glimpses of other delights. One summer he appeared at Torquay, the best of the south coast seaside resorts, with an American accent and a large American automobile, saying that he was a Pan-American Airways pilot. He became very popular, and when there was a town carnival he was asked to drive the carnival queen in the procession, which he did, bringing out a scarlet and gold uniform for the occasion. He gave the right impression of being very good-humoured about doing something which he could not, of course, really like doing.

It is an obvious enough story. He suffered from the neurotic's incapacity for love and could not compensate for that lack by exercising power, so pretended to be powerful. But it was much more than that. The idea of flight had had some treatment in his mind which made it tremendous. When Mr. Humphreys, listing his lies, asked him whether it were not true that he had pretended to be a pilot though he had failed his tests, he was convulsed with grief and fury as he shouted back that he had not failed his tests, he had never taken them, he was not allowed to take them, because he had concussion. "You have no right to say I failed," he cried, as if Mr. Humphreys were in some magic way killing him by using those words. He too had his religion, he could not bear to have it violated, he was a fervent worshipper. That was to be seen in his apartment, which was a temple of flight. The upper parts of all the walls were obsessionally covered with photographs of planes, of aviators, of air battles, with parts of planes, with cartoons about flyers. Many boys and girls are infatuated with flying, but their rooms are not quite like these, though the fetishes are the same. In his apartment there was a wall on the staircase to the upper floor which took the light. On this wall there were arranged such pictures and such plane parts, and a medal. They were arranged in a pattern like the outline of a great bird with wings. This was not planned; it was an achievement of the daemon within Hume, who had ideas about flight beyond the sphere of aeronautics, who allowed, indeed, some pictures on his walls which were neither of planes nor aviators, which were of birds with strong wings, wild swans, wild geese, creatures of dazzling plumage, cleaving air so high and pure that it is not air at all. Hume had mistaken the nature of his spirit. This was not denial, it was affirmation.

Purity is the justification of flight here. You rise and leave your abhorred mother and the orphanage far below. Above the pictures and the plane parts on the walls was a cartoon representing a pilot as a knight in armour, saving the world from evil. There was no indication anywhere in the apartment that Hume was attracted by the idea of murder. There were on his shelves no detective stories, only books, mostly of a high standard, about flying and adventure. But there were in these pictures hints that added up to a broad statement that a man had lived here who would find it ecstasy, the perfect realization of a fantasy which had absorbed him from childhood, to take a corpse, reeking emblem of our human corruption, defy its nastiness by exposing it to the purification of flight, and cast it down through the clean air into the clean sea, which would keep it and cover it and annul it forever. It was extraordinary that somewhere an unknown man had found it pleasing to his soul to kill and cut up an enemy, thus giving Hume an opportunity to do the equally strange thing that pleased his soul; but not more extraordinary than that the corpse should ultimately have been picked up by Mr. Tiffen, who was as strange as these others in his great goodness, and therefore was able to pity Mr. Setty in a way that performed the miracle Hume had thought the air and sea would do, and took the horror from the crime.

It must not be thought that Hume got his ecstasy for nothing. He had had to win it by great courage. He had either been connected with the RAF or posing as a flyer for about twelve years, but not till the last year had he taken flying instruction sufficient to get a licence. Then he only got a civilian "C" licence, which enabled him to fly solo but included only one hour's instruction in navigation and none at all in night flying. It was the opinion of the airfield staff that he had no gift for flying, and in any case he must have lacked practice. In his work as an electrician he showed a curious mixture of flashes of unusual aptitude combined with an unusual unhandiness and failure to grasp essentials. It is to be noted that the times of his two flights with Setty's body over the sea, running into the evening, are fantastically long; he should have been able to do the job well before dusk fell. He landed in the most odd places, twice coming down south of the river when he wanted to be north. He owned to the police that he blundered about, losing his bearings, misjudging his height so that once he nearly flew into the water. It was bad weather. It was sheer accident that he did not die for his ideal.

Surviving that phase of danger, he tried again for martyrdom. When he was telling the story of how the three men had given him the parcels his life depended on whether he was believed; but his desire to alienate his hearers grew here to a perverse climax, and he told the story so that nobody would wish to believe it. When he was describing how he had handled the third parcel, how, as he lifted it, it made a gurgling noise and he saw a pool of blood under it, he said, "It put the fear of Christ up me," and leered. There was nothing spontaneous in the brutality of his speech. He was using the name of Christ in the hope that some believers would consider it blasphemy, he was speaking of the dead flesh with planned callousness so that he should affront the pitiful, and he was feeling a sensual pleasure at the thought that he was disgusting people so much that presently they would turn round and hurt him, perhaps to the ultimate degree. He worked still further to that end by altering the time when this incident had occurred to an hour different from the one he had given in his original statement, thus making it less easy to believe. At such moments his plump face lost masculinity and youth; he might have been a smiling middle-aged woman dressed as a man. He was invoking chaos, and it came. But he did not appear a murderer. It was impossible to imagine him leaving the world of fantasy long enough really to kill a man. But the three men he described as leaving the corpse with him, they too seemed to belong to the world of fantasy.

It is true that there were two witnesses who confirmed the existence of the three men. One was a retired army officer who seemed odd to English eyes, because he was exactly like the American idea of an Englishman. Tall and rigid, with a long and fastidious face, and a voice strangled with punctiliousness, he gave evidence that he had once lived in the mews where Mr. Setty had his garage, and that it had rapidly degenerated from a citadel of respectability to a haunt of spivs. His head went back, his nostrils dilated. One saw the gipsies come in, some in black and some in yellow. He was of opinion that among the spivs there had been two called Maxie and The Boy, and one who had answered to the description of Greenie. This took us not very far; but the second witness was to take us much further. This was a man in his early thirties who described himself as a writer. He was an attractive young man, with thick golden hair, a sensitive face, and a well-bred voice. Before he gave evidence he looked round the court with a diffident smile which told that he liked being liked. He gave evidence which, if it were accepted, went far to making Hume's story credible. He said that he had been in Paris the year before, and had got into touch with a gang engaged in the smuggling of arms into Palestine and automobiles into Britain. Two strong-arm men attached to this gang were known as Maxie and The Boy and answered to the description given by Hume. He had got into this company, he explained, because he had met a man in a nightclub who had offered to cash some travellers' cheques for him, and so he had gone back with him to his hotel, at which place the obliging gentleman was arrested by the police; and the mere fact that he had been present at the arrest had made the other members of the gang accept him as one of themselves. He had collected a great deal of information about them and had sent a report about them to both the French Sûreté and the British Embassy. This last statement could be so easily verified that it compelled belief in his evidence. But alas, this was —let him be known as Philip—a poor soul born to vex a respectable family, well known to every contemporary amateur of crime by reason of his frequent convictions. Yet he is no criminal, merely one of the wild asses of the world, and nobody, not even the police, is ever very angry with him, though, to be sure, larceny and forgery and bigamy cause some inconvenience. It was most strange that he should have come out of safe obscurity and visited Scotland Yard, which for him was putting his head in the lion's mouth, for the purpose of giving testimony in support of Hume's story of the three men. He had never seen Hume in his life before, but there was a bond between the two of them. For Philip's first conviction and Hume's only conviction had been for the same offence: for unlawfully wearing military emblems and representing himself to be a member of His Majesty's Forces. It is most probable that Philip did not know this when he volunteered to give testimony for Hume. These two naturally flew in the same flight, in bad weather and poor visibility, losing their bearings and diving so deep that the waters rushed up at them.

It would have been better for Hume if his wife had mentioned the three men when she murmured her evidence. But she, like the charwoman Mrs. Stride, gave testimony that wrecked both the case for the prosecution and the case for the defence. She declared that she had been in the apartment throughout the night when, according to the prosecution, her husband had stabbed and cut up Mr. Setty, and had seen and heard nothing unusual; but with equal, gentle firmness she declared that she had seen no three men in the apartment at the time when Hume said they had visited him. And her evidence was certainly true, for she had not sought to prove that she was away from the apartment on the night of the murder, which a perjurer in her position would certainly have done. Yet many people regarded her with suspicion. Even if Hume had merely received the parcels and put them in the coal cupboard, wouldn't she, the housewife, have been bound to know something about that? And why hadn't she asked her husband why he suddenly wanted the dining-room carpet cleaned, and where the rug in the hall had gone? These questions showed the prevailing ignorance of nearly all men and the more articulate kind of woman regarding the common lot of the inarticulate woman. A mother only three months past a dangerous confinement, who was feeding her baby and was worried about its illness, would be just getting round to the things she had to do, and would not be worrying about the coal cupboard, which was below eye level, and could only be inspected if she went on her knees. As for the carpet, it was light green, they had tried to buy a dark green one when they were furnishing and had been unable to get one, so they had taken the lighter one and had promised themselves to have it dyed as soon as it got dirty, and it was dirty by this time, it had been down for over ten months. She had not asked why Hume wanted it dyed at that particular moment for the same reason that she had failed to ask where the rug had gone, because she was the kind of woman who accepts everything that men do. The creatures are irrational, but they are useful, and it might impair their usefulness to vex them with reasonable propositions. The disappearance of the rug, moreover, had appeared to her, when she hazily thought about it, as possibly to be explained by her husband's habit of pawning things, which often sent her possessions away on temporary holidays.

But the suspicion that many men and some women felt about Mrs. Hume was derived not from dissatisfaction at her explanations of her conduct, but from their own reactions to her intense femininity. Her face, her body, her bearing, and, above all, her soft, preoccupied voice, made an allusion to something outside the context; and they believed this something to be the truth about the murder. One might as well suspect a tree that has blossomed because it is spring of making signals to another tree. What her whole being was alluding to, definitely though with dignity, was sex: the whole process, not short-circuited. When her eyes darkened, and she knitted her delicate eyebrows and then smoothed them out again and smiled, the suspicious imagined that she was thinking, "How terrible it was that night I helped him to wash out the bloodstains in the apartment, but thanks to the lawyers I have got out of all that trouble scot free." But those who knew her, and these included some not unskilful in extracting secrets, were aware that at such times she was pondering such thoughts as these:

"This apartment is not very convenient now we have a baby. I wish we had a proper house, with a garden. Then I could put baby out in her pram to sleep in the mornings. And I could hang the diapers out to dry, instead of putting them on that horrible pulley outside the window, which is so stiff and heavy. Also, it would be more convenient for keeping the pram; I have to leave it on the stairs now, and people have to push past it. But I must not grumble. After all, Golders Hill Park is just up the road, and it is a very pretty park. It is a big house with beautiful gardens, and the London County Council has taken it over and keeps it just as it used to be before; you might think you were visiting a friend's home. It will be nice, taking baby up there in the summer, when the band plays. And they have a little zoo there, with kangaroos. It will be amusing when baby is old enough to notice them."

Her thoughts were not of this simplicity because she was stupid but because she was a pragmatist and these were the thoughts which were most useful for her to think in her present situation, while she was the mother of a young child. It was very difficult to make people believe that what seemed interesting and exciting to her about her life at present was not that her husband had been caught disposing of a corpse, but that she had just had a baby. Yet, when the bloodstained facts of history are considered, it is apparent that this must have been the standard feminine attitude throughout the ages.

She was a troubling figure to anybody who had begun to doubt the value of life as a thing in itself, who had decided that life ought to be rejected if it were this and not that. Passive and yielding and drowsy with the fatigue of doing all that has to be done for a young baby, she had the massive resolution of a battleship or a bomber. She meant life to go on, whatever it was like. That was how she came back into the case, at the very end. Her husband's counsel, Richard Levy, had made a closing speech that put him in the first rank of criminal lawyers. He was already well known at the commercial bar, where the great fees are made, and much esteemed by his fellows; but this speech took him a stage further. What he did for Hume was not to expatiate on his story of the three men but to prove that the prosecution's story was at least as vague, and cite the evidence of Mrs. Stride and Mrs. Hume as proof. It was a superb speech, as free from humbug and tricks as Euclid, and it lived in the memory by its logic and lucidity. It showed the strength of the best sort of Jewish mind, which

224

becomes majestic as it pursues an argument, because justice is the product of sound argument, and Jehovah is a just God.

Nevertheless its majesty moved Mr. Christmas Humphreys to one last transport of what looked like indecorum but was acute spiritual distress. He could not abide the use that Mr. Levy made of Mrs. Hume's testimony that she had seen no murder done in the apartment; he had used it as conclusive proof that no murder had been done. Mr. Humphreys said, "I am not prosecuting Mrs. Hume. I am not defending her. She is first and foremost the wife of the man she loves. There is a law older than the law of England or any man-made law; a man and a wife who love one another stick together. I do not say that Mrs. Hume had no part in this murder. I say I have no evidence whatsoever that she had any part in it. I certainly do not agree necessarily that she had no part in the cutting up of the body and the tidying up of the apartment. That is entirely a matter for you to consider if you wish." These were strange words. They suggested to the jury that they should consider whether Mrs. Hume was guilty of murder or of acting as an accessory after the fact, though she had not been charged with either offence nor given an opportunity of being legally defended against such charges, and the jury had no means of expressing its conviction of her guilt, or, what was more important, her innocence. This left Mrs. Hume at the end of the trial in a position in which the process of justice should never leave anybody. This was peculiarly unfortunate, as there was not a shadow of evidence that she had committed any offence whatsoever. But there are philosophical divergencies which go deep. "Now let the unravished heart arise, and find Communicable light," Mr. Christmas Humphreys remarks in one of his poems. But Mrs. Hume was the female whose heart, not to be ravished by any calamity, found communicable light and communicable shadow too, and went on producing life in its unreformed state.

When the jury disagreed and had to be discharged there ran through the court the relief which is always felt when a man escapes conviction on a capital charge, a relief which is not so much of the mind as of the bones and blood and nerves, feeling for their kind. But it was succeeded by distress. For one thing, it is in England something of a scandal, reflecting credit on no person connected with the trial, when a jury disagrees on a murder charge. It happens very rarely; nobody at the Old Bailey that day could call to mind more than two such cases in the last fifty years. Theoretically the Director of Public Prosecutions should not charge a man with a capital crime unless it has got enough facts to shape a story which a jury can either believe or disbelieve. But this odd crime had made it impossible for the prosecution to stick to this theory, for there were so many facts which made it look as if Hume had murdered Mr. Setty that it would have been giving a licence to murderers not to bring him to court.

There were, however, deeper reasons for discomfort. The position of man is obviously extremely insecure unless he can find out what is happening around him. That is why historians publicly pretend that they can give an exact account of events in the past, though they privately know that all the past will let us know about events above a certain degree of importance is a bunch of alternative hypotheses. But they find such hypotheses. Here, however, was a crime that was not in the past but in the present, and was much simpler than any important historical event. But it remained a secret: a secret which was in the hands of a talkative spiv, yet was unbreakable. If we could not find out the nature of a monstrous act which we knew to have been committed in the insubstantial shelter of Hume's flat, we were more helpless than we had thought, and anything could creep up on us. It also made for misery to contemplate Hume. It seemed a symbol that two judges had sat on the bench, coming out of different centuries to try him, the one so like a medieval churchman, the other so visibly a man of our times, liberal and reasonable, and that there was no verdict. Hume could not be thought of as a coherent person, and made limbo a real place.

The legal situation created by the disagreement of the jury was tidied up within a few minutes. Another jury was sworn in, and Hume was again charged with the murder of Mr. Setty, and asked to plead, and he pleaded not guilty; then the prosecution announced that it intended to offer no evidence, and the judge directed the jury to return a verdict of not guilty. This procedure was not automatic. Two days later another jury, in the North of England, failed to reach a verdict after the trial of two men on a

226

murder charge which lasted thirteen days, the longest murder
trial that has ever taken place in Great Britain. The men were on
trial again within a week, and one of them, a man named Kelly,
was condemned to death and the other was acquitted, within a
fortnight. But there was plainly no use retrying Hume's case. Not
that he went free. There was another indictment against him
which charged him with being an accessory after the fact of murder; and he pleaded guilty to this offence, having confessed to it
in his statement, and was sentenced to twelve years' imprisonment. Then came the last strange feature of the case. It did not
come to an end.

We all waited for more to happen. Hume was a man who would
have to talk, who would have to go on making drama. In prison
it would be safe for him to talk. He had said that he had wanted
to go to the police and tell them about the part he had played in
getting rid of the body when the news of Mr. Tiffen's find on the
marshes had been published in the papers, but had been frightened into silence by a telephone call from the three men who had
left the parcels with him. It might be perfectly true that from some
quarter he had been threatened; he would be protected from such
intimidation now. That he should have a new story to tell became more certain as certain facts about the old one sunk into
our minds. In fact there had been three men, Mac or Maxie, The
Boy, and Greenie. It was slowly realized that the description of
Mac or Maxie quite closely fitted one of the policemen who were
in the police station where Hume was examined; and as for The
Boy and Greenie, there is a novel, by Graham Greene, called
Brighton Rock, which had been turned into a film. The chief
character is a nasty little gangster, who, like Hume, had been
brought up in an orphanage, and he was known as The Boy and
as Pinkie.

But, though there were rumours that Hume had made a statement in prison, nobody has been charged with the murder of
Mr. Setty; and Scotland Yard has indicated that in its opinion the
case is closed. But in our minds it is still open; and the individual
members of the various organizations which cooperated to bring
Hume to justice find it hard to stop talking it over. The features
of the murderer behind Hume are so mysterious. For one thing,

they are so trustful. It may be that Hume himself never met him face to face, but he knew the identity of his agents, and whether they were Maxie, The Boy, and Greenie, or anybody else, they left a trail which could have been followed back by Hume himself or by the police. Who was the man who could devise a cunning and intricate murder that but for the whimsical pull of the moon on certain tides would have gone for ever undetected, and confided the execution of it to a flying man who could only by a miracle have performed the flying essential to the plan, and who habitually gossiped and lied and boasted? Nobody could do anything so mad. But somebody had done it; and the behaviour of the witnesses was to give, before the case slipped down into the depths of memory, evidence that no course of action is so mad that some human being will not adopt it.

One day the crime reporter who had been haled before the court because of his letter and telegram to Mrs. Hume was sitting in his office when there came in, with that shy smile which told of such a strong desire to be liked, Philip. He carried a telegram which he said he had received at his London lodgings. It was from the gang, and it threatened him with revenge. What gang? And why did anybody want to revenge themselves on him? Why, Philip explained, the gang in Paris. They were angry with him because he had gone into the witness box and told how he knew Maxie, The Boy, and Greenie. The crime reporter was nonplussed by the reappearance of these characters. Pulling himself together, he expressed sympathy, regretted that he could do nothing about it, and advised Philip to go to Scotland Yard and tell them about it there. They went out and had some coffee and a chat, and Philip went off into London with a charming wave of the hand. The crime reporter never expected to hear anything more of the matter. But Philip took his advice. He went to Scotland Yard, where they took little interest in the telegram but looked at him sadly. Now he had come back to see them they could not help arresting him for a new charge that had been brought up against him since he forced his way into the limelight by giving evidence in the Hume case. He had been committing bigamy, and he got two years for it.

Up in Golders Green, Mrs. Hume was still living in the apartment, not because she was insensitive to the tragedy which had taken place there (whatever that had been) but because of the times. The apartment was under the Rent Restriction Act, so she got it for just over three dollars a week; and even if she had been financially justified in going out and looking for a more expensive one, the housing shortage was still so acute that it would have been difficult to find one. No fine feelings can disregard such solid facts. Now her sister and her little niece were living with her, but otherwise her domestic arrangements were much as before. The charwoman, Mrs. Stride, had presented herself on her usual day and had said that, if Mrs. Hume did not mind her working for her after she had given evidence against Mr. Hume, she would be pleased to continue to give her every Wednesday. When Mrs. Stride was asked by any of her other employers or in any of the local shops whether it was true that she was still working for Mrs. Hume, she was accustomed to reply with dignity, borrowing locutions used only in old-fashioned and majestic establishments of a sort not now found in Golders Green, that she was proud to do her best for Madam and Miss Margaret. By Miss Margaret she meant the six-months-old baby. But it would be unsafe to draw from this manner of speech any conclusion regarding Mrs. Stride's view of social problems. It is her moral nature which is asserting itself. She will have no cruelty practised on the innocent and the unfortunate.

In that household also the Hume case is not closed. But it is not the same case that continues to perplex the outer world. What puzzled Mrs. Hume was not the identity of the man who sent the parcels to her husband: that was just somebody male doing something unusually silly and horrid. It was the identity of her husband, the identity of her home. Nothing in her life was what she had believed it to be, not even the dog. A short time after the trial she found herself telling a visitor how this cheerful mongrel, part Alsatian, part collie-dog, had come to belong to her husband. When he was in Europe with the RAF in 1945 his squadron took over an airport which the Germans had abandoned, and found a paddock in which the German airmen had left their dogs; and he and this mongrel had taken an instant fancy to each other, so he smuggled him back to England in his plane next time he flew home. That was the story she repeated, as she had heard him tell it again and again, to her, to their friends, to strangers, to anybody who was moved by the dog's jolly character to ask where he had got it. Now it suddenly struck her that the story could not be true. Her husband had not been an RAF pilot, he had taken no part in the liberation of Europe, he had been by then a civilian. This made the dog a double mongrel, part Alsatian and part collie, part real and part phantom. She looked at it doubtfully, fearing that if she patted it her hand would go through it.

She felt a like amazement about her husband. Not, it must be emphasized, about his involvement in the murder. Women of her type resemble artists in their failure to feel surprise at the exceptional event. What amazed her was the incongruity between the facts which the police told her about her husband and what she herself knew about him. Of her own knowledge she was for the most part silent; she has a great faculty for silence. But sometimes she spoke of merits that he had, such as his great kindness, not merely warm and impulsive, but responsible and enduring, towards the men he had employed in his radio business. She did not deny that what the police said was true, she simply made a claim that what she knew was also true. It was a pity for her sake that she was not more sentimental and bemused, that she would have to go in a state of stone-cold emotional sobriety to all the prison visits which lay ahead of her; and indeed those visits went worse than could have been imagined, and later, because of them, she was granted a divorce. But these matters did not, of course, touch on the really important point. The baby upstairs was putting on the right amount of weight now. It was everything that a baby should be. Her mother would bring her up so that she was an attractive girl, very like any other attractive girl. The snarl in Hume's genetic line would be disentangled.

The mystery which involved him with Mr. Setty will be written about as long as there is a literature of crime; but it will exist only on the printed page. Day by day, through the years, somewhere in the outer suburbs of London, its practical effects will have been quietly smoothed away, and it will be as if it had never happened.

Greenhouse with Cyclamens III

(1954)

GREENHOUSE WITH CYCLAMENS III

The Lake of Lucerne presented its usual paradox: mountains and a wide expanse of water were pretty as a kitten, as iced petits fours on Rumpelmayer's counter. It seemed a pity we were there because one of our party was attending a congress of economists. For economists are the fortune-tellers of our age, as psychiatrists are the exorcists, and though their claims are extravagant, or the world would not be as it is, they are not quite baseless. It is much more difficult to count than to read or to write, and these are people who can count better than others, and are therefore likely to have a better understanding of those parts of destiny which go by numbers.

But destiny is very rarely determined by numbers, since man is perpetually deforming his calculations, either because he is too stupid to add and subtract, or because he wants to practice a fraud for his own profit, or because he wants support for some theory learned by the easier art of reading, or because he is suicidal and wants to be ruined. Numbers triumph in the end, for the sum of wronged husbands' assaults on their wives' lovers is a trifle compared to the terrible revenges that two and two wreak on those who pretend that they do not make four. But they take time to effect their vengeance, and it is the interim period which defeats the economists' power of prophecy. It seemed better to cry over spilled milk and read history; and there was a book at hand which threw a light on the moralistic experiment of our times which had most ambitiously attempted to prevent the spilling of milk in the future. Hans Fritzsche, Goebbels' radio chief, one of the three Nazi leaders who were acquitted at Nuremberg, had given his account of the trial in a book named *The Sword in the Scales.*

After Fritzsche's horrid exodus from jail with Schacht he was convicted under the denazification laws and released in 1950, on condition that he should neither speak in public nor write for publication during the rest of his life. Yet this did not prevent him from publishing this book. It was described on the title page as having been "told to Hildegard Springer," a former colleague of his at the Ministry of Propaganda, whom he married after his release. This is a transparent evasion of the law, and one that could have been prevented only by imposing a restriction on the liberty of a person who is not a convicted criminal but related to one. But in any case it would have been a pity to suppress this book, which throws a bright light on Nuremberg and on the possibilities of affecting human conduct by international action.

Fritzsche got into the dock and out of it by sheer mediocrity. In the past, illustrated papers used to publish photographs of exalted personalities momentarily involved with the obscure, and print underneath captions identifying the Duke of This or the Duchess of That "and Friend." The proper caption for the photograph of the Nazis and their Fritzsche should have been "Beelzebub and Friend." He was himself not in the Beelzebub class, and he really knew nothing about the Beelzebubs except that they were on the crest of the wave. He served the monsters, but never discovered what monstrosity was, and therefore never became a monster, though doubtless he would have chosen to suffer that change had he ever discovered the trick. But the judges could find nothing in any of his administrative actions or his broadcasts which made him a participant in the gross crimes committed by the men who stood beside him in the dock. This may seem impossible, but reference to the trial records will show that the conclusion was just enough. His broadcasts were banal twitterings, which were of use to his employers because they suggested that the Nazi movement was controlled by normal citizens.

But he was so much of a Nazi that one of his chapters troubles us as if Goebbels were still about. The twenty-seventh chapter, "Funk and the Reichsbank," is a thumping lie that bears the hallmark of his master. In this Fritzsche sets about whitewashing Walter Funk, one of the defendants sentenced to life imprisonment, a soft and platitudinous creature, a Mr. Chadband so credulous that he was taken in by himself. Originally a journalist, he became Hitler's press chief. His evidence was genteel and pretentious: he tried to win the court's sympathy by describing how Hitler liked listening to him playing the piano, and on one occasion broke up a large press conference in order that he should enjoy this pleasure. But it was certainly not Funk's musical talent which led to his rapid elevation to various posts of a financial and economic kind. For our comfort it should be noted that there were many important posts which no decent German with genuine qualifications would consent to fill under Hitler.

Funk ended as President of the Reichsbank, and Fritzsche described how at Nuremberg the American prosecutor charged him with having in that capacity accepted certain deposits from the SS, and when, after some pressure, he admitted this, Mr. Dodd, the American prosecutor, charged further that these deposits consisted of loot stolen from the inmates of concentration camps. In quite convincing terms Fritzsche described Funk's surprise when the prosecution then showed a film in court.

> We saw projected on the screen before us the horrible pictures of what the Americans found in the strong-room of the Frankfurt offices of the Reichsbank. We saw soldiers enter the building and the big safes swing open. Huge tightly packed bags with the imprint Deutsche Reichsbank dropped to the floor; powerful men needed all their strength to lift them on the tables. Then the seals were solemnly broken and the contents poured out: rings, bracelets, earrings, trinkets; jewellery of every conceivable kind, from simple brooches to great tiaras, coins, banknotes, studs, sleeve links, and above all false and gold-capped teeth in their thousands. We sat flabbergasted.

After some pages which portray Funk as a martyr in the hands of the heathen, and the men in the dock as his fellow martyrs who wondered how the heathen, heathen though they were, could

235

be so excessively heathen, Fritzsche went on to describe the evidence given at the trial of a man named Puhl, who had been concerned with these SS deposits, by an official of the Frankfurt branch of the Reichsbank. This witness asserted that at the time of the city's occupation by American troops the strong-room and all the safes of the bank had been completely empty, and that he had handed it over in that state to the occupation authorities.

> The witness was then questioned about the film which, according to Mr. Dodd's statement, had been made immediately after the occupation of Frankfurt. To this he answered that he knew all about it, because he had been personally present during its production. A few days after the occupation some U.S. lorries had pulled up at the door of the branch and the manager requested to hand over Reichsbank bags which were then filled with gold teeth, jewellery, etc., taken from the lorries and put in the empty safes. After these safes had been filled cameramen appeared and made a film of their contents.

There the chapter ended. The statement was so stark that it was hard not to believe the suggestion that the Americans faked the film in order to bring a false charge against Funk. If it were a lie, it was such a huge, naked, projecting lie that surely nobody would have the impudence to tell it.

But it was a lie. Or rather the story was true as far as it goes, but it did not go far enough. Simply it omitted to explain that the objects in the lorries had been found in the Merkers salt mines by American troops, with indications that they had been deposited by the Frankfurt branch of the Reichsbank; that they were returned to the vaults whence they had come, which was natural enough, as it was very necessary to put them somewhere under lock and key; and that they were then photographed as a matter of routine.

The whole story was based on a single slip made by Mr. Dodd. In alluding to this film he spoke of "materials that were found in your Reichsbank vaults a year ago." He either meant to say "photographed" instead of "found," or suffered a confusion which was purely momentary. For he did not dispute the statement given in evidence by Puhl, "I had the impression that the things of which we are talking had been put there expressly for the purpose of taking the film," although he interrupted to correct various other statements made about the film. There was, of course, an initial improbability in the story which should have discredited its starkness; it is unlikely that the Americans would have allowed Germans to be present while they faked a film. It was also incomprehensible why they should have faked a film about these deposits when they had two directors of the Reichsbank and two of its officials to give lengthy and detailed testimony regarding them, and when there was a large amount of documentary evidence. This last was extremely voluminous, owing to the circumstances of the case. The SS account was lodged in the name of an imaginary depositor called Max Heiliger, and there were seventy-seven deliveries of the bloodstained loot. The jewellery was sent by the Reichsbank to the Berlin Pawn Shop, and the gold and dentures and spectacle frames went to the State Mint to be melted down. Later the Pawn Shop and the State Mint were glutted and could not handle any more stuff, so the goods were not unpacked when they arrived at the Reichsbank but were stored as they had been sent. All this involved a mass of correspondence, which was found by the Allies. There was therefore no need to bolster up the case against Funk by forging a film, particularly as it was not used as proof of any charge, but was simply shown to the witnesses in order that they should testify whether they recognised these goods as typical deposits made by the SS. From first to last Fritzsche's story was simply a whiff of what Whitman called the stale cadaver, rising from the tomb of nazism.

It is disquieting to realize just how hard it is to ascertain that this story is a lie. The tiny proportion of the interested populations who were able to attend the trial are under no special advantage in detecting it. No memory would carry the minute details of which this lie is fabricated and which reveal it for what it is. It is impossible to consult the files of any newspaper for a full report, since there was none. Fritzsche complained self-righteously of the irresponsibility of the world press in giving so little space to the trial, "though it was of considerable political and international significance." This was due to the shortage of newsprint. Anybody who now wants to learn the facts can, of course, obtain the transcript of the trial published by the Allied governments. This, as issued by Her Majesty's Stationery Office, is in twenty-two parts and costs just under seven pounds. To follow any of the main issues of the trial, such as the case against the Service defendants, it is necessary to have all twenty-two parts under one's hands; and even to check this Funk story three have to be consulted. The documents, which are about as bulky and costly, have been published in an incomplete and unsatisfactory form. Those put forward by the Soviet prosecution are not available; the documents put forward by the other Allied prosecutions have been left in their original language, though certainly the British and American prosecutors usually dealt with them in a translated form. Those who can afford to buy these publications will have to find eight feet of bookshelf for them.

It is indeed a pity that this material is not accessible to the general reader. Let us face it, these trials have set up a dozen itching abscesses of ignorance and hatred in the public mind. Some trials drew on the Allied tribunal's suspicion of fascist sympathies which were sheer bunkum, by a process that was a threat to law itself. Certain German criminals were picked up by the invading armies, and the war correspondents sent home stories about them which were honest in intention but erred because they were written in haste. When those criminals were brought to trial there often turned out to be no legal proof that they were guilty of the graver among the charges first brought against them. There was usually good ground for suspecting that their guilt had been as black as that, but no evidence of the sort which our pernickety courts required; and we went to war to preserve just such pernicketiness. The criminals were then charged with the lesser offences which could be proved, and if their judges found them guilty they gave them appropriate sentences. Then the public, which had read the war correspondents' stories but not the transcripts of the trials (because the newspapers had no space to print them), shrieked that the sentences were too lenient and the judges pro-Nazi. This did not further the ends of civilization. Other trials, again, were attacked by people belonging to some international caste, such as the bureaucracy, who thought they saw their interests threatened by an attempt to burden their German fellows with the guilt of an action for which their employer, the state, should have been held responsible. The trial of civil servants, known as the Ministries or the Wilhelmstrasse trial, at which a number of civil servants including Weizsäcker were charged, was much better than its critics pretend. Weizsäcker should not have initialled an order for the deportation of three hundred French Jews; and Puhl, the Reichsbank official who gave evidence in the Funk trial, put up a typical defence when he claimed that he was actually obliged to accept gold teeth wrenched from the jaws of corpses by their murderers by the Reichsbank law, which provided that the bank must effect all banking operations for the government "insofar as they are within its competence in accordance with the present law." It was never part of the German law, even under the Nazis, that innocent persons should be murdered and their corpses mutilated.

Other trials were vaguely attacked by the inverted humanitarianism which pretends that everybody in a court of law is a foul criminal with the single exception of the man in the dock, who is so sinless that any evidence unfavourable to him must be perjured. As the lapse of time between the alleged crimes and the trial of the accused persons lengthened, more and more opportunities were offered to such humanitarians, for not the utmost judicial integrity can war against the staling of evidence. Two of the trials simply took off and left the earth, becoming phantasmagoric, chapters out of *The Mysteries of Udolpho,* not trials at all.

As for the great Nuremberg trial, the trial of Göring and the Nazi leaders, it is an ugly focus of infection. To discuss it with any knowledge of what actually happened during the case is as sure a way of earning unpopularity as to talk of American affairs in England with an understanding of the American Constitution; here the point at which the informed excite most irritability in the uninformed is the conviction of the Service defendants. The uninformed wished to believe that the Nazi generals and admirals were tried for obeying orders, such orders as might have been given by any Allied government to its generals and admirals, though this is not true in any single case. So fervently do the uninformed wish to believe this that the belief must serve a deep need; and in fact cynicism about the Nuremberg trial does for survivors of the Second World War just what cynicism about the Treaty of Versailles did for the survivors of the First World War. If in 1918 we were guilty of blockading Germany after the cessation of hostilities and giving it over to famine by greedy reparations, if in 1946 we were guilty of condemning the Nazi leaders on false charges, then we are no better than our enemies. If we are no better than our enemies, who, it is admitted, were vile, then it would be hypocrisy for us to go into war on a moral issue. This will not merely prevent us from waging an aggressive war, it makes it ridiculous for us to defend ourselves. What can it matter if the inhabitants of another country come over to rule over us, when they can be no worse than we are? This is a mechanism which will come into play whenever a victorious power engages in large international action after a war. It might be called a defence mechanism, but it can defend nobody against anything. Many English people resorted to it in the twenties and thirties, but Hitler declared war all the same.

❖❖ 3 ❖❖

But it would not matter what uses fatigue and timidity had made of the Nuremberg trial if the noble end contemplated by its promoters had been realized: if it had given a demonstration of the Rule of Law in all its beauty to a Germany which had seen its courts hopelessly degraded by the Nazi regime. But *The Sword in the Scales* shows that that hope was grievously disappointed. The procedure at Nuremberg did not impress Fritzsche and his fellow prisoners, it revolted them; and, indeed, it revolted many Germans who saw the trials or read the transcripts even when they were strongly anti-Nazi. This was due to a real national difference, not to be wiped out by an improvisation such as the Nuremberg trial. The procedure adopted by the tribunal was a compromise between the English and the American procedures, as the French and Russians claimed no concessions to their national practice. So the routine of examination-in-chief and cross-examination and re-examination was in force, and it might nave been imagined that this machine, which we find works so well, would be recognized by everybody concerned as efficient and convenient and fair. But the chapter in which Fritzsche deals with the Nuremberg procedure, which is the most honest in the book, is entitled "A Duel with Handicap," and he begins straight away with a protest against what he felt to be a shameful injustice.

It was only when a prisoner was in the witness box that he began to understand one of the strangest features of the trial—the evidence given on oath by the accused in his own defence. The tribunal had borrowed this curious practice from Anglo-Saxon law. In Germany it is customary for the judge to examine the accused, who is not admitted on oath and to whom the law imputes the right to, so to speak, lie in his own defence. Thus the accused is not bound to speak the truth save by the dictates of his conscience and the fear of appearing untrustworthy to the court. So far as the questioning of the prisoner is concerned, German advocates and public prosecutors can do no more than supplement the judge's personal examination.

This may seem a naïve complaint against a beneficent provision of the English law, which seemed a victory for justice when it was put on the statute book fifty-five years ago. But in fact Fritzsche was expressing a resentment which would seem reasonable enough to his compatriots, all his compatriots, whatever their political complexion. Indeed, it would seem the more reasonable to them the less Nazi they were, for what the British-Americans took away are what are considered the basic rights of accused persons, and, as the Nazis took away these rights, anti-Nazi Germans felt hopeless confusion at seeing the Allies also disregard them. Though the German in the dock cannot give evidence on his own behalf, he is not asked to plead guilty or not guilty; and though he is questioned by the judge, who both examines him and cross-examines him, he is not put on oath. Moreover, he can refuse to answer all questions or any question, without needing to plead, as he would be obliged to do in a British court of law, that if he answered he would be forced to incriminate himself;

and judges and lawyers and juries are very conscious that it is not the intention of the law that they should draw any conclusions from such refusals. They feel, it is said by those who should know, rather more strongly than English judges and lawyers and juries feel it, that they must not nourish suspicion concerning a witness who exercises his right to avoid self-incrimination. The German system can, in fact, put up quite a pretty argument that it is as fair to the accused person as the English and American system: it gives him a very good chance to get away with the ball if he can steal it. A German lawyer or journalist (however anti-Nazi) who went to Nuremberg and saw a fellow countryman under indictment being examined and cross-examined by counsel, under risk of prosecution for perjury if he lied, must have felt exactly the same sense of outrage that an English lawyer or journalist would feel if he attended an international tribunal and saw a fellow countryman prevented from giving evidence on his own behalf and being questioned, often with open hostility and incredulity, by the judge.

But the Germans were shocked by another feature of the Nuremberg procedure. Fritzsche stated it in a ridiculous form; but the grievance was there. He was indignant because he was lodged in a prison cell during his trial instead of being allowed to live in a hostel and come to court daily; and it is plain that all the defendants thought it scandalous that they were detained in jail before they were convicted. It was, of course, sheer impudence of the Nazis to quarrel with the justice that overtook them on any ground, since they had done their best to murder justice; and it is probable that had the Nazis not been jailed some fanatics would have tried to rescue them. But there is some substance to this complaint. It is one of the injustices inherent that it is impossible to handle persons awaiting trial without inflicting on them hardships which are a reproach to the community if these persons are proved innocent. In Great Britain and America we deal with this problem by allowing accused persons out on bail; but if any man cannot find bail or seems likely to run away or threatens to commit new crimes, he has to endure imprisonment under conditions nearly as disagreeable as those which punish the convicted.

The German conscience has always, except during the Nazi regime, been much more tender on this point; and they avoided detention wherever possible and treated detained persons with greater consideration. There can be no doubt that many anti-Nazis were shocked because the defendants in Nuremberg were kept in jail, on jail diet and in jail clothes, and under the supervision of warders during their trial. Some might even have expected that at least the admirals and generals and diplomats would be allowed to live in some dignified form of house arrest; for most Germans, even when they are anti-Nazi, revere rank. Here, again, proceedings which the British and Americans took as normal and inevitable must have been regarded by German spectators as an abuse of the power given by conquest.

But there is a more disquieting suggestion in Fritzsche's pages. It seems that not only the defendants but their counsel were slow in understanding the English and American theory of the function of the prosecutor. They did not understand how a lawyer could be a public prosecutor and yet not act under the instructions of the court. Fritzsche wrote:

> Our German lawyers, too, were often under the impression that an attack on the prosecutor implied an attack on the bench; they failed to realize that such an attack was considered perfectly legitimate, since it was aimed only at their opponent in this species of legal duel.

Certain incidents in the early stages of the trial suggest that this was true; and it means that the German counsel, who in taking part in a trial conducted on British and American lines were as much at a disadvantage as a pianist who is suddenly called upon to give a violin recital, at times did not feel free to bring forward arguments in favour of their clients which they believed to be valid, because they thought that this would exasperate the judges, in whom they assumed a determination to convict. Thus, through no fault of the authorities, there were certain moments when the defendants did not receive a fair trial according to the standards we had hoped to impress on the Germans.

But truly the courtroom at Nuremberg was a tank filled to the brim with misapprehension. Fritzsche tells an illuminating anecdote regarding the appearance in the witness box of an SS leader named Bach, who gave evidence for the prosecution:

> As the witness was conducted down the hall and out by the central door he had to pass the corner of the dock where Göring sat. As he went by the Field Marshal rose and said *"Schweinehund."* He spoke quietly, without the least sign of emotion, but loud enough for the whole court to hear. The blood rushed to Bach's face and he stopped short in his tracks; but he did not turn his head and left the court in silence. The insult was not translated over the microphone, but everyone who was not familiar with the expression inquired what it meant, even the judges leaning back to question the two interpreters who always sat behind them.

Alas, it is unfortunately true that there are a number of beautiful and subtle German words which we cannot adequately translate—who amongst our most gifted linguists could find a perfect English equivalent for *Wesen* or *Gemüth* or *Sittlichkeit?* But all of us know the meaning of *Schweinehund,* and what worried the judges at that moment was the problem of conducting the trial if these crazy barbarians in the dock started barracking the witnesses. Fritzsche's anecdote is alarming because it shows not only that the defendants were so far off the mark as to think that the judges were awed by Göring's panache, but that none of their lawyers understood the situation either, for if they had, they would certainly have explained it to their clients with a view to indicating what sort of conduct they had better avoid. Again, it must be asked whether the defendants would properly be defended by counsel who did not understand the court before which they were pleading. It is written that when the Lord saw men building the Tower of Babel, He said, "Now nothing will be restrained from them which they have imagined to do. Go to, let us go down, and there confound their language, that they may not understand one another's speech." But the confusion which circumscribes us goes deeper than language. All of us had our earphones, there was not a person in court who did not understand the literal meaning of every word that was said. Yet there was this welter of misunderstanding, this frustration, this incapacity to demonstrate the Rule of Law anything like as clearly as had been hoped.

But of course it would be absurd to take Fritzsche's book as the last word on the Nuremberg trial. He could hardly be expected to acknowledge that the world was under a necessity to find some way of punishing the Nazi leaders; that a gaping hole would have appeared in our moral system had it been possible for villains to commit a vast number of vile crimes in their own and other countries, and to escape punishment because they had created ruin so general that it had consumed all courts of law. Civilization could no longer have been regarded as a viable idea if Dr. Frank, the governor of Poland, could not be punished for breaking Polish laws simply because he had murdered Poland and the corpse was incapable of prosecuting him. And it would have been too much to ask of Fritzsche that he should appreciate the service rendered to history by the Nuremberg trial.

This was immense. Many thousands of documents from enemy archives were submitted by the prosecution, and as they could be challenged by the defence their authenticity was guaranteed; and the witnesses annotated them and had to prove their annotations under cross-examination. Though they are not now easily accessible to the general reader, they are there for the student; and the lawyers had to act with a haste that was all to the good. The historians would have taken them to their studies, shut the doors, and dealt with them at the slow pace of scholarship, and scholarly prejudices and obsessions would have struck deep roots and grown a quickset hedge about the facts before the work was done. The glands of some don might have a second springtime, or even a first, while he weaved an erotic fantasy about Göring; and a don of the other sort, that shines on television, looking for a unique stance, might find it in a thesis that Goebbels was a man of elevated character who might have saved Europe had it not been for the machinations of the British Foreign Office. Indeed, as the Allies drew apart and each went back to its party strife, the Nuremberg documents might have suffered the fate which was later to overtake less important but still interesting material. It does no good to history when a ministry takes out of its files a batch of documents and, instead of issuing the texts as a government paper, gives it to a writer to use for his own personal profit as material for a book to be sold through the ordinary commercial channels. This might easily amount to bribing a writer to twist the evidence for a policy favoured by a government, or by a minister, or by a caucus of civil servants within a ministry. Hence, if the Nazi archives had not been aired at Nuremberg, enthusiasm for the European Defence Community might have produced some pleasing pastel portraits of the Service defendants that would be taken as accurate, and a contrary view might have taken us out of the field of Daumier to the terrible microcosm of Hieronymus Bosch when the policy veered towards appeasement of the Soviet Union. Though the printed record of the truth is hidden from the general reader, its existence preserves him from much mischievous special pleading.

But for the rest the Nuremberg trial must be admitted as a betrayal of the hopes that it engendered. Its makers devised it as well as the times allowed. Conducted by officials sick with the weariness left by a great war, attended by only a handful of spectators, inadequately reported, constantly misinterpreted, it was an unshapely event, a defective composition, stamping no clear image on the mind of the people it had been designed to impress. It was one of the events which do not become an experience.

To lay down *The Sword in the Scales* and look round at the economists on the hotel veranda taking some time off between their congress meetings, was not to lose sight of the international situation. Englishmen were among them, and Frenchmen and Belgians and Dutchmen and Scandinavians and Italians; and though none of them was doing badly, or they would not have been there, they all looked poor beside the Americans. It seemed natural that this should be the pattern, and it was startling when it changed. But there was one nationality not at first represented. The congress was to last a week, and the latter half was to be devoted to an inquiry into the economic condition of Germany; and on the third day German officials and journalists arrived, who bustled in with the air, modest yet consequential, of not being the performers but of being essential to the performance, like the men who run into the ring at horse shows and put up the walls and hurdles for the jumping competition. The next day came the performers, conscious of being a people of state, and on the last morning the star, the Minister of Economic Affairs himself, descended on the congress, bright as courting Jove. But by that time the miracle had already been effected. By the side of the Germans the Americans were looking poor.

Suit for suit, tie for tie, shirt for shirt, briefcase for briefcase, the Americans and the Germans were running level. Both had the best of everything; but the Germans had better than that. Their grooming spoke of a wealth of shaving sticks and brilliantine and toilet water in a country where, four years before, there had not been enough soap. Their confidence spoke of productiveness that had risen to one and a half times what it had been before the war, with a standard of living only slightly below the British level. But the extravagant glory that shone from them came not from their prosperity but from a conclusion which they were drawing from that prosperity: a conclusion that gave them a happiness which all other people of our age lacked. It took some spectators back to the early twenties. In those days it was believed that the golden age had dawned and would not end. An American newspaper owner, who had also vast industrial interests, was showing some European guests round his newspaper building, and had some difficulty with a Negro elevator man, who proved to be new, from the South, and illiterate. One of the guests, an educationist, said, "Ah, yes, you Americans have your problems like the rest of us." The newspaper owner looked brutal in his contempt as he said, "No, we have not. You have all the problems there are over in Europe. But here in America we have nothing to do but just go ahead and get rich. We shall be a country with no history." Since the crash of 1929 no American capable of attaining any sort of distinction would have used those words; but it could be believed that they might come very naturally to the lips of these Germans. It was because they felt rich as Americans did before 1929 that they seemed richer than the Americans of 1953.

It would not have surprised those strong and ruddy men that

we were afraid of them. But they would have mistaken the nature of our dread. They would have imagined that we feared them as industrial rivals who would drive us out of the world market, or as conquerors in another war. It would be hard for them to believe that, not in panic, but in weariness, we feared lest, for a third time, their gross addiction to defeat should reassert itself and seek to drag us into a common tomb. It was not that a revival of nazism seemed probable. The illustrated paper *Der Spiegel* operates on a very shrewd estimate of the greatest common mental measure of the German population, and it reviewed *The Sword in the Scales* in the spirit of a family that has heard that Cousin Sam, who had coshed Grandmamma and emptied Father's till, was to be let out of Broadmoor. But all the same the German people are subject to bad dreams, and though that nightmare might not return they might be visited by another; and it was these dreams which alarmed us, and not their daylight selves.

In that greenhouse which now proved to have been the only solid building in Nuremberg, the one-legged man who grew enormous cyclamens with the help of a child of twelve was certainly frightening, but not because he grew enormous cyclamens. He terrified because his absorption in industry left a vacuum in his mind which sooner or later would be filled. If no religion or philosophy or art came to bind this man's imagination to reality, then the empty space would be flooded with fantasy which would set him at odds with life. Above the greenhouse the Schloss had soared like a huge doll's house, designed to house all the characters out of Grimm's Tales; and some of those tales are very brutal. When men do not put away childish things in time, they turn on their tracks and seek the sources of death, such as the Nazis unsealed for them. But the Germans had a right to propound that we had no right to fear them; for they had lifted from us part of our moral guilt for the plight of the displaced persons and the refugees and expellees. In their reckless and speculative prosperity they had provided for these homeless people as we could not have done.

But surely there was no need to fear that the story would take such a turn again, for millions of Germans had now the opportunity to spell out for themselves a faith that came from reality, and that would bind them to it. The resistance of Berlin and East Germany was continuing, and even in Switzerland it still seemed good. That was a severe test: the genius of that country chooses neutrality and conformity and a quiet life, and only those who never saw a bombed city will sneer at the choice. But even in this sunlit town by this blue lake, where the unholiness of unnecessary rebellion was brilliantly apparent, the moral compass twitched and told us that not here, but in a ruined city to the north, and on the now coarsely husbanded plains running to the east, there was more sacred territory. There the Germans and the Russian peoples were enlaced in the darkness cast by an absurd political relationship, like snakes sleeping through the winter under a rock. But they were not sleeping; the entangled coils were sliding back and forth in contact that was an argument. Dumbly they were discussing what government should be, which is to say that they were discussing what life is.

Prewar Germany had not thought enough about government and life. It had produced an enormous number of books on these subjects, but just as there are some events which become experience and many more which do not, so there are some books which become experience and many more which do not. But that the discussion had been inadequate is proved by the simplicity with which the Germans granted the Nazis licence to perform operations which inevitably degenerated into tyranny and massacre. Western Germany was the heir to prewar Germany, and very like it, and the fears that might be felt about its future would have been lightened had Western Germans been able to share in the experience of Berlin and East Germany. But they had hardly more chance of coming within range of that revelation than if it had been made in Iceland or Madagascar. Few of them could travel into the area; and the constant arguments between the Western Allies and the Russians in Berlin, and the censorship of news from Eastern Germany, made all journalism concerned with those parts tedious to all but specialists. Years must pass before the ferment settles down and any true and convincing works of art are precipitated.

It seemed a fresh proof of the idiocy of Potsdam that it prevented the man in the greenhouse at Nuremberg from learning the lesson Berlin might have taught him. But it was that same idiocy which gave Berlin the power to teach. The Berliners were given two experiences of totalitarianism, which demonstrated that it was its principle which was wrong, and that no matter who applied it the result would be pain; and it was the second experience, which gave them a chance of contrasting totalitarianism with the democratic system represented by the Western Allies, which counted, because they were then shut up by Potsdam in a small circle of privation with little else to think about except this contrast and its consequences. Rarely in any age has its peculiar problem been investigated under conditions more likely to lead to the discovery of the truth, and less favourable to the diffusion of that truth.

But destiny cares nothing about the orderly presentation of its material. Drunken with an exhilaration often hard to understand, it likes to hold its cornucopia upside down and wave it while its contents drop anywhere they like over time and space. Brave are our human attempts to counteract this sluttish habit. Brave were the economists who met together and tried to set the world's ledgers straight; brave the Western Germans who inscribed the neat pattern of industry on a patch of earth known to be specially unstable; brave the Berliners and East Germans who set about understanding the problems of the state when international action had wrecked the state to which they naturally belonged; brave the mediocre Fritzsche who tried to put down how happenings looked to people who had never quite known what was happening; and brave the men who, in making the Nuremberg trial, tried to force a huge and sprawling historical event to become comprehensible. It is only by making such efforts that we survive.

The Better Mousetrap

THE BETTER MOUSETRAP

❖❖ 1 ❖❖

In the summer of 1952 the detection of a Soviet agent in London uncovered a hidden well of emotion in the British people. On June 13, in King George's Park, Wandsworth, some officers of the Special Branch of the Metropolitan Police surrounded two men who had been sitting for over half an hour on a bench and were then on their way out to the park gates, and they told them that they were suspected of committing offences against the Official Secrets Act, and must come to the local police station. One of the pair was a young man of twenty-four, William Martin Marshall, a radio telegraphist in the service of the Foreign Office, and a native of Wandsworth. Through the bare preliminary reports and the blurred press photographs the fact stuck out that William Marshall was gangling and vulnerable, over six feet and still a child, the kind of child that climbs out of its perambulator and crawls onto the railway line. He made no reply to the police officers. The other man was a stocky, balding, impassive, middle-aged Russian named Pavel Kuznetsov, who gave them the not at all disarming answer, "It is up to you to prove your suspicions," and at the police station claimed that he could be neither detained nor searched, and produced a certificate of diplomatic immunity showing that he was a third secretary at the Russian Embassy in London, but pointed out that it did not give him his proper rank. He had recently been promoted to second secretary.

With a blandness which later excited the Soviet Embassy to a protest, the police searched Kuznetsov, as they tersely put it, "before this information could be checked." Twenty-five pounds were found on him in pound notes, and some documents, which were interesting but not what the police had hoped for, since none of them led back to the man in Foreign Service employment with whom he had been arrested. Again, through the bare preliminary reports a fact stuck out. Kuznetsov was not behaving as a man of his position would have been expected to behave in this predicament. He was guilty of indecision and inconsistency. He complained to the police that he had been arrested when he was walking in a park, which is no offence against the law. Then he simplified his complaint; he had been arrested when he was walking in a park with a man whom he did not know. In Marshall's presence he persisted that they had been strangers till that day. But when his statement was read back to him he withdrew the amplification and went back to his first complaint: he had been arrested when he was walking in a park. Then he returned home, to his apartment in a converted Victorian house in a fading part of West London, where he lived with his pretty wife and his little son.

With Marshall the matter was much more straightforward. In his wallet they found a copy, written in his handwriting, of a confidential document which he had been given for the purposes of his work, and in his diary they found Mr. Kuznetsov's telephone number, and two groups of initials which looked like notes of the appointment which he had been keeping when he was arrested, and of another which he had arranged to keep in the same park at a future date, July 8. Both these appointments were bracketed with the words, "Day off." Marshall was employed at Hanslope Park, the out-of-town establishment which the Foreign Office maintains fifty miles north of London in Buckinghamshire. The boy also made a long statement in which he named seven other occasions on which he had met Kuznetsov during the last six months, and claimed that these were merely incidents in an innocent friendship, in which no question of loyalty was involved. But the police charged him under the Official Secrets Act with having communicated to Mr. Kuznetsov information useful to an enemy, and of obtaining secret information.

During the twenty-five days that passed between Marshall's arrest and his appearance at the Old Bailey, it became evident that Marshall had excited far more public sympathy than any other person ever charged in Great Britain with espionage. Many

Britons of unquestionable loyalty held the opinion that, if he were a traitor, it was because he had been subjected to intolerable persecution, which must inevitably have stung to reprisal all but the oldest and wisest. This opinion was based on a single passage in the statement he made at the police station.

It appeared that William Marshall was the son of a bus driver, and had, on leaving high school at the age of sixteen, gone to a nautical college in Wales, and been trained as a radio telegraphist. He had no success in finding employment when he had completed his course; and, indeed, he must have looked fragile cargo to send to sea. On being called up for military service, he joined the Royal Signals and was sent out with them, first to Palestine, then to Egypt, where he was stationed in the heat and the flies and the political unrest of Ismailia, a lakeside town between Port Said and Suez. Out there he heard that there was such a thing as a Diplomatic Wireless Service, in which he might get a job. When he returned after two years he was given a government grant to continue his studies in radio telegraphy, and then was taken into the Diplomatic Wireless Service. At first he was sent back to Ismailia for some months, and there was an odd incident on his return. He had been told that he was to eat in the officers' mess of the regiment with which he worked in liaison, and he had presented himself for dinner in a sweatshirt and flannel trousers, both very dirty. After he had appeared in this guise for three nights he was sent down to the sergeants' mess, where they could be trusted to deal more forthrightly with this breach of etiquette, which was also, in the climatic conditions, an offence against hygiene. As he was a dandy, and as the instinct of all other men of his sort in these circumstances had been to smarten themselves up for the evening meal, this was strange; and some of the men in the sergeants' mess, though not in the officers' mess, had put it down as probably "a piece of bloody Communist rot." It is to be observed that it is not the conduct of a man working under normal Communist instruction in the underground, or even of a man who would be chosen for underground work. He was then recalled to England to work at this out-of-town establishment of the Foreign Office at Hanslope Park.

At the end of 1950 he was offered a post at the British Embassy at Moscow; and it was by the passage which described what happened to him next that he won the sympathy of the British public.

On December 31 I flew to Moscow. I was a misfit at the Embassy from the start. The people were not in my class and I led a solitary life. I kept to myself and spoke to as few people as possible. I did my work as well as I could and just waited for the time to go home. I was disgusted with the life at the Embassy and began to take an interest in the Russian way of life. I was impressed by the efforts of the Russian people and their ideals. They seemed to be building a society which gave the biggest scope to human endeavour. But they have a long way to go. When I came back from Moscow in December 1951 I was as friendless as when I arrived there.

These sentences exercised a liberating force on the British public mind. Just as the translation into English of Freud's works broke down a taboo among the well-mannered, who thereupon began to acknowledge frenetically that they detested most, and not infrequently all, of their relatives, so these sentences in young Marshall's statement suddenly unsealed the lips of an even larger section of the community, which, it appeared, could not abide diplomats. It was evident that most Englishmen and Englishwomen thought that no young man not born into that vicious tribe could possibly endure a more horrible experience than having to spend a year abroad at an Embassy among ambassadors and secretaries and attachés and the like. He had been committing offences against the Official Secrets Act, had he? Well, no wonder.

Horrible visions haunted them. Some saw a vast palace in Moscow, where the parquet floors were so highly polished that the gilded furniture seemed to float on a tawny lake, and anybody might slip and fall down. There would be in any case lots of little tables standing about to trip over, with things on them that would break. In the most superb room of all, under chandeliers dripping pompous irradiated stalactites which would permit nothing to go unseen, is a table surrounded by lackeys not only fearsome in powdered wigs and frogged liveries but proud, very proud, and showing this pride by a lifting of the eyebrows and dilatation of the nostrils. This table is covered with an exquisite tablecloth, on which it would be easy to spill things, and laid with wineglasses and silver obviously far in excess of all reasonable requirements, obviously in hopes of trapping outsiders who do not know the rules of the game.

At this table sit a number of persons who are, with one exception, all diplomats and diplomats' wives. Oddly enough the diplomats are all in morning dress, as terrible in their striped pants as an army with banners, while their wives, fit mates for these arrogant tyrants, with noses running down in a straight line from their foreheads, like the Greek statues, are in full martial décolletage, with diamond tiaras. The one exception is William Marshall. Delicate and overgrown, he sits ill at ease and ignored. Suddenly a tremor runs through the assembly. The stripes of the pants of the shuddering diplomats waver like lines on a television screen, and the tiaras on the haughty heads of their shuddering wives emit flashes of prismatic brilliance. The lackeys sneer in perfect time; they have often rehearsed it. Marshall has used the wrong fork. Or rather, Marshall has used the wrong fork again. Small wonder that the wretched boy's eyes go to the window, where, in spite of a snowstorm, male and female Russian comrades are to be seen, driving tractors and building hydroelectric dams, not in striped pants, not in tiaras.

Such was the picture of Marshall's life in Moscow as many Britons saw it. It illustrates the operation of the time lag in popular myth-making, for of course it is true that had Marshall had to come to close quarters with typical diplomats of the past, such as Lord Castlereagh, who represented England at the Congress of Vienna in 1815, he would indeed have been made to feel himself "a social misfit." There is also some contemporary justification for the public attitude, since many diplomats are rude, and must necessarily be so. The present complexity of international affairs taxes human intelligence to its limits, and often beyond. Hence the policy of any Foreign Office is bound to be frequently wrong. Its diplomats are, however, bound to defend it; they would be not worth employing if they found themselves able to go about admitting that their country and organization were wrong. But there is very little to be done in the way of defending a position which logic and accomplished fact indicate ought to be abandoned, except by showing insolence toward the attackers. It would be very hard for any diplomat to keep up an argument claiming wisdom for the advice that was given to the late Mr. Ernest Bevin when he was Foreign Secretary, without lapsing into discourtesy. Diplomats, therefore, suffer an occupational risk of rudeness. Yet William Marshall's case cannot have been as he stated it and as the public imagined it.

"The people were not in my class and I led a solitary life. . . ." The British Embassy in Moscow is housed in a vast palace built in the time of the Tsars by a sugar king. The ground floor is used for offices, and in the great rooms above, the Ambassador and his family live and entertain, and some senior members of his staff have their own quarters. Apartments in the city are found for some married members. All round the garden of the palace are stables, laundries, cottages, storerooms, and the like, which have been turned into comfortable accommodations for the rest of the staff; and it was here that Marshall lived. This is an unusually large Embassy; with wives, the community numbers just under a hundred. Of these only a small number were diplomats, and the rest were clerical and technical employees, stenographers, cipher clerks, radio operators, pilots, and the like. Today in Britain it is not easy to say how strong class feeling runs and what divisions it sets up for itself. But it would be safe to say that people who have been to the same sort of school feel comfortable together. The diplomats would probably have gone to public schools, and of the others, the clerical and technical employees, some from needy homes might have got there on scholarships. They would for the most part be the products of secondary schools. This means that Marshall was one of quite a large group with which he could have felt on equal terms.

Quite certainly he did not lead a solitary life. That he was not allowed to do, any more than a patient who is known to have taken an overdose of a sedative is allowed to fall asleep. He was reckoned to be in a certain danger for which company was an antidote, and so he was forced to have company, just as the drugged patient is forced to drink cup after cup of black coffee and walk up and down. The trouble about the British Embassy in Moscow is that people there are apt to feel as if they were in a mousetrap. In the garden there are tennis courts and a swimming pool is shared with the Finns, but the summers are short, and at other seasons of the year there flows into the vacuum of unusable leisure the same malaise which afflicted the Allied armies of occupation in Germany in the first years after the war. But all the constraining elements which operated in Germany pinch more tightly here; all the compensations diminish to vanishing point. There is a worse climate, no playgrounds in the forest or in the mountains, and an unlearnable language. When you cannot go home, when home is a long way off, when the times do not ask you to work hard enough to exhaust yourself, when you do not understand the people of the country and it can be seen from the way they look back at you that they do not understand you, then you may feel that you are a mouse in a trap. It is said that this claustrophobic fancy is increased in some because the British Embassy stands on a little island with a canal at its back and the river Moskva in front. In winter all this water is frozen two feet deep.

There is a risk that people who give way to this fancy of being in a mousetrap may find themselves inside a real one. Not many have turned their backs on their own people and gone over to the service of the Soviet government, but enough have done it to prove that this is something which can happen to people who are in no way exceptional, except in the degree of their temporary misery. The cause may have little enough to do with respect for the Marxist theory or Soviet administrative performance, which alone could justify such conversion. An obsessional hatred of the other members of the staff, such as sometimes inflames a sailor against his shipmates during a long voyage, may spread until it includes all the hater's countrymen and his country itself. Or the evident mass and might of Russia, stretching away in all directions from the British pinpoint on the artificial island, may make a timid soul feel that the next war is as good as lost and he may as well go over to the victors in good time. There was a hysterical refinement in this local danger. There were a certain number of British people in Moscow who were not at the Embassy and had nothing to do with the Embassy, though some of them had once been familiars of the Embassy. Three of them lived together in an apartment; one was Ralph Parker, formerly correspondent of the London *Times,* now working for the Soviet government. These people were terrifying to contemplate for a simple and primitive reason which had nothing to do with Marxism. If you had begun to want to go home and knew you could not go home until the end of a fixed period, then the sight of these men filled you with a sense of claustrophobia; for they would never be able to go home. And there are those who, having heard of others suffering an ugly fate, even the fate which they most fear, have to contrive it for themselves. Hating heights, they hear of a man throwing himself from Beachy Head or Brooklyn Bridge, and after brooding on the news, go to that place and go again, until one day they are drawn down into the depths. A mousetrap can also exercise this perverse charm.

Great efforts are made to avert the melancholy and distress which are apt to afflict many members of the Embassy staff, if only for a few days. So there is much encouragement of sociability, which is supervised with great efficiency by a welfare officer who is by all accounts not merely genial by profession. She is remembered by many as a kind and gay person, who has a genuine preference that people should be happy. Marshall was able to go to a great number of parties and club meetings when he was in Moscow, a good many of them given in conjunction with the American Embassy; and at them he was often an object of a special solicitude. It was said quite often, "There is young Marshall, looking very miserable, we must try and get something going for him." Nobody else evoked quite such a sense of pity. This was partly because his appearance suggested that he was in bad health. He was so tall and narrow-chested, and he was very pale, with a chalky pallor intensified by the darkness of his hair, which he wore long and sleeked close to his oval head. Actually his pallor meant nothing. It was a family characteristic, shared by his mother and his brother, who were notably robust and energetic, but any stranger must mistake it for the result of severe illness or shock. As for looking miserable, he was, and always had been, miserable. He was miserable as a child, when he was evacuated from London during the blitz; he had hated it in the country when the cold came, having known till then only the mitigated winter of the city. He had been miserable in the army, in the unmitigated summer of Egypt. He was now writing home to Wandsworth that he was miserable in Moscow.

It is now remembered that Marshall's air of ill-being caused the British Ambassador and his wife to make inquiries about him more than once. Sir David and Lady Kelly were in all respects unlike the diplomats and their wives seen by the British public in their vision of the shaming of Marshall at the ambassadorial table. They would be unlikely to notice if Marshall or anybody else had used the wrong fork, for they were absorbed in livelier interests. Both are aristocrats who are forcing the unwilling age to give them as entertaining lives as their forebears enjoyed, through the use of their remarkable talents. Sir David's mother was a member of the Irish branch of the great Rhineland family of Ahrenberg, as old as any in Europe, which was deprived of its estates and titles by Napoleon and then scattered over many lands; and his father was a brilliant Irish professor of classics who died young when he was teaching in an Australian university. Sir David went through St. Paul's School and got a scholarship at Magdalen College, Oxford, and after doing well in the First World War went into the Foreign Office. There he advanced in a formidable fashion, always giving the impression that he knew what he was doing, and after he left Moscow and retired from the service wrote an autobiography which showed that that impression was correct. His wife was a Belgian aristocrat, a direct descendant of St. Jeanne de Chantal, the founder of the charitable order of the Visitation, and kin to Corneille and Madame de Sévigné; her sister is a leading ear, nose, and throat specialist in Brussels; she herself is a topographical photographer of high professional standing, and writes travel books which bring the story back complete with its tail feathers. It is significant that it was in her book on Turkey that there was first told to the general reader in England the horrifying tale of what happened to the treasures Schliemann dug out of the ruins of Troy and gave to the Berlin Museum. At the outbreak of war they were packed in crates and hidden. Some are still lost; but the pottery served the need of some German peasants in the season of privation who were finding it hard to observe a local custom of breaking cups and plates at a local wedding. Lady Kelly found this terrible postscript to the *Iliad* in an article in the *Turkish Automobile Club Bulletin*.

People like this are very busy. To save themselves time they sieve reality and the petty falls through and they worry no more about it. They did in fact notice Marshall. They would be too able, too impeccable, too energetic, were it not that both their faces were clouded, not by weakness or indecision but by imagination. They turned their clouded faces on young Marshall and asked whether he were ill, whether he was usually as he looked. They were told that he seemed to be in normal health; when he was in the army he had had a bad attack of pleurisy, but it had left no aftereffects. As for being miserable, he had no real troubles, so far as could be seen, but was one of the worrying sort. Of all the Embassy employees, those who made the best adaptation to Moscow life were the retired petty officers of the army and navy and air force, who did all the stewards' work. They were drawn to this difficult post because the special allowances were high and they wanted to provide generously for their families, and they found the exile not such an ordeal after the years they had spent at sea and in foreign stations. These men kept a kindly eye on their younger and less hardy colleagues, and one of them reported of Marshall that there was no harm in the lad at all, and his main trouble was the very reverse of a fault. He fell over backwards trying not to be a sponger. It was noticeable over his smoking. If anybody gave him a cigarette he could not rest until he had repaid the loan; and should this be impossible for any reason, had his friend suddenly gone home on leave, he would fuss and fret. He was also inordinately distressed when the authorities inadvertently overpaid him by five pounds. Well, it was to be hoped that the lad would never learn the meaning of real trouble.

The Ambassador and his wife, it is remembered, smiled and agreed. Soon afterwards Sir David's sixtieth birthday brought him to the retiring age, and he and his wife went back to England, two or three months before Marshall was due to return. Nobody then suspected that Marshall was about to meet trouble, for he seemed too simple to invite it.

It could easily be imagined that he might be completely happy in his parents' little house in Wandsworth. He enjoyed coming home in the evening and playing his gramophone records of light music; he had two hundred of them, very neatly kept in a cabinet, with a catalogue written out in his spidery, feminine handwriting. He also enjoyed making silk mats. At some period of his adolescence, whether at the nautical college or when he was ill in the army, he had been taught this handicraft and had practised it ever since. It is fairly simple; on a cardboard framework one makes a warp and woof of fine threads, then uses another thread and a crochet hook to form them into a network. He took out to Moscow quite an amount of material for making such mats. There is an accumulation of them in his home, all extremely fragile and made of some sort of rayon with a high iridescent sheen, in colours which would be chosen by someone who liked opals and mother of pearl. His parents have begun to be a little anxious about this hobby of their son's, in case it should give an impression that he is effeminate, and they say he is not that at all; and indeed one does not often meet women who have a passion for making silk mats.

The hobby did not seem so strange when it was realized that his parents spent a great deal of time making things with their hands. In the little garden in front of their house they had broken up the flower beds with elaborate concrete borders which have the charm of a child's sandcastle. They did all their house-decorating themselves. They lined their sitting room with romantic wallpaper, on which a group of forest trees are green against a mysterious blue night. The paint they applied to the woodwork is prodigally laid on, with a skilful, creamy finish. Everything is ritually clean, the paint, the brass fire irons, the linoleum, and gives back the light. On the floors are rugs they have made, deep in pile and strong, even violent in colour. They love embroidery, they prize immensely a small framed panel of Indian needlework, representing butterflies, sewn in blue silk and outlined with gold thread. There is a great deal of furniture in the house. It is a truism to say that a poor home can produce a greater effect of abundance than a rich one, but the reference is usually to spiritual wealth. Yet it is also true that there are people who have little money but attract to themselves a plenitude of material goods, by some process much more magical and effective than mere good management.

Mr. Marshall, a small, quick, talkative man of fifty or so, was a bus-driver until a V-1 wrecked him and his bus in the last year of the war, and since then he has drawn a disability pension, and done odd jobs at home, though an injury to his back recently put an end to that; his wife had a part-time job taking charge of a news-agent's shop in the afternoons. They let one of their upstairs rooms to a maiden lady. The household income could not be large, yet there was no sign of want, nor even of anxious thrift.

This was partly because of the exquisite state of repair in which every object in the house has been kept, but there is more to it than that. Mrs. Marshall was a Ceres-like figure. She was pale like her son, but she was full-bodied, and moved with a slow, matronly grace. Her hair was dark like her son's, but it had turned white at the ends, so that the curls she wore about her temples and ears and the nape of her neck looked like a Greek headdress. She had a pleasant unhurried voice. The greengrocer would instinctively give her the largest and reddest tomatoes; and she would choose in any shop what was most luscious and durable, and if she had to save to pay for it, would do so serenely, trusting in the bounty of life. Things would come to her; and her husband would talk things towards himself.

These people could not imagine what happened to their son. He cared, they thought, for nothing but his home. He had, they say, no friends, and took no interest in politics. They had been quite unprepared for his arrest. He had told them he was going out to dinner with a friend and had said to his mother, "Oh, Mum, this is a tin-pot place we live in. I've been to the Railway Hotel and they don't do a dinner at night, and I've been to the Spotted Horse and they don't do a dinner at night, and I'll have to take this chap right over the other side of the High Street to the Star and Garter, because they do a dinner every night." She had asked him if he would not bring his friend home after dinner and play records to him, and he had answered that he thought his friend would have to go straight home. But when the police brought her son into the sitting room that evening she thought that he had dined with two friends instead of one, and that they had come back to listen to the records, and she rose and held out her hand to them. It made her angry to remember that. She was not the

kind of woman who would forgive policemen for arresting her
son just because they were only doing their duty.

The whole thing started, they said, in Russia, with the miserable time he had had in the Embassy at Moscow. No, he didn't
like the life there. He didn't like the life there at all. Mr. Marshall
compressed his lips, shut his eyes, wagged his head, implying
many things. Mrs. Marshall, her great chocolate-coloured eyes
full of tears, nodded in confirmation. It was not the sort of thing
that their son was accustomed to. There were continual parties.
Cocktail parties. The sharp sound of the words, flung out after a
preparatory pause, recalled that there had been an age long ago
when a cocktail was considered an immoral drink, as different
from sherry as concubinage is from marriage, and a cocktail party
meant an assembly of people who had abandoned normal restraints. A change in custom in one group may take a very long
time to become known among other groups. There was indeed
no reason why a household like this, which either drank beer or,
more probably, only soft drinks, should ever have learned that
cocktails had long since become respectable, and that cocktail
parties had for many people moved up to the position formerly
occupied by tea parties, of social functions too stereotyped to be
anything else but tedious.

But although there was plainly some illusion here, there was
as plainly some truth. All exiled communities drink too much.
We all know the prisoner's plea that getting drunk was the quickest way out of the grimness of Manchester. But it is also, as many
a man found in Germany, the quickest way back to hideous and
beloved Manchester out of the beautiful and abhorred alien corn.
Yet most witnesses agreed that the drinking in Moscow was on a
modest scale, far below army of occupation standards, and was
constantly checked by the authorities. Still, it was probably enough
to shock the child of this innocent household, which took its pleasure rug-making.

Drinking parties, said Mr. Marshall angrily; and his wife
sighed that the boy had been forced to go to them, had been
bullied into going to them. Thus did they see the efforts which
had been made to render their son's exile tolerable and to keep
him out of a certain mousetrap. There was also, Mr. Marshall

continued, the social difficulty. All the time he had felt that he
was a misfit and that the other people at the Embassy looked
down on him because they had all been at public schools and he
had only been at a secondary school. The father did not seem to
have heard that the majority of the other employees at the
Embassy would have been at just the same sort of school as his
son, and looked vague when it was put to him. It appeared possible that there had not been very much talk between this boy and
his parents. This man and woman with their active hands had
made this small, bright, warm, crowded cave in the darkness of
London; and the boy had sat in the cave, enjoying the sharp,
quick tongue of his father and the comfort of his mother, listening to his tinkling records and making his silk mats, and speaking
of little things such as the failure of the Railway Hotel to do a
dinner at night.

The father hurried on, trying to build up a personality for his
son which the strangers would recognize as guiltless and precious.
It was in Russia, he was sure, that the mischief had started. Not
that the boy had become a Communist out there. For he had no
interest in politics. But the jealousy had started, the jealousy
which had made certain people determined to get him into
trouble. Oh, anybody could see what it all meant. For of course
the Russians had come to notice that the boy was not like the rest
of the pack at the Embassy. The Russians aren't stupid, they
would get on to a thing like that, it would stick out a mile in their
eyes. So when they realized he was different they gave him all
sorts of special privileges, showed their appreciation in all sorts
of little ways. One thing was that they arranged for him to pay a
visit to the Kremlin. Well, it was not everybody who got that attention, so of course the people above him were jealous. His son
had known that, and had even realized that they had gone so
far as to have him followed, and had just laughed at it all. That
showed that there had been no harm in his friendship with
Kuznetsov. He had gone on seeing him long after he had known
they were watching him.

But of course young William was innocent. Mr. Marshall knew
that for certain. He had gone to see him in prison, and had found
him in hospital, and he had stood beside him and asked, "Son,

have you been doing anything you shouldn't have done?" Now, he and his son were friends, real friends, and the lad was always straight with him. If he had been guilty he would just have told him right out, "Dad, I've had it." The father imitated how his son would have looked up at him and humorously shaken his head as he said it. But he had not used those words. He had said, "Well, Dad, it all depends on what they make of it." Mr. and Mrs. Marshall agreed with each other that that made it quite clear that the boy had done nothing.

These people had been thinking of their son's arrest, and of nothing else whatsoever, for nearly three weeks. It was hard to accompany them into the twilit world where their fears and hopes were kneading their memories of what the boy had told them into new shapes, which they trusted would be amulets to keep away misfortune. With surprising abruptness Mr. Marshall announced that his son was sexually normal. He had, indeed, been very much in love with a girl and had hoped to marry her. But recently he had told her that that could never be. This was because he had by then been to Moscow. There he had seen how international affairs were handled. Mr. Marshall shrugged his shoulders contemptuously to convey the horrid substance of his son's knowledge. Even to those who are most repelled by many Foreign Office policies this condemnation seemed too sweeping.

Of course, Mr. Marshall continued, we were bound to have a war, the way they were muddling things. Then the atom bomb would go off; and there was no sense in bringing children into the world just for that. Anyway, till then he would have nothing to offer his wife except life in an Embassy. And the boy knew what that was. Not fit for a decent girl. The degradation of a diplomatic environment was mentioned after the atom bomb, and it was clear that that order was adopted for the sake of keeping the worst to the last, of avoiding an anticlimax. Even to those who are most fatigued by the drinking of exiled communities it seemed that he was not being quite just. Had he been speaking of a young woman who had been kidnapped to Chinatown and infected with the opium habit, and for these and other reasons might as well be dead, his tone would not have been different, and it would greatly have astonished Sir David and Lady Kelly.

For a moment it seemed desirable that they should be in this room. Surely they would by their presence have dispelled this bad dream of a debauched coterie which had humbled the Marshalls' son and ruined him for childish motives. Sir David would have given them wise and drastic advice on the course that would best serve the boy's interests; Lady Kelly would have understood that the couple's pride in the framed panel of embroidered butterflies and their passion for rug-making established them as distant kin to the builders of the Russian churches and the Turkish mosques which her taste and technical skill had commemorated. Their acute minds would have circled the house and the cloud of imagination on their faces would have thickened, and they would have perfectly understood the situation. Yet the Marshalls had, of course, no particular desire at that moment to be understood. What they wanted was to get their son out of prison.

From the doorway they said again that their son took no interest in politics. Outside, the summer dusk had lifted in that last moment of false daylight which comes before the dark falls, and there was a staring whiteness in the sky. It could be seen that the Marshalls lived in the kind of street which is in our age a conduit of political danger. It was eighty years since the English passed their first great Education Act. Practically everybody in the street was the child of parents who had some schooling, and was himself easily literate. People who could not learn at school or forget what they learned there do not succeed in living in this decent and orderly street of little houses, they lived in still smaller houses. But if they learned much more than was taught at school, if they went on to the universities, or if they were clever in industry or commerce, they were apt to move away into larger houses. Those that remained here were sensitive to print, they were within the radius over which complicated ideas broadcast themselves. Some considered these ideas with deliberation and good sense, some ignored them, some embraced them too eagerly and insisted that they be immediately applied. Round the corner from the Marshalls there lived a man who was coughing out his life and gave such moments as he could wrest from tubercular death to the service of the British Fascist party as it has survived the war, addled and minuscule. He read the wrong books and did not quite understand what he was reading. This happens in such little streets as these, all over Europe, and it is apt to lead to one form of totalitarianism or another.

The trial took place on July 9 and 10, and it was not one of those which takes place in a self-engendered theatrical glow. There were not many people in court and few of them were notable, save the Earl of Athlone and his wife, Princess Alice. The Earl is the brother of our Queen Mary, and resembles her in at least one endearing respect. Their aged and massive bodies are like weathered towers in which there lives a child who has not yet outgrown its wonder of the world, who, being well brought up, does not pry, but could not open its eyes a speck wider. It happened that at the time of the Abdication, the Crystal Palace, our vast Victorian fun fair, burned down, and for all that Queen Mary was heartbroken she would let nothing do her out of a good fire, and officials had to conduct her on a thorough tour of the smoking ruins. The same interest in the spectacular had brought the Earl to this trial. He and Princess Alice, a slender white-haired lady noted for her amiability, leaned forward in their seats, fascinated by this young man, who was a new kind of fire, who could by treason burn and make ruins. But so obviously had poor William Martin Marshall neither heat nor light, so obviously was poor Tom acold, that the royal pair lost their awed horror, visibly relaxed, and sent out to him rays of grieved benevolence, as if he had been a cripple in some hospital.

He did indeed draw the eye. Three among the several counts of the indictments charged him with violating the Official Secrets Act by communicating to Pavel Kuznetsov information about the British Diplomatic Wireless Service, which was calculated to be or might be directly or indirectly useful to an enemy, at interviews which all took place in public. But it seemed impossible that he could ever have been a spy, that any foreign power could have considered him for one second as a possible informer. He had the most fatal disqualification for cloak-and-dagger work. He had a distinctive appearance which made him recognizable instantly and from a great distance. Not only was he very tall, and thin to a point that roused concern for his health, he had sloping shoulders, sloping as steeply as the shoulders of any Gainsborough beauty, at an angle not often seen in the male physique. He had a long neck, and a very pale face which was long and thin and had a peculiarity of moulding which did not amount to a deformity but was very noticeable. There is an area beside the ear, below the cheekbone and above the jaw, just over the parotid gland, which in thin people is always flat or concave. In him it bulged in a slight protuberance which was faintly pitted in the centre. He was neither repulsive nor ridiculous; he was simply a magnet for the sight and memory, like an albino or a person with an unusual shade of red hair.

 2

At the trial of William Martin Marshall, telegraphist in the British Diplomatic Wireless Service, his family showed that he was very valuable to them. Mr. Marshall was dressed with the dreadful neatness which distinguishes the male relatives of accused persons, which reveals how the morning broke for them, how they came out of sleep in a small room and slowly realized that this was the day, and got up and splashed punctiliously in the hand basin, and brushed their hair and knotted their ties anxiously before the small mirror, scraping together the best of themselves as a sign to the judge that the whole thing is a mistake, the wrong family has come into court, that all its members, without a single exception, even the apparent one in the dock, belong to that section of the community which cannot in any circumstances be justly sent to prison. He looked angry and his lips were compressed. It was a great hardship to him that he could not use his special talent in the service of his son and talk the case out of court. Throughout the trial his lips were constantly moving.

His wife was as carefully arrayed, but she was refusing to behave well, she was openly showing her distress. This was not because she lacked self-control but because she was the sort of woman who refuses to knuckle down to men. Nobody was going to find her admitting that there was anything in the male claim to have devised a machine called the law which automatically produced justice, because she knew that justice cannot be done unless the truth is first established, and she knew further that truth is made up of minute fragments which it is hard enough to piece together as a whole, even though one gossips all day, and which could roll away and scatter in the corners if they were brought into open court. Though she was punctiliously neat she had come bareheaded into the Old Bailey, which was a breach of convention but aesthetically proper; she and Hecuba and Andromache would not wear hats. The peculiarity by which her strong hair was dark at the scalp and white at the ends, where she curled it about her temple and ears and the nape of her neck, was very noticeable. She looked like an illustration to some legend telling of a vigorous woman on which some unseen power, winter or death or extreme grief, suddenly laid its hand.

She was being soothed by her husband and her younger son, Ronald, who was revealed as one of the deep unmedicable causes of the misery felt by the man in the dock, which had been noticed by his colleagues in Moscow. For Ronald was very like his older brother, but with differences that made him good-looking in a comfortably ordinary way. A reporter had questioned Miss Jones, headmistress of the infants' department in the Wandsworth school where the two boys had started their education, and she had no recollection of William at all but remembered Ronald; and had later sought out the choirmaster of the church choir in which both boys had sung, and to him William was "a quiet lad, not in the cricket team, as his young brother was." Women like his mother are not so wrong in their sceptical attitude towards the law. The court would have regarded what Miss Jones and the choirmaster said as irrelevant.

The trial was tormenting to the Marshall family and difficult for the spectators to follow, because much of the evidence was given by Security officers in closed court, and then we had all to sit in the shadowy corridors. Some Indian women lawyers walked up and down in green and lilac and silver saris. There were Indians at Joyce's trial, there have been Indians at all the treason trials. They have cast off British government, yet they retain their delight in the law which was the instrument of that government; they adore its intricacies, its protocol, the obsolete and dusky and airless caves where it practices its mystery. A Negro barrister's

271

luminous black skin and rangy stride made a new and picturesque costume of his white wig and flowing gown. He settled
down on a bench with two of his compatriots, and their chatter
propounded the riddle of Negro speech. The voices of African
Negroes have a quality not found in European voices but are just
as different from the voices of American Negroes. There is much
more sensuousness and joyfulness in the American Negro's
voice; people are torn from their homes and packed in ships and
sent thousands of miles to work under the whips of slavery, and
their children speak for ever afterwards as if their lips were but-
tered with rich food and laughter were as often with them as
speech. Strange is the course travelled through the centuries by
alien peoples; but as we went in and out of the court the case confronted us with another more disconcerting type of strangeness.
We saw a known routine reversed, and men who were adepts in a
certain craft acting as if they were novices.

As soon as William Marshall had come into the dock it had
seemed unlikely that any foreign power should have wished its
agents to engage in activities which it desired to keep secret with
this odd-looking boy, who was so pale and tall and thin, so easily
identifiable by the most curious moulding of his cheeks and the
steep angle of his sloping shoulders. Every moment he spent in
court made it appear less likely that the police had lied when they
described him as showing signs of nervousness when he was being watched. They need not have been close to him to have
made such a report. As he sat and listened to the evidence he continually pursed his lips, then pouted them, then abruptly compressed them and puffed out his cheeks, and finally tried to wipe
out the grimace by stroking his mouth and chin with his very long
fingers. Considering that strain had this manifest physical effect
on him, it was against all probability that the Soviet espionage authorities should have chosen one of the Embassy staff to handle
him.

It does not seem likely that Embassy officials often deal with
such matters in these days. Very sensibly, the standard Communist routine provides that all espionage should be carried out by
three persons. The first is the "source," usually a national of the

country in which the espionage is carried on, and the second is "the contact," who takes it from him, who also is usually a native. The third is "the agent," who is often a Soviet national and employed in a Soviet organization and delivers it to the local Soviet espionage headquarters. This routine was varied in the case of the atomic spies, whose communications were regarded as so important that the contacts were cut out and they were handled directly by the agents, even though these were Soviet diplomats. This was not too rash a step, for it was during the war and the Russians knew that the Allies were treating them with complete confidence, and rightly divined that these diplomats were not shadowed. But it is now known that Nunn May handed over his information straight into the hands of Lieutenant Angelov, an assistant of the military attaché in Ottawa, and that Fuchs's first contact was Simon Kremer, secretary to the military attaché at the Soviet Embassy in London. There is therefore little doubt that the British authorities shadow Soviet diplomats, and the temperamental bias of the Soviet authorities must lead them to exaggerate rather than minimize the amount of shadowing that is done. It is therefore not to be understood why they sent a second secretary to deal with a source whose appearance was God's gift to any detective.

But even if it be granted that they had to take William Marshall as a source, because for some reason they needed a radio telegraphist at the British Embassy at this particular moment so badly that the certainty of early detection did not matter, and even if it be supposed that Marshall himself had somehow come to know Kuznetsov and insisted on dealing with him and nobody else, their choice of meeting place leaves the matter still enigmatic. Spies usually meet in private houses or in country lanes if they think they are a long way from having excited any suspicion; or, if there is any doubt, in crowded streets or bus stops or subway stations, or in large saloons. If there are any documents to be passed the encounters will be very brief. Much of the information Marshall was accused of handing over, such as the code letters for the various stations, could have been written down on paper. But Marshall and Kuznetsov met for leisurely meals at restaurants,

273

at eight different restaurants, of which six were exactly the places one would have thought spies in general, and these men in particular, would avoid.

On January 2, shortly after Marshall had returned from Moscow, they lunched at the Berkeley, which is the London equivalent of the Colony, and three days later they dined at the Pigalle, a fairly grand restaurant which puts on a floor show, not far from Piccadilly Circus. They might easily have met Sir David and Lady Kelly at the Berkeley; and the Pigalle is the sort of place that a young diplomat might easily go after the theatre. At neither would one expect to see a young radio telegraphist. It might be thought that Kuznetsov was trying to soften Marshall by giving him luxurious tastes, but that was evidently not the plan. For nine days later they lunched at the more popular Criterion. After that there were longer intervals between their meetings, because Marshall had gone to work at Hanslope Park and got back to London only on his leaves. It was three weeks before they dined together again, this time at Chez Auguste, in Soho. After dinner they went to a hotel in the Bloomsbury area, frequented largely by prosperous businessmen from the provinces. Three weeks after that they lunched at the quiet and conventional Royal Court Hotel.

Not one of these restaurants was a mere nosebag. All of them were in the metropolitan nexus. Later Marshall and Kuznetsov were to eat in Kingston and in Wimbledon, and in such places a restaurant draws on a small, enclosed, local world, which will often find no clue to a stranger. But at these first six appointments the two exposed themselves to the scrutiny of a sprawling and well-informed system. At any one of them it was possible that people at the next table might be diplomats, or Embassy employees, and even probable that they might from time to time have attended a diplomatic reception. At any one of them the waiters belong to the upper circle of their profession, which has its own unwritten "Who's Who," far meatier than the printed version. At any one of them a table has to be booked. If Kuznetsov did the booking, it would be rash of him to give his own name, still more rash to give a false one; and if it were Marshall, the question might be asked at any moment, "Who is this young man who is going about with the second secretary of the Soviet Embassy?"

It was so little surprising that Marshall had landed in the dock that it was very surprising. It was comprehensible enough that when Inspector Hughes of the Special Branch told how he had arrested Marshall and found the copied document in his wallet and searched his room in his parents' home, there was no joy of the chase in his tone. Marshall's counsel put it to him that the young man had a blameless record and had been given an excellent character when he left the Forces, and the Inspector drearily agreed. But he added with sudden and grim emphasis, "Better than normal." It was not clear what he meant. It might have been that he had been nauseated at having had to watch for months this pitiable young man shutting himself up in a mousetrap. It might also have been that that character was framed in such strong terms of recommendation that, now Marshall had got into trouble, it appeared possible that at some point there had been fiddling with his papers. Perhaps without his knowledge, persons who wanted to plant him in the diplomatic wireless service had seen to it that he could produce a character which would make him seem an exceptionally desirable candidate. It was, after all, out in Egypt that it had first occurred to him to seek employment in that service.

But that was dissolved in the general doubt. This oddly reckless pair had behaved in a way bound to arouse in any reasonably cautious person the suspicion that Marshall was a criminal; but it seemed not at all certain that he was going to be convicted of any crime. There were two counts of the indictment which related to the copy of the document which was found in his wallet. One charged him with unlawfully obtaining the information in the document, for the benefit of a foreign power; but the judge announced early in the trial that he was going to direct the jury to acquit Marshall on this charge, since it was information which had been given him in the course of his duties and he had made no effort whatsoever to obtain it. It was in fact the copy of a notice which was put up in each of the bays in which the radio telegraphists worked. Another count charged him with recording that information for the benefit of a foreign power, and there seemed little doubt that he could be found guilty of this offence, since an expert graphologist had testified that the copy was in his handwriting. But even this was not certain. Since it had been found in Marshall's wallet, and there was no evidence that he had ever taken it out since he originally put it in, it seemed possible that he would be acquitted of that charge with its imputation of a desire to help a potential enemy, and that he would be charged again with the very much lesser offence of wrongly retaining the information. But the gravity of the case, the element in it which made his parents' distress reasonable enough, lay in the three other counts, which charged him with having on three dates communicated information to Kuznetsov which could be useful to a foreign power. And there was not a particle of direct evidence that there had been any such communication at all.

On the first date, April 25, Marshall had been seen to go to the Thameside town of Kingston. There he met Kuznetsov, lunched with him at the Normandie Restaurant, and went with him to a public garden by the river, where they sat on a bench for an hour and twenty minutes. Marshall was seen to take some papers out of his pocket, and he appeared to be explaining them to his companion; and he sometimes made a drawing on some paper laid on his lap, as if he were illustrating his explanations. If anybody halted in the neighbourhood of the bench he put away the papers; and when he left his friend and went home he looked nervous and worried. That was all the detectives could say. Nobody had overheard what he said or seen him give any papers to Kuznetsov.

On the second date, May 19, Marshall met Kuznetsov in Wimbledon High Street, close enough to his home in Wandsworth, and spent two hours with him in a restaurant. But neither then nor on their last meeting, in King George's Park on June 13, was a word of what they had said taken down by the detectives, nor did any papers pass between them.

It seemed quite likely that he would be acquitted on these major charges until he went into the witness box to give evidence on his own behalf. There he damned himself. He was in all things a contrast to his parents. His swaying, fidgeting height shot up out of the witness box like the rootless saplings that grow out of the crevices of bombed buildings; it did not seem possible that he should have been the child of this amply made woman, this compact and vigorous father. The boy shifted from foot to foot as he testified in a high, weak voice, which the judge and the counsel found hard to hear. This reluctant trickle was different from the slow, full river of sighs and persuasive murmurs and passionate exclamations with which his mother had tried to suggest his innocence, or the cascade of words with which his father had tried to sweep away his guilt; and it was flowing in the opposite direction.

He told an incredible story of how he had come to know Kuznetsov. He said that when he had come back from Moscow he had found that he had failed to return a pass issued by the Soviet government which all British Embassy personnel had to carry in case they were stopped in the city. Though it had been issued to him by the Embassy officials, he did not hand it back to the Foreign Office, and accounted for this absurdly, by saying that he "did not want to involve the Foreign Office" if he should have handed it back before he left Moscow. He returned it to the Soviet Embassy in Kensington Palace Gardens, and not by post. He took it himself, and when he explained the purpose of his visit to the doorman, he was taken in to see Kuznetsov. He implied that this was the first time he had ever met him; but it is to be noted that Kuznetsov had been sent from London to Moscow the previous autumn and had been there during the last three months of Marshall's service in the British Embassy there. With him he had a conversation which immediately engendered a feeling of friendship. "We found," he said in his statement, "we had a good deal in common and we looked at life in the same way. I told him I was still working at the Foreign Office and we agreed to meet again." He gave the duration of this conversation as a quarter of an hour.

In his statement he also said, "I gave him my address and told him I could not possibly meet him at home as my parents would not agree to such a proposition." Since he had also asserted that this friendship with Kuznetsov was of a perfectly innocent and personal nature, unconnected with the passing of information, he was cross-examined as to his reason for making that remark. He answered, "I told him that because my people's political views are opposed to my own." Neither the prosecuting counsel nor his own counsel had asked him whether he was a Communist, and it had not appeared in his statement. His vague complaint of feeling a social misfit at the British Embassy had not been accompanied by any avowal of Communist sympathies, and most people who had seen a vision of him being snubbed by arrogant diplomats and had thought of him as spying out of resentment against this humiliating experience saw him as doing it impetuously, as a young clerk who has had a talking-to from the boss might buy the *Daily Worker* for a few mornings. The authorities had in fact had no suspicions regarding him. But he had now made it quite plain to the jury that when he went to see Kuznetsov he had already championed the Communist cause so definitely that it had caused disputes at home. The voices of his parents, asserting that he took no interest in politics but was absorbed in his records and his film magazines and his silk mats, sounded through the memory and now seemed touching and sacred.

Marshall made two more serious slips. He claimed that for the most part he had talked with Kuznetsov on political subjects: on the Russian way of life, on the division of Germany, on the war in Korea, on the unrest in Malaya. He explained that when he was sitting with Kuznetsov on the bench in the public garden at Kingston, he had been showing him papers on which there were written "general summaries of the news" and that the drawing he had shown him was "a map of parts of Russia in connection with the division of Germany." This was, of course, heart-rending stuff. It would be unlikely that the second secretary of the Soviet Embassy, an able and experienced man of middle age, should have spent an hour and twenty minutes listening to "general summaries of the news" and looking at maps of Russia set before him by any radio telegraphist of twenty-four—least of all by this radio telegraphist, whose every word betrayed a simplicity of mind so great that its effect was as disconcerting as complexity; whatever he said he made the listener think back along winding routes in search of the naïve misapprehension on which his view was based. The attorney general suggested to him that on the papers there had been written the call signs of a number of wireless stations, and that the map he had drawn showed wireless circuits. This he denied, and he was asked again if he maintained that all he and Kuznetsov had talked about was Germany, Korea, and

278

Malaya. Tossing his long head, he answered in a tart and reedy tone, "Yes, and we exchanged cultural information on Moscow."

This perfect specimen of *Daily Worker* English dashed and depressed the court. Such words would come naturally only to a young man who had taken a linguistic tan from exposure to the fierce rays of Communist prose; and it takes time to get a tan. This had, of course, no evidential value, and it should have had no effect on the jury, though God preserve any of us from saying "sibboleth" for "shibboleth" quite so clearly when we are on trial. But Marshall's third slip was something which the jury had properly to take into account. When he was asked about the copy of the secret document found in his wallet he said, pouting, that he knew nothing about it. Peevishly he insisted on oath that he had not written it, that he had never transcribed the notice which was put up in his bay, and that he had no notion of how the copy came to be in his wallet.

He had asked the court to clear a high hurdle. To accept his story one would have had to believe that the police had obtained this document and specimens of Marshall's handwriting and given them to a reliable forger to make a copy which could be fathered on Marshall, and then, after taking all that trouble, had planted it on the wrong man. For they would have had a watertight case had they found it on Kuznetsov, but instead they found it on Marshall. It might be argued that the police shrank from the delicate international situation which would have been created had they found evidence that a Soviet diplomat had been acting as a spy; but they had shown no signs of shrinking from that hazard; they had, on the contrary, been advancing towards it with every sign of delighted appetite. They had, after all, searched Kuznetsov, after he had announced that he was second secretary of the Soviet Embassy, as they blandly said, "before this information could be checked." It was quite impossible to swallow Marshall's story; and it was no surprise to anybody that the jury found him guilty of the charge of having copied the document.

The general necessity for public trials can only be realized when a particular necessity forces the judge to clear the court for part of a trial. The remainder never quite makes sense, just as the face of someone whose eyes or lips are hidden is not really

a face. All the evidence regarding the contents and importance
of the secret document which had been copied, Marshall's work,
and the meetings at Kingston and Wimbledon, were given *in camera,* and the counsel's speeches showed a corresponding evasive-
ness. So, too, was the judge's summing up, which was delivered
on the morning of the second day, after a night which, it could be
seen, had been sleepless for the Marshall family. They were all
much more markedly themselves than they had been before: the
father went about with his jaw protruding and his fists carried
clenched and forward, as if ready to spar with the spirit of the
Old Bailey; the mother was Volumnia; the son, dutiful and vigi-
lant, followed them like a stretcher-bearer. The judge's summing
up lasted till noon, and then the jury retired. It was obvious that
they would take some time to consider their verdict, but Mrs.
Marshall stayed in court, splendidly but not self-consciously
grouped with her other son, while her husband stood in the corridor and sipped from a glass of water, as if it were poison he
were forcing someone else to drink. There was certainly reason
for them to hate someone, after their son's appearance in the witness box. For he had not been rehearsed. Even had he been
wholly innocent of the charges, it must surely have occurred to
Kuznetsov that he was a dangerous friend to an employee in the
British Diplomatic Wireless Service, and that some day the boy
might be questioned about the acquaintance; and he might have
warned him to keep silent about his Communist sympathies. If
Marshall were guilty, then Kuznetsov's negligence was even more
shameful. He should have been warned that if any copies of documents were found on him he should admit to having copied them
but deny having shown them to anybody, thus getting away with
a lesser offence and enabling kindly people to think that he might
be a credible witness and speaking the truth when he denied the
graver charges.

After an hour the jury came back and the foreman announced
that they had found a verdict of guilty on all four counts that remained, but added that they wished to add a rider, as the British
call a recommendation added to a verdict. Riders are not encouraged in the English courts, for they are felt to be an encroachment
on the constitutional powers of the judge to pass sentence accord-

ing to his own unfettered discretion, so the judge replied that it was preferable that a plain verdict of guilty or not guilty should be returned, and the prosecuting counsel concurred. But the foreman gently insisted. "We ask," he said, "that the prisoner be shown the utmost mercy. We feel that he has been led astray." The object of their pity was shifting his balance from one foot to another, pouting his lips and biting them back, and giving every now and then a simultaneous toss of his head and slight twist of the hips, and indeed it was unbearable to think of the full weight of justice descending on him.

The judge announced that he would hear some further details of the case and give sentence after the luncheon adjournment, and with a shrug Marshall turned to go down the steps inside the dock to the cells. Mrs. Marshall ran forward and beat on the glass panel that surrounds the dock, calling to him, "Keep your chin up, boy." Marshall looked at her. It was the first time during the trial that he had looked at any of his family. He gave her a faint smile and made a motion, faint also, of his hand towards his father and his brother, then turned back to the warders and went down the steps. A family who were in a position to say to a son, "We told you so," but had not said it, might find itself greeted in just that way by their son when their prophecies had been so completely justified that he was far too humiliated to thank them for their forbearance.

As Mrs. Marshall left the court she cried, "There is no British justice." She protested again when she came back after the adjournment, and the court was cleared again, to enable the judge to hear some evidence about the contents of the secret document which had its bearing on the problem of how much leniency he might show. She turned her back on the door and took up a stand beside the dock, with a defiance not the less genuine because she knew she would be led away. So in the Balkan mountains the superb sheep dogs often stand in the way of an automobile till the last minute, registering hate of the modern things though they know quite well that at the last minute they will have to yield. She went out, and the day became tinged with farce; for it is farcical when a member of the Secret Service is called to give evidence and is being so secret just at that moment that he cannot be found. Then we were all in court again, and Marshall was asked if he had anything to say before sentence was passed on him. With childish irony he replied in his unresonant voice, "I have. The learned jury in their wisdom have found me guilty of the offences with which I am charged but I still say I am innocent." He thought he was parodying the pompous jargon of the law, and had an impression that the word "learned" is sometimes used at trials, and so it is; it is sometimes applied to judges and to counsel, but it is never applied to the jury, for the whole point of juries is that they are unlearned, they are chunks of laity. The mistake was a measure of the lightly furnished state of the boy's mind.

The judge then told Marshall that he had been found guilty of grave offences but went on to say that he was prepared to assume that they had not been committed for the purpose of gain. This was probably correct. Marshall said in his evidence that when he and Kuznetsov dined together Kuznetsov paid for the meal and he paid for the drinks, and if, as he said, they drank wines, this might be the heavy end of the load. He was a spender, far beyond the habit of his kind. Foreign Office employees are paid well for Moscow duty, and while he was in Russia his salary and allowances amounted to more than a thousand pounds a year, on which he paid no tax. This would be double, or more than double, the sum on which most of his neighbours in Wandsworth would be keeping their families. There were few opportunities for spending money in Moscow, so most of the employees sent large remittances home to their families. But Marshall did not do much of that, not because he was ungenerous but because his parents had no feeling that he ought to contribute to their upkeep. Some time after he returned to England it became apparent that his father was going to be prevented by the injury to his back from going on with his odd jobs, and then he told his mother that he intended to make her a regular allowance. She objected, "I don't like taking your money, boy," and he answered, "Don't be silly, Mum, you might just as well have it. If you don't take it it will all go on records and books."

But it should have been no strain for him, for he must have brought home the bulk of what he earned in Moscow, and though he was paid much less in England he was living in a hostel in a provincial town, where, again, there were few opportunities for spending money. But when they arrested him he had only fifteen pounds left in his savings account. There had been at work the idiosyncrasy which had impressed his fellow employees at Moscow: his pressing sense that he had to return every cigarette given him as soon as possible, as if he were a bankrupt whose creditors were so universal that he could accept nothing lest it add to his vast obligations, and could never pay out enough to discharge his debts. He was indeed to pay out, under our eyes, a great fortune; all that might have happened to him between the ages of twenty-five and twenty-eight. For he was sentenced to five years' imprisonment, which with the usual remission would work out at that.

It took a long time for us to learn this, for the judge had to explain to the jury that though they had asked him to be lenient he could not let Marshall off with a trivial sentence, because the information in the copied document was really important, its disclosure might endanger the lives of many of his fellow countrymen; and he had also to make it clear that on the other hand he felt justified in giving much less than the maximum sentence of fourteen years, because of the testimony put forward by Security officers to claim that Marshall had probably not realized the significance of what he had done. Evidently the judge felt the full horror of shooting this sitting rabbit. So he went on and on in a maze of sentences, while Marshall played cat's cradle behind his back with his long fingers, always swaying and shifting his weight from foot to foot, and rolling his small mouth round and round over his teeth. All this time Marshall's father was watching the judge with his eyes narrowed and his chin protruded, in a trance of hatred; and the aspect of Marshall's mother, who had risen to her feet, accused everybody of sin except her son.

He twitched his shoulders petulantly, and a final violent grimace passed over his mouth. Again his parents approached the back of the dock and smiled up at him through the glass panel, but this time he would not look at them at all. "I stood beside him and I asked, 'Son, have you been doing anything you shouldn't have done?' Now, I and my son are friends, real friends, and the lad is always straight with me. If he had been guilty he would have told me right out, 'Dad, I've had it.' " Mr. Marshall's picture of a happy relationship hung like a transparency in front of the sullen lad, turning his back on his father and mother as he went down the steps inside the dock to the cells. Briskly the court passed on to the consideration of another case, but Mrs. Marshall continued to stand by the dock, weeping without false shame, sure of the appropriateness and sound sense of her tears, till her husband and her son led her away, out into the corridor, down the stairs.

The automobile that was to take the family back to Wandsworth had to be fetched, and they waited on a bench in the vestibule, a gloomy oblong hall struck by sideways shafts of dusty light. Mrs. Marshall's dusky pallor and the white curls round her dark head shone in the shadows; she was of a different and more dramatic substance than the vague figures about her. The journals in which her son's plight was discussed and deplored were to publish page photographs exploiting another such contrast of human whiteness against obscurity, another such melodramatic example of chiaroscuro. The young son of Sir David Kelly was during that morning married at Brompton Oratory to one of the eight children of Lord Howard of Glossop and his wife, the eleventh Baroness Beaumont. There were eight bridesmaids drawn from the old Catholic families; and they had been photographed as they waited for the bride, sitting on a bench in the aisle. Their young faces and bare arms, their light dresses and the fillets in their hair, the sheaves of flowers on their laps, were bright against the blackness of the church. To the instructed they represented enclosed purity, an almost insolent cultivation of integrity not possible to those who had to go about the world on its business. But it was painful to think how differently they would appear to Mrs. Marshall should her eyes fall on that photograph. For according to the fantasy which had given her comfort, these young girls were smeared with guilt by association, fatally compromised by contact with the world of diplomacy, which had revolted her son's fastidiousness and driven him into dangerous courses.

Most trials result from a collision between a fantasy and reality. In this trial the fantasies were growing rankly and were potent and disturbing, because they made allusions to reality ranker than any disclosed during the proceedings which were supposed to establish what was real. There was this wild indictment of the diplomatic world as an Alsatia; but this pointed a finger, if a shaking one, in the direction of the truth. A diplomat had behaved badly, and his misbehaviour was due to the nature of diplomacy. Kuznetsov had done worse than merely fail to coach Marshall in what he ought to say. It had been in his power to get Marshall acquitted, and he had not done it. For if he had come forward as a witness and had assured the court that he had in fact found pleasure in young Marshall's company, and had been edified by his views on the division of Germany and Korea and Malaya, and had exchanged cultural information on Moscow with him on a park bench, it would have been difficult for a jury to convict Marshall, particularly if Kuznetsov had spoken with a certain warmth. But nothing had been heard of Kuznetsov since a couple of days after Marshall's arrest, when a Soviet Security officer had called at his apartment and driven him and his wife and his little boy to the Soviet Embassy, where he had remained ever since.

That was considered by many to absolve him from blame for his desertion of his friend. They went on to say, "Poor chap, he'll be sent home now, and then his days won't be long in the land, considering how he bungled the job." But that conclusion was perhaps not entirely correct. It is possible to regard the trial as the result of reckless incompetence, which ventured on a change of plan when it was too late; to suppose that the acquaintance began in honest friendship, at which time Kuznetsov saw no reason why he should not be seen with Marshall in London restaurants, and that the thought of espionage only developed later, and drove the two to suburban trysts which offered real cover and would have been safe enough if they had not already attracted the attention of the Security organizations. But the trail they left round the suburbs leads away from that supposition.

It was on April 25 that Kuznetsov and Marshall met at Kingston, that charming riverside town where the Thames looks like the Seine, and the flowers and shrubs and trees grow richly in the good alluvial soil. The two men met in the town centre, which is on flat ground near the river, and there Marshall was unfortunate, for he became involved in the temperamental peculiarities of a family named Bentall.

Eighty-five years ago a young man named Frank Bentall, the son of a storekeeper in a small East Anglian port, was given some money by his father and told that now he was twenty-five he must buy himself a store of his own. He bought a blanket store in Kingston High Street, and did so well in his first year that he bought the business next door and engaged two assistants. He, and his son Leonard after him, prospered mightily, and were devoured by an ambition. They wanted the little store which had been bought in 1867 to grow until it filled the eye, the eye of the individual, of the town, of the county. Nothing else would do. It had to be that store magnified. Otherwise they would surely have moved to another site, which must have been more convenient, wherever it was, for no other part of the town was so cluttered up with properties resistant to transfer, such as schools, vicarages, church halls, and public houses. But they wanted the visible miracle, so they built new quarters for the educational and ecclesiastical authorities and went on bidding through the decades for the other coveted premises, joining the separated houses as they absorbed them by a network of underground passages and overhead galleries. Had they been Americans they would have built a skyscraper, as like as not in a prairie town, and against all reason, with nothing between them and the horizon but cheap land, just for the hell of it, just to make the town more interesting by topping it with a challenge to probability. But the soil on the site to which the Bentalls were tied by their infatuation is for fifteen feet down a water-logged soup of Thameside sand and gravel, which had to be converted by chemical means to artificial sandstone before it could carry a modern building only a few stories high. They had to build their skyscraper horizontally.

When Leonard had wholly conquered the block in the main street where the store had started, his ambition went round the corner, and he began to acquire properties in a narrow and gloomy lane called Wood Street. One of his colleagues objected that there were no shops there and it was impossible to imagine that it could ever become a shopping centre. Leonard answered, "If you live long enough you will see in Wood Street one of the finest buildings in the county and the road one of the best in town." He went on to recite what was afterwards identified as a quotation from Emerson: "If a man write a better book, preach a better sermon, or make a better mousetrap than his neighbour, though he build his house in the woods, the world will make a beaten path to his door." Thus he showed, as his colleague was later to comment, a remarkable prophetic gift.

Today the Bentall store is by English standards a very impressive concern. It employs three thousand people, and it has crept all along one side of Wood Street, which makes a right-angled turn, so that it now covers three of the four sides of a large island site. This expansion has only been possible because it draws on much more than local trade. The merchandise is good and solid, but the place is also a good entertainment in itself, there is a curious circus air about it, and therefore many customers come from all the towns and villages for a long way out on the country side of Kingston, and quite a number from London itself. This means that there are always crowds of far more than the usual suburban density looking at the windows with the leisureliness of shoppers out on an expedition.

Across the road from the store in Wood Street, just opposite the right-angled turn, the Bentalls have bought an odd site to use as a garage and a car-park, and in order not to waste a speck of street frontage they have built on it a two-story building, which is the Normandie Restaurant. Like everything the Bentalls have created, it takes the eye. It is not beautiful, it is not ugly, but it hits the retina, it has to be noticed. It is set catercornered to the store opposite, so anybody who wants to watch it can hide among the window-shopping crowds on both legs of Wood Street. No continuous pavement runs past the restaurant. To the left of the restaurant is the entrance to the garage and car-park, to the right the exit. To get to the restaurant it is necessary to cross the street at one of three points, all close together. These crossings would never be used by any pedestrian who had not the intention of going to the Normandie. There could not be an easier place to watch.

On April 25, when Marshall and Kuznetsov visited Kingston, it was Friday, a popular shopping day, and there were plenty of people on the pavements to give cover for detectives. The pair went into the Normandie at one o'clock. The sole entrance opens into a bar, from which a narrow staircase with a sharp turn leads into the restaurant itself. There is no other way of getting in or out of the room. Upstairs the men took a table facing the door, which was visible from every other part of the room, for it is not large. Marshall's party, though he did not know it, occupied a seventh of the available accommodation. For there were twenty-one tables, and he and Kuznetsov had one table, the officers from the Special Branch were sitting at another, and a third was taken by the party of police from the Soviet Embassy, who, though Marshall did not seem to know it, were always present at these meetings.

Marshall must have been very happy at this lunch. He was with his friend. He was defying authority. Possibly he thought that he was saving the world. Certainly the Normandie's claim to be contemporary and dashing would please the part of him that pouted against Wandsworth because the Railway Hotel did not do a dinner. The food at the Normandie is well cooked and quite imaginative by English standards. If Marshall paid for the drinks, as he said in the witness box he always did on these occasions, he may have gratified his taste for spending money, for there are some good wines on the list.

After having eaten their meal in this goldfish bowl Marshall and Kuznetsov walked away down a narrow street known as Water Lane, in which no boy of ten playing at sleuthing could have lost his quarry. They had before them an unusually large choice of retreats where they could have talked quietly and kept at a distance from any eavesdropper. A short bus ride would have taken them to Richmond Park, and within walking distance, just over Kingston Bridge on the other side of the Thames, were Bushey Park and Hampton Court Park. Instead the two men went to Canbury Gardens.

This is a riverside strip of greenery which solves a problem grave enough for a town relying for much of its income on people who come to enjoy its prettiness but also has its industries. Canbury Gardens masks the gasworks and electricity plants of the town and distracts the attention of the pedestrian from the covered dock where the barges discharge their cargoes of coal into an elevator. The Gardens run along the river for less than a quarter of a mile, and the depth is never more than a hundred and fifty yards and is at some places as little as fifty. There is a line of plane trees on the garden side of the towpath, with benches between them where one can sit and look over the glassy Thames at the opposite bank, where the weeping willows droop to their reflections, and the Georgian mansions are mellow in the green shade of the tall wet-rooted trees. But there are never at any time many people sitting about in Canbury Gardens. Mothers with babies and very young children find pleasure there, and so do the elderly. But it is the river that captures the fancy here, and most people follow the towpath, looking inland only occasionally to see the bright flowers and shrubs. There are tennis courts on the town edge of the Gardens, but the players usually enter them by a special gate.

If the two men had taken a bus to Richmond Park or had crossed the river to Hampton Court or Bushey, they could have found an open space and set down their coats on the grass and spread out maps as if they were hikers talking of routes, and it would have been hard for the detectives to find an excuse for getting near enough to see what they were doing. In Canbury Gardens they sat down on one of the benches between the plane trees. They were therefore silhouetted against the waters of the Thames, and, as the bank faces westward, against the afternoon light. Marshall's sloping shoulders and his long narrow head must have been crassly identifiable, and when he took papers out of his pockets and showed them to his companion, and when he drew maps for him, not a shade of the explanatory gestures could have been missed. It was ten days after Easter Monday, on which date Canbury Gardens goes into its summer routine, so there were piles of deck chairs set at various points from which visitors could pick up as many chairs as they needed and set them down where they pleased. The detectives following the pair could have stationed themselves on the lawns behind Marshall and Kuznetsov, at any distance from them which seemed most prudent, without doing anything which seemed remarkable. There were only two or three benches which could not have been covered by people sitting on deck chairs behind them, and these were overlooked by the windows of a tea house, which was open.

We know little about the next meeting of the two men, which took place on May 19, not very far from Marshall's home, just outside Wandsworth in Wimbledon. The evidence regarding it was given in closed court, and Marshall could not remember the name of the restaurant where they ate. But it appeared that they met in the open street in heavy rain. There comes to mind a note made by Ragov, the organizer of the Canadian spy ring, on the margin of a contact's report on a meeting with the scientist Durnford-Smith: "Was a torrential downpour; but he nevertheless came. Give instructions not come in the future in such weather, it is not natural." Marshall and Kuznetsov did not even behave as two men keeping an appointment in a storm would be expected to behave; they did not give each other a perfunctory greeting and then hurry off to shelter. It seemed to the watchers that they went through a curious conspiratorial ritual, that they met and passed without a sign of recognition, then turned back and went off together into a doorway. Marshall denied this, and indeed, from his demeanour in the witness box, it could be believed that at that moment, peevish under the pelting rain, tense in his knowledge that he was defying authority, he might have weaved and fluttered so that the watchers were perplexed into inventing interpretations of his conduct which had no real basis. As Kuznetsov must have noticed long before, Marshall was constitutionally unfit for underground work. Yet on June 13 the two men met at a trysting place which was even more exposed than the Normandie and Canbury Gardens, which could have been chosen, surely, only by someone who was saying, "Take him. Oh, will you never take him? Take him, take him now."

◈◈ 3 ◈◈

The place where William Martin Marshall and the Russian diplomat Pavel Kuznetsov met on June 13 was very close to Marshall's home. It would have been quite impossible for Marshall to shake off any detectives who might have been shadowing him (as indeed they were doing, and as Kuznetsov must have suspected them of doing) during the short and direct walk which took him to King George's Park. The particular section of the park he sought was not the one prudent men would have chosen. Originally the park was a strip of open land alongside the river Wandle, about three quarters of a mile in length and between two and three hundred yards in breadth, which was continuous grassland, though cut into sections by two roads and several fenced and asphalted footpaths. Since the war a colony of prefabricated houses has been planted on one of the interior sections, so that there are now two separate King George's Parks, one on the north side of this settlement and one on its south. Two men who desired to talk in secrecy might well have arranged to meet within this colony and walked along its winding roads, or in the northern park, where there are a children's playground, a swimming pool, and a restaurant to attract crowds, several entrances, and a good many seats along the path which runs right round the grassland. But Marshall and Kuznetsov chose to go to the southern park, which is quite simply a playing field and nothing else. It is a rectangle of flat ground, about eight acres in extent, and there is not a yard of it on which a man might find cover. It is grass, save for a cinder track which runs along the western edge from a gate in one of the transverse roads to a gate in one of the transverse footpaths. Ten trees are planted along this cinder track, and they shadow three benches. On one of these William Marshall sat himself down with his friend Kuznetsov.

The scenery around him defined his plight. Behind him flowed the river Wandle, separated from the park by a narrow strip of vegetable gardens. This stream, which looks as it might be thought water could not look, old and battered, had been the subject of continual pollution through the centuries. Cloth-dressers and hatters working on its banks for the London market accused each other of fouling it in the year 1376. Today it is clean enough; but all the same, as it flowed past the park where Marshall met his friend, the wreck of a baby carriage, stranded wheels upward on a knot of driftwood in midchannel, shook perpetually as its submerged springs were jostled by the current. This neighbourhood is not pernickety about tidiness. Farther

291

along the river on the opposite bank are some industrial plants, none of them large. In London most of the great glossy corporation factories are north of the Thames, and to the south of it there are the family-size factories, and the tough little workshops, which are sometimes rickety and inefficient, but often do a limited job very well and sometimes hit on a mechanical idea that crosses the river and makes its fortune. But just behind this part of the park the opposite bank is taken up by a line of houses that are a survival of Dickens' London, the eternal London, old and snug, with backyards cluttered up by hobbies. In one yard a rabbit fancier has stacked home-made hutches into skyscrapers of a miniature animal town; in the next a little dog sits barking most of the day on the tilted seat of an armchair short of a leg, among piles of doors and posts and planks which nobody but an unusually infatuated amateur carpenter could cherish; in another, outside a minute and crooked workshop, an old bicycle gesticulates with twisted handlebars from the top of a scrap heap. In such houses lively individualists, pottering away at their private pleasures, have to some degree acquired an understanding of scientific method. They are not delivered helpless over to what is said to them on radio and television and written for them in the papers. They have their own experience of cause and effect.

If the men looked to the right they saw twelve prefabs which had been allowed to trespass on the western edge of the park, which backs on the transverse road. These are of the frankly temporary sort which have been put up all over England since the war, and are white, white like a strip of bandage applied to a long wound in the town, except for the black sections of dismantled Nissen huts which serve as wash houses at the back. Their raw new gardens project into the park, uncluttered by rabbits or timber or metal. The tenants of such houses have often been bombed out and lost their livestock and their lathes and their carpenters' tools. Not least among the losses suffered by Britain under bombardment were the informal laboratories of the backyards, where generation after generation had learned by practice the essentials of biology and mechanics. It is not cheap nowadays to repair such losses, and the younger tenants are unlikely to start these hobbies, not only because of the high cost, but because they were evacuated to the country during the raids and were separated from their parents and were never taught by Daddy to proffer the right sort of lettuce leaf to the twitching muzzle or how to hold a chisel; and since then they have been packed into the over-crowded houses of relatives and long for tidiness above all things. So their gardens are empty and orderly, and their amusements are public and standardized, films and radio and television, football matches and the pools. They love their houses, they live peace-ably, they are good citizens. But with their hobbies they have abandoned their traditional approach to scientific method. Now they must get all their interest, and nearly all their knowledge be-yond what their schools give them in childhood, from what they read and hear. They are not only sensitive to print, they are de-pendent on it, and they are less able to defend themselves by criticism than their fathers were, unless they do in truth become intellectuals.

If the two men looked straight across the park in front of them they saw some small neat castles, apartment houses built by the London County Council in the sound tradition of housing which it has followed throughout this century. Here are people who are even less handy and less scientific than the tenants of the pre-fabs; they have not even raw new gardens to fill with annuals or walls to cover with creepers; they must get every scrap of knowl-edge out of books. Nor can they make friends casually over the garden fence; they must purposely build a society on the basis of common interests, discovered at the Co-Operative Stores social or the Union Branch meeting. Here, in fact, the working class is manufacturing a new middle class. This is turning out to be not at all unlike the old, even to political compactness; it is said that the odd eccentric Tory in these apartment houses is quite un-popular. The successes of this new social enterprise are often spectacular; but the inauguration is not easy.

If the two men turned their heads to the left they looked across the last section of the park, which is planted with vegetables, at a region covered with low factories and workshops above which tower schools of an obviously outmoded pattern. When a society has staked its all on book-learning its hope must lie in lavishness of education; but Hitler has hamstrung all such ambitions.

Young Marshall's spirit ranged uncomfortably over these several planes of a community which was passing through a transitional stage. His parents belonged to the old traditional London, and he had inherited from them the individualism which made him ready to question authority. It was a pity that they had turned to handicrafts for their hobbies, for though they had robustly used their fingers to make a strongly coloured and ornate home, their son had only developed his taste for weaving silk mats, which obviously had not satisfied the demands of his inner nature and was unlikely to win him social prestige. No doubt he felt as if he belonged to the more modern world of the prefabs and the apartment houses by virtue of his occupation as a radio operator, though here there is an obvious irony. Though radio telegraphy is a recent discovery it is already clear that it will soon be superseded by more recently discovered methods of communication; and as the technique is easy to master far too many young men enter what is in effect a dying industry, which will not prepare them for any other occupation. Young Marshall was, indeed, in danger of becoming within a few years as obsolete as the clothdressers and hatters who had fouled the river behind him in the year 1376. It may have been some sense of his imminent plight which had drawn him towards communism. But it is possible that the determining consideration which brought him to this bench was of quite a different nature. He was a kindly lad; he had spent the earlier part of that day mending the vacuum cleaner which belonged to a spinster neighbour. He probably thought of himself as doing Kuznetsov a good turn not different in nature.

It was on the bench nearest the gate to the footpath that Marshall and Kuznetsov seated themselves. Again the young man was tempted into a small and exposed position, even smaller and more exposed than Canbury Gardens. The path was only about two hundred yards long, and he could not stray from it, for it was seven o'clock and the expanse of grass in front of him was covered with children having their last game before supper. All three benches could be watched from behind by anyone who cared to enter the vegetable gardens on the lip of the Wandle. These were allotments—that is to say, they were rented out by the local authorities to enthusiastic amateur gardeners with no gardens of their own; and this was the very time of day when such people were at work. A detective could loiter there, smoking a pipe and looking wisely down at the celery and up at the beans, or fiddling with a fork or a spade, and keep two men under his eye without doing anything out of the ordinary. But the pattern of the hunt had hardened into a simpler form. The detectives settled down on the bench that was farthest away from the one on which the two men were sitting, near the gate into the road. After ten minutes they decided they would like to be nearer and they moved to the middle bench. When the two men rose to leave the detectives closed in on them. This must have been, in a sense, premature, for they had not seen Marshall pass any documents to Kuznetsov, which is what they must have wanted. But perhaps they moved in to prevent an open scandal, for it was obviously only a matter of time before the pair, in their dogged search for conspicuous meeting places, would arrive at the vestibule of Scotland Yard.

When Kuznetsov was released from the police station, the Soviet Embassy having confirmed his claim to be on its staff, he left behind him a situation of very definite colour. He had made a clumsy assertion that Marshall was a stranger to him, and he had as clumsily refused to set it down in black and white; and he had done nothing to prevent Marshall from telling a story which was bound to be incompatible with what he had said. He went straight home to the floor of the Victorian villa which he occupied with his wife and child; but nobody was surprised that he slept there that night and no other, and that a Soviet automobile came the next day and removed him and his wife and child to the Embassy. It was assumed that the thunder and lightning of Moscow had descended on one of its servants who had failed in an assignment, and that he had been segregated to his shame until he could be sent back to Russia, there, no doubt, to realize something less than his normal expectation of life. Yet it is not impossible that this assumption was mistaken. Certainly Kuznetsov was ultimately repatriated. But to those who have visited the Normandie Restaurant and Canbury Gardens and King George's Park it seemed that failure might not have been his portion in this affair; that through his contact with Marshall he might have achieved as spectacular a success as he was likely ever to enjoy in all his life.

Kuznetsov's departure from Britain was not according to protocol. At first the British Foreign Office took it for granted that the Soviet Embassy would send him out of the country as soon as the court had found Marshall guilty; but when it was seen that he was not taking steps to get on the first Polish boat to leave after the trial, a formal request for his repatriation was handed to the Soviet Ambassador, Mr. Zarubin, who had not yet been replaced by Mr. Gromyko. Kuznetsov sailed on another Polish boat, the *Jaroslav-Dabrowski,* from London Docks on the night of Thursday, July 17, seven days after the end of the trial. The delay exasperated the British public, which regarded it as a wanton insult. But this was unjust. Kuznetsov had had to wait till his successor was sent from Moscow, and the business of handing over his files to the newcomer must have demanded more than a day or two. For it appeared that Kuznetsov was a more important person than had been supposed. Indeed, though it seems incredible that anybody trained in police work could have made the glaring errors which led to the detection of his meetings with Marshall, it is said that he was the London representative of the MVD. He must have worked quite hard during that month he passed at the Soviet Embassy, and been unable to find the pleasure that Russians usually derive from that handsome establishment.

For Russians find their Embassy very pleasant, for both sensuous and ideological reasons. Since Queen Victoria left it to go to Buckingham Palace, Kensington Palace has been, what it is now, a refuge for needy royalties and court families; and in the 1840s it was realized that its grounds were far larger than was necessary for the palace's needs. So in 1845 the kitchen gardens and paddocks which lay behind the palace, on the extreme western edge of the parkland, were put on the real-estate market, in the form of some thirty building sites, each suitable for the erection of a really large villa surrounded by its own grounds. Most of the sites were laid out to form a wide avenue running north to south, though a few, which were considered not so grand, were round the corner, out in Bayswater Road. All of them were grouped under the name of Kensington Palace Gardens, which has kept for a hundred years a certain plump and golden significance. These sites were enormously expensive and were sold as leaseholds for a period of ninety-nine years.

Rates were high. The sizes of the houses and gardens meant that their tenants employed from ten to twenty-five indoor and outdoor servants. Moreover, as the cost of building rose (and in the last thirty years it has risen by one hundred per cent), a heavier and heavier burden was imposed on the leaseholders by the terms in their contract with the Crown, which insisted that they keep their houses in the pink of repair. It was, therefore, from the beginning, a sign of great wealth to live in Kensington Palace Gardens, and as the cost of living rose it became the sober truth that nobody could maintain a household there who was not a millionaire in pounds. Today if one gives a taxi driver an address in Kensington Palace Gardens he is as likely as not to respond with a knowing nod and the words, "Millionaires' Row"; and the millionaires have got a good return for their money. The setting is delightfully verdant; there is also a charming sense of consequence in residing here. It is in the Crown precincts, the avenue is a private road, and there are porters in the livery of the Crown Commissioners posted at each end to turn back pedestrians and drivers who have no business with the residents and are trying to use it as a thoroughfare from the north to the south side of the parklands. There is probably not a quieter and greener place to live in London, or, indeed, in any other great capital.

In the old days there were quite enough millionaires in the British Empire, though not always of British birth, to fill the street. But after 1918 a cold wind blew along the avenue. A certain number of leaseholders who, before 1914, could have afforded to live in any conceivable habitation except the Vatican, had to get out of their houses. It might have been that the war had hit the system so hard that it was cracking. There was an apparent recovery in the early twenties, but this was cancelled by the economic tornado which broke over Britain at the end of that decade. Many people feared that the capitalist system was going to collapse immediately; and therefore it seemed significant when, in 1930, the Soviet government moved into this estate which had been planned as a realization of the rosiest dreams of capitalism. It became a tenant of the Crown and set up its Embassy at Number 13, an enormous edifice on the favoured east side of the avenue, which had till then been known as Harrington House.

It was built in 1852. The dramatic appearance in its halls of Mr. Kuznetsov after his release from Wandsworth Police Station might have been designed as a celebration of its centenary. It was specially ironical that this particular house should have been acquired by the Soviet government. The house had been built by the fifth holder of the Earldom of Harrington, which had been created to reward one William Stanhope for public services rendered as Secretary of State during the second quarter of the eighteenth century. His correspondence with the British Ambassador in Russia shows that he was hardly able to spare a moment for the consideration of Muscovite matters, so absorbed was he in the obviously much more important problem of appeasing the kingdom of Spain, which was then considered as the permanent great power of Europe. The fifth Earl of Harrington, Leicester Stanhope, is known to many more people by his features than by his name, for when he was a child he sat as the model for a charming painting by Sir Joshua Reynolds called "Sprightliness," which shows him beating a drum.

This was an omen. He was sprightly, he covered no end of ground, and he created a continual disturbance. At first his ghost must have been delighted by the sale of the house he had built to the Soviet government, for he was a romantic radical. He was an army officer, and was one of the first to raise the acute modern problem of how far a professional soldier should engage in political activities. He served out in India and supported the beginnings of the Indian nationalist movement. Later, like Lord Byron, he went out to fight as a volunteer in the Greek War of Independence, but he was far further to the left than the poet, for he advocated a republican form of government for liberated Greece, which Byron refused to do. Ultimately the Turkish government complained so vehemently of his intervention that the War Office forced him to return to England. But though he was all for revolutions he belonged to the Puritan type of reformer, and during the ten years of life which remained to him after he moved into

Harrington House he constantly brooded ecstatically on the State of Maine, for he was an ardent prohibitionist, and he regarded the Maine liquor law of 1851 as the first legislative step towards the establishment of the earthly paradise; and the lavish supplies of vodka and champagne for which the Soviet Embassy parties are celebrated must have warned his ghost that this was not the revolution which he had so eagerly expected.

But there was another and more spectacular irony in the choice of this particular house. It is not like its neighbours. Except for a fantastic outcrop of stage scenery which the Indian Prince of Baroda topped with oriental cupolas, most of the houses in the avenue can be described as big houses and are just that and nothing else. But Number 13 presents clearly and with touching faith an idea which was proved an illusion by the ruin of Europe. It mirrors the imaginative prepossession which pro-German Queen Victoria and her court imposed on her age. Designed in the German Gothic style, it is loaded with pious copies of every recorded type of Gothic ornament, with tracery and oriels and quoins and crockets and cusps, and it originally sported a soaring Nuremberg-ish pinnacle on the roof. Every brick and stone of it refers to the innocent fairy-tale country which sent us the Prince Consort, the pleasing custom of the Christmas tree, *Heilige Nacht,* the story of Rumpelstiltskin, *Baumkuchen,* the music of Mendelssohn, and the legends of the Rhine, sober, industrious, and peaceable Germany, beloved by Carlyle and Matthew Arnold; the same country which waged the two world wars, which devoured millions of her own young, cost Britain more lives than had been lost in all previous wars, and killed more Russians than all the Asiatic invaders who hacked their way across the steppes throughout the Middle Ages.

In consequence of these events the Soviet Union has occupied Kensington Palace Gardens. This was not fully achieved until after the Second World War. When Hitler ended peace, Britain and the British Commonwealth had got back on its feet after the economic tornado of the late twenties and early thirties, and in 1939, though there was a sign of weakening of the system in the presence of the Nepalese and Lithuanian Legations in the avenue, most of the houses were still occupied by millionaires. Among the

299

Soviet Ambassador's neighbours were the Duke of Marlborough, the Marquess of Cholmondeley, whose wife belongs to the great Indian family of Sassoon, Sir Alfred Beit, the owner of heavy holdings in South African mines, Sir Charles Seligman the banker, Sir Berkeley Sheffield, an industrialist who was among other things a leader of the paper trade, Sir Harry Oakes, the Canadian oil king who was afterwards murdered at Nassau, the Duchess of Marchena, daughter of the Spanish lady who married Sir Basil Zaharoff, Alfred Chester-Beatty, who owned mines all over the world and was a famous collector of manuscripts, Daniel Fooks, who had interests in the Far East, and G. R. Strauss, a Socialist M.P. who was a minister in the last Labour government, who had inherited his house from his father, a North Country metal broker.

Today all these residents have gone except Lord Cholmondeley, the Duchess of Marchena, the widow of Mr. Fooks, and Mr. Strauss, and few of their sort have come to fill the gap. Against nineteen houses in private occupation in 1939, there were at the time of Kuznetsov's misadventure nine. Of the rest two were bombed and three were for sale; one was still occupied by the Nepalese Legation; the premises vacated by the Lithuanian Legation were taken over by Syria, and the Lebanese Legation was next door but one; the French Ambassador had his official residence in Number 11, which belonged to the Duke of Marlborough; and the Soviet had retained Number 13 and acquired three more houses. One of these, Number 5, listed in the telephone directory as the office of the Soviet Film Agency, is among the less impressive houses outside the main avenue, round the corner in the Bayswater Road. But the other two are among the supreme manifestations of the spirit of the place. Number 18 was once the residence of the great Baron de Reuter, who with Cagliostroish, wizardly air exploited the invention of the electric telegraph by founding Reuter's News Agency, and thus revolutionized newspaper and stock exchange practice; and it afterwards belonged to Leopold de Rothschild, the head of the English branch of the family, one of the brilliant and amusing Jews who, by charming King Edward VII, helped to get the English monarchy to set its face against anti-Semitism. Number 10 is even more splendid, and is on the east side of the avenue, with a superb terrace looking over Kensington Gardens. It was for many years owned by an exuberant financier with gold-mining interests in South Africa, named Leopold Hirsch. He added to its vastness by clapping another story on top of it, a feat which recalls the line of Milton, "Elephants endors'd with towers"; he used to disturb the calm of the district by walking about his house and gardens singing the Lieder of Schubert and Brahms in a voice as huge as his fortune and his home. It is now listed as the office of the Soviet naval attaché.

These houses have proved to be key positions. The estate is now alien territory. It might be thought that it must have been that for a long time, with all its tenants bearing such names as Marchena and Reuter, Baroda and Rothschild. But, indeed, when the place was theirs, it was as English as the Tower of London or Westminster Abbey. The parties of children which used to be seen hurrying along the avenue at the close of any afternoon, in the care of nannies or mademoiselles or Fräuleins, on the way home to tea from a dancing class or an hour spent sailing model yachts on the Round Pond in Kensington Gardens, all looked like the children in *Punch* drawings, no matter what their names might be. But now the avenue might be outside the British island, might be part of an area whose nearest frontier was, say, in the Soviet Sector in Berlin. The tedium and complication of the Russian Security system hangs over the place, not very thickly, but as visible as ground mist. There are at all hours of the night and day bored policemen yawning up and down in front of the four Soviet mansions, and private ownership of the avenue itself is now insisted upon to a tiresome degree. The two gates at each end had in the old days always been open for traffic, now one was sometimes closed; and whereas the Crown Commission porters used to carry out their duty of checking traffic in an easygoing and sensible way, they are now forced to keep strictly to the letter of the rule. Hence there was, in this tetchy time towards the end of Stalin's reign, constantly performed a comedy which might have been written by Gogol. The porters held up every vehicle and asked the driver which house he intended to visit. If the number given was 10 or 13 or 18, the porter asked the name of the person to whom the visit was to be paid and telephoned it to the central switchboard of the Soviet Embassy to see if the visit would be welcome. Very often, if the vehicle was a commercial van with goods to deliver, the driver's pronunciation of the name of the Russian official which was on the invoice, and which was itself often misspelled by the clerk who filled in the invoice, was not recognized by the Russian switchboard operator when it was repeated over the telephone by the porter; and then orders were given that the van was not to be allowed to proceed. This invariably exasperated the driver, who felt, reasonably enough, that if he took his crate of electric-light fittings or his bale of blankets to the house from which they were ordered, inquiry might have led to the person who actually wanted them. He was apt to regard the porter in his Crown Commissioner's livery as the instrument of privilege, and probably hostile to the cause of the revolution; and often altercations started during which a queue formed up behind the van, composed of visitors anxious to fulfil their engagements with the Ambassador of France, Mrs. Fooks, or Lord Cholmondeley.

The Soviet Embassy carries the enormous staff of one hundred and eighty employees (as against the staff of thirty-two which the British employ at their Embassy in Moscow), and there are over seventy Russian officials working at various agencies whose lives centre in the Embassy. Many of these have their families with them, so there are not infrequently to be seen strolling in the avenue groups of dark and thick-set men and women with their children, all, even to the tiniest boys and girls, clad in the stiff, rectangular type of tailoring by which Soviet citizens can always be picked out against a Western background. These people are instantly likeable, because of the manifest warmth of the affection they bear one another, and because of the humour which plays about their eyes and lips. They have also (which makes them neither more nor less likeable, for it is something which may alight on any nation when its turn comes round) the air of conquerors treading conquered ground. They walk with the same slow complacent lurch as the occupation troops in Germany; and they too stare at the passers-by, not insolently, not even unkindly, but as if the passers-by were blind and could not see them stare. The Russians know, of course, that according to the book of the rules there ought to be a military victory to seal such a conquest, but their kindliness and their pride lead them to nourish a hope that that necessity has in this instance been obviated. For surely they would not have been permitted to pitch their camp in this stronghold of capitalism were not the system about to crumble into ruins, were not their enemies even now so far confounded that they could not think it worth while to muster their forces for what must inevitably be defeat.

This view is illusory. The decay of Kensington Palace Gardens means simply that there have been two wars lately, and that the community has altered its way of spending its wealth in the last few decades. If these houses are no longer private homes, it is largely because servants' wages and the cost of fuel—which means miners' wages—have risen enormously; and if the duty of keeping these houses in the state of repair required by the Crown has become a burden that can be borne by few, it is because builders' wages also have risen and because the labour and material available for constructional purposes are now being diverted to other forms of building, such as prefabs and the London County Council apartment houses which surround the park at Wandsworth where Marshall and Kuznetsov were arrested. Nor would it be safe to deduce from the state of the avenue that the plutocracy of the West had carried within their loins the seeds of their own destruction, and that the families who had sold their houses had let their property fall from hands palsied by degeneracy. The Harringtons still do their duty as agriculturalists in the North of England, and the son of the South African millionaire to whom they sold their house now farms and directs various corporations in South Africa. In no wise do they resemble the men of Nineveh and Babylon, of Tyre and Sidon.

Indeed, the Soviet government had done no more by its choice of quarters than take four white elephants off the real-estate market. But the myth of its significance is strong among the Russians, and it must have profoundly affected Kuznetsov during the weeks he passed in Harrington House before his departure from England. Whatever interpretation he placed on the story of his meetings with Marshall, he must have spent those weeks in a state of apprehension. If the superficial interpretation be correct, and he was simply an unfortunate man who had had too much luck and had managed to rise very high in the MVD in spite of his unusual lack of talent for police work, and he had not intended the Special Branch to discover his meetings with Marshall, then there was good ground for the popular belief that his return to Russia would take him to some extreme form of punishment. But if the right interpretation be that which comes up through facts when they are stared at for any length of time, and Mr. Kuznetsov was not stupid but obedient and conscientious, and a model police officer in every way, and the Special Branch had been intended to detect his relationship with Marshall and arrest him as a spy, then he still had reason to fear the worst. He could not be as sickeningly sure of his ultimate end as he would have been if the superficial interpretation was correct. But he may well have felt sick with uncertainty.

For there could be only one reason why Soviet Intelligence should have wished to seduce the awkward and inept child William Martin Marshall: to put him on a salver and serve him up to British Intelligence, to divert its attention from another and more valuable agent, possibly not British at all, who was working on so nearly the same field as Marshall that the British and American Intelligence authorities would think, having arrested Marshall, that they had stopped the leak which had been troubling them and could relax their vigilance. So far so good for Kuznetsov. He could not have trussed Marshall up more competently had he been a professional poulterer and the lad a Christmas goose. Kuznetsov had even put in some fancy touches on which he was able to congratulate himself; prodigious cantrips on his way to his appointments which looked the very thing a not-too-clever spy would do if he were trying to throw detectives off his trail. But the other agent, the agent who was not Marshall, must be very valuable. He must indeed be enormously valuable if to cover him Soviet Intelligence deemed it worth while to stage this prolonged and elaborate farce, which involved the withdrawal from his duties of such a responsible official as Kuznetsov, even though that might be only for a time. But whether it would only be for a time must have been one of the questions which worried Kuznetsov during those weeks. The ways of Intelligence being what they are, there would be British and American observers in Soviet

Russia who would have their eyes on Kuznetsov. If he was to be visible, at liberty and in good condition, then these observers would say, "What, is that not Kuznetsov? Why is he walking about at his ease after he made that catastrophic blunder? Can it be that the Marshall case, after all, was not what it seemed?" There would be no simpler way for the Soviet government to convince them that the Marshall case was exactly what it seemed on the surface than by punishing Kuznetsov severely, by punishing him for a long time, by finding, if it were possible, a form of punishment which would lull foreign suspicions for ever. It is to be noted that when the Soviet government accuses persons of conspiring against it, such as Rajk, the witnesses who testify that they conspired with them are afterwards treated as if that evidence were true, however patently false it may be, and are punished accordingly.

Often Kuznetsov must have lifted his head from his work and sent his thoughts along the avenue to the gates where the porters in the Crown Commissioners' livery turned back or let pass the incoming traffic. For him the hinges of the trap worked the other way. He had been allowed to go back to his flat once to pack up his luggage, but only once. Not possibly could he get out of Kensington Palace Gardens again until his colleagues took him down to the docks. In ordinary circumstances a foreign diplomat can walk out of his Embassy and seek asylum with the British authorities. But as it would have been very natural that he should want to do this, and as nothing was more certain than that the British authorities would have refused to receive him unless he approached them in the candid spirit of another Gouzenko, he would have been unwise if he had betrayed any desire for fresh air and exercise. He was suffering a form of imprisonment oddly crude for such an elegant residential area, but, of course, that incongruity may have counted for him as a consolation. Such Russians as he, able and resourceful and disciplined, place themselves at the disposal of the great organization which has taken over their country because it claims to be able to compel success, and they belong to the breed of the successful. It is well known that success depends on efficiency; and efficient management cuts its losses, sacrifices the smaller profit to the larger, scraps without hesitation the equipment which has had its day. Now that Kuznetsov found himself relegated to the category of the cut loss, the smaller profit, the obsolete equipment, he could comfort himself by reflecting that the management which was jettisoning him had the justification that it was in fact efficient; it had penetrated into the stronghold of British capitalism, it could be assumed that it had achieved its object and that the West was dying. If, as his mind ranged along the avenue, he thought of the men in the buildings occupied by the Embassies of other countries, who were certainly not in a state of detention and fear like himself, he probably despised them as children of a less glorious race, who would be spared great misfortunes only because nothing great of any sort would ever meet them on their road.

Often, during those days of high summer, he may well have had less heroic hours of consolation, have fallen into drowsiness, forgotten that he must soon start on a journey, and abandoned himself to the pleasantness of the place, pretending, perhaps, he was going to be able to stay there as long as he liked. The rooms in the Soviet Embassy buildings are quiet and cool, and there is no reason to fear the ghost of the fifth Earl of Harrington at Number 13, for he must surely have fled his old home for ever during the Second World War, for there was only one cause as dear to his later years as prohibition, and that was Polish Independence. Unhaunted, these rooms would exercise the spell which is cast by the whole avenue. All these houses were built in the age when it was thought that there was enough of everything to go round, and the illusion in the architects' minds controlled their hands and still influences our eyes. It is impossible to remain for long among these serene masses of masonry without beginning to believe that all is well and will continually grow better. A conniving myth is told by the view from the windows, which blends the scattered treetops of Kensington Gardens and Hyde Park into a woodland where there might revel a company of beings in the dress of another age, dancing and speaking to one another always in verse. Kuznetsov must have often thought that Kensington Palace Gardens would have been a very agreeable spot indeed, if only people had not kept on coming to it.

He might have finished his career in peace if there had never come to this door the gangling boy, William Martin Marshall, twitching and pouting as if the old system were a harsh wind blowing on purpose to spite him, swaying and languishing as if he were courted by the new system. And in these later hours Kuznetsov might have been able to forget him had not the boy's father also availed himself of the damnable accessibility of Kensington Palace Gardens. For the intrepid bus driver, who believed so fervently in the power of speech, who was of the opinion that if one spoke of things happening a certain way one could make them happen that way, did all he could to have his wish and talk it out with the man who could have saved his son from jail. He made the journey from Wandsworth with his wife, in his pocket a letter he had written to Kuznetsov, urging him to make a statement which would make it clear that he received no information from his son. He took it to Number 13, leaving his wife to wait outside. They both struck those who saw them as having aged by years since the trial. The letter was taken from him, and he was put into a small room. After an hour the letter was returned to him, and he was told that he could not see Mr. Kuznetsov, and was sent away. His appeal must have struck any Soviet official as light-minded and naïve, like a hysterical proposal to raise a sunken submarine by some device which ignored the mathematics of aquatic pressure.

But if it came to Kuznetsov's knowledge it must have distressed him, for he was by all accounts an affectionate father himself, and during the last few weeks his five-year-old son must have seemed peculiarly dear to him. Misha was not with him in Kensington Palace Gardens. The Soviet Embassy has a country house for its employees, Seacox, fifty miles southeast of London near Hawkhurst in Kent, which it acquired for thirty thousand pounds. The little boy was sent down there when he and his parents were removed from their flat in Holland Villas Road. It is not known when his father saw him again. For Kuznetsov was alone when he left England on the *Jaroslaw-Dabrowski* on July 17. Though it might be supposed that the passages on a Polish ship would be at the disposal of the Soviet government, it was announced that there was only one cabin free and that therefore his wife and child must follow later. They sailed on August 5 on the *Beloostrov*. When they arrived at Moscow station Mrs. Kuznetsov looked eagerly round her, then burst into tears. Apparently she had hoped that someone would meet her whom she did not see. This may have been her husband. But other people came forward and took her away. Nobody was sorry for the Marshalls and the Kuznetsovs, for pity had long ago gone out of fashion.

Mr. and Mrs. Marshall visited Kensington Palace Gardens not once but three times; so wise was Emerson, so true was his saying, admired by Mr. Bentall of Kingston, "If a man write a better book, preach a better sermon, or make a better mousetrap than his neighbours, though he build his house in the woods, the world will make a beaten track to his door." The Soviet Embassy might as well have been in the woods, so far as Mr. Marshall was concerned. To a lively inhabitant of Wandsworth, which is warm and moist with close-pressed current life, there can have been little enticement in Kensington's wide and disappointed streets, where nearly every house is used less handsomely than was intended, and life seems to be draining away down the unnecessarily broad gutters. He cannot really have expected that things would have gone well with him there; if there had been any possibility that Kuznetsov could speak he would have spoken long before. But Mr. Marshall was not a free man. He was in the custody of his own fatherhood, and when his jailer bade him go with his wife, who was in the custody of her motherhood, into this alien and formal area for his son's sake, he had to obey. They were, though they could make this journey across London, as much prisoners as the man they visited and as their son.

It is to be wondered that Kuznetsov should have had a son, knowing that the door might shut on him at any time as it had shut on the others. Mr. Marshall, too, had known well that there were nets and pits and that many a man had been caught before he could think of the words that would get him out. But the city which was traversed by the Marshalls, which encased Kuznetsov's growing sense that something had gone wrong, was inscribed with a larger writing of that riddle. In winter the irrational process is disguised, but in summer, when children rush out of all the houses, it shows, naked and astonishing, the persistence of the human race in begetting and giving birth, in being born. In many gardens behind the little houses washing was hanging on the lines, even when it was not Monday and therefore not washing day at all by British tradition; there were rows of diapers pegged out square and white. Across a gravel path a wooden horse painted with blue spots lay on its back, the red cart it drew sticking up into the air at the authentic angle of serious accident. On the next lawn a tiny boy stood in front of cricket stumps, opening his mouth in an earnest circle as he held his bat straight and waited for an imaginary bowler to send along the ball; and in the next again, a fat little girl lumbered round and round, twirling a stick with a paper star on it. Among the shrubberies of an orphanage children in blue overalls ran and leaped as if they had not been deserted. There were many of them; there were specks of blue coming and going among the farthest trees. In the streets the air was loaded with a warm haze, smelling of dust and sunbaked bricks and mortar, which was a dry tickle in the nose and throat, yet left sweat on the skin; so down by the Thames the naked boys stood on the mud under the embankments and sunned themselves, their spare bodies erect like flames and white against the grey stone, or slid out among the diamonds of the sunlit water, shouting to other boys who shouted back from boats.

On the other side of the river the grey pavements, whitish under the excessive light, were scored with chalk marks for hopscotch, and hop, hop, hop, the little players went, lively in spite of the heat, as those cannot be who are older and have had summer after summer sucking the marrow out of their bones. In deck chairs, on the shiny blond grass in the parks, adults lay with closed eyes, their faces piteous, as if they could not support the weight pressed on them by the massive sunshine. Past them hurried children, on their way to bathe in the pools, or to hurtle themselves about on the slides and swings and whirligigs in the playgrounds, or to have a game of cricket with a curled-up coat laid on the ground for stumps. The children cried out exultantly as they went, crying without cease, as people in religious processions chant continually, that they were children, that they were with other children, that all of them were alive. If there should come to earth travellers from another planet where there is justice and all goes by reason, it must amaze them, how humanity makes a

309

beaten track out of nothingness to this curious prison where there is no end to captivity and giving into captivity. They would wonder why the orphans in the shrubberies, the naked boys on the mudflats, the children in the parks, lifted up their voices like confident prophets, and why the adults lay still under the sun, as if they saw through their closed lids a vision which made it safe for them to rest. They might wonder if humanity knew something as yet unstated, which makes it not folly to be born. But it can be said of this larger mystery only what can be said of the lesser mystery in which William Martin Marshall was involved: the facts admit of several interpretations.

Rebecca West was the pseudonym of Cicily Isabel Andrews, British journalist, novelist, and critic, perhaps best known for her reports on the Nuremberg Trials that are part of *A Train of Powder*. Born in 1892 and the daughter of an army officer, she was educated in Edinburgh and later trained in London as an actress. Beginning in 1911 she contributed often to left-wing publications and gained a reputation as a fierce advocate for woman suffrage. She wrote five novels which attracted less attention than her social and cultural writings, the most important of which were *Black Lamb and Grey Falcon*, an examination of Balkan politics, culture, and history; *The Meaning of Treason*, about William Joyce and the role of the traitor in modern society; and *A Train of Powder*. She died in London in 1983.